# ASIATIC MONOGRAPHS.

# ASIATIC MONOGRAPHS.

## Vol. III.

# NEW RESEARCHES INTO THE COMPOSITION AND EXEGESIS OF THE QORAN

By

HARTWIG HIRSCHFELD, Ph.D., M.R.A.S.

ISBN: 978-93-5128-704-9

First Published in 1902
Indian Reprint in 2017

*Published by*

Kalpaz Publications
C-30, Satyawati Nagar,
Delhi – 110052
E-mail: kalpaz@hotmail.com
Website: kalpazpublications.com
Ph.: +91-9212142040

**Cataloging in Publication Data—DK**
Courtesy: D.K. Agencies (P) Ltd. <docinfo@dkagencies.com>

**Hirschfeld, Hartwig,** 1854-1934**, author.**
New researches into the composition and exegesis to the Qoran / by Hartwig Hirschfeld (Ph.D., M.R.A.S.).
pages cm. — (Asiatic monographs ; vol. III)
"First published in 1902"—Title page verso.
Includes index.
ISBN 9789351287049

1. Qur^an.—Criticism, interpretation, etc. I. Title. II. Series: Asiatic Society monographs ; vol. III.

BP130.4.H37 2017 DDC 297.1226 23

## ADDITIONS AND CORRECTIONS.

Page 13, last line: The term "Hanifa" occurring in my article on Abd Allâh b. Ubaiy in the *Jewish Encyclopedia*, Vol. I. p. 44, is an unauthorized alteration for "Hypocrites."

Page 15, line 8, *read* Numb. ix. 8.

Page 22, rem. 11, *read Lehre.*

Page 29, rem. 52, l. 4, *read* Tishrîn; *ibid.* l. 6, *for* [illegible] *read* [illegible]. See *J. Q. R.* XIII. p. 232.

Page 45, line 22, *read* styled.

Page 70, line 2, *read* in several.

" " last paragraph: The prophetship of Josef is, at all events, hinted at in *Súra* xii. 15.

Page 73, line 32, *read* with narrative.

# PREFACE.

The critical study of the *Qorân* has advanced but little since Professor Nöldeke, forty years ago, published his book which combines learning, acumen, and judgment in rare perfection. Its authority has been such, that many of the most important questions of *Qorân* criticism were regarded as finally settled in its pages.

There is, I hope, no arrogance in the assertion that in matters of research no such thing as a final decision of every disputable point exists. Each fresh attempt that promises to bring us a step nearer the truth, therefore, deserves encouragement. As regards the beginnings of the *Qorân*, it is probable that the truth will never be completely revealed, and the seeker must be satisfied with attaining a certain degree of probability. One thing cannot be denied that, in spite of the splendid efforts of Weil, Nöldeke, Sprenger, Sir William Muir, and others, new questions and difficulties crop up in the old fields, whilst the most important episodes in the career of the founder of Islâm absorb the student's search-light rather than reflect it. For instance, students as well as others, by a kind of tacit agreement, are content to look upon the chief factor in the missionary power of the Arab prophet as a frenzy or nervous affection, which assumed the form of fits. The historical evidence for this belief is, however, exceedingly slender.

What is the interest we take in the history of Islâm? If the dawn of a new religion is an event of importance, that of a monotheistic one demands the closest attention. The chief questions are whether it arose spontaneously, or whether we can follow up its development from its very beginnings. These doubts are only too often set aside with the phrase: "Islâm arose in the light of history, and its importance for our recognition of the origin of religion is therefore very great." This is, however, a double delusion. Islâm is not an entirely spontaneous growth, and though it came to life in historical times (and in not very remote ones either), the circumstances accompanying its birth are hidden in impenetrable darkness. Of the mass of material handed down by professional Moslim makers of history only a very small quantity is of any scientific value.

Another favourite idea is that the prophetship of Muhammad furnishes us with a reliable image of Biblical prophetism, and allows us to peep into the inner working of their calling. This is true to a certain extent. If we place the characteristic features of both side by side, the points they have in common, as well as the differences, will soon become apparent. The main point is enthusiasm, with which were combined moral courage and self-denial. The first difference is that of degree. Whilst with the prophets these qualities remained stationary during the whole of their careers, they diminished in Muhammad in proportion to his increasing influence. Biblical prophets had no policy of their own, whilst Muhammad's attitude during the Medinian period of his life was largely political. "Obedience to Allâh and His Prophet" is the watchword of all those years, but since the former was only present *in abstracto*, this meant obedience to the Prophet alone. And he was very exacting in this matter. Finally, in contradiction to his predecessors he did not trouble about the nature of the means he employed, so long as they enabled him to achieve his aim, and in several cases did he not flinch from distorting the truth.

In spite of all this, Muhammad is a most interesting personage, and probably the most suitable man his country could have produced for this great monotheistic reaction against a decaying paganism. This is the main reason why we study the work of his life. We can do him more justice, if we measure him according to the moral standard of his age and country. There is absolutely nothing superhuman in him. The important lesson to be derived from Islâm is to see how the great teachings of the Bible worked themselves through a channel of very ordinary clay into a broad and living stream. The *Qorân*, the text-book of Islâm, is in reality nothing but a counterfeit of the Bible. Its chaotic condition is in some way indicative of its contents. It is full of points not yet used for the study of the life of its author, and of problems as yet undiscussed, and which I by no means claim to have exhausted. Future students of the *Qorân* will no doubt unearth more interesting matter.

In concluding these brief preliminary remarks I desire to express my gratitude to the authorities of the British Museum and India Office Libraries for the loan of their books and MSS., to the Council of the Royal Asiatic Society for the distinction conferred on the work by their publication of it, and to Prof. T. W. Rhys Davids for the kindly interest he took in the same.

*London, 27th December* 1901. H. HIRSCHFELD.

# TABLE OF CONTENTS.

## CHAPTER I.

### GENERAL CHARACTER OF THE QORÂN.

IBN KHALDÛN on the miraculous character of the Qorân — Definitions of Islâm and Qorân — Translations — Muhammed, author, but not editor, of the Qorân — Maxim of "Abrogation" — Meaning of the term "Arabic Qorân" — Qorân, the "Speech" of Allâh — Transcendental character of the Qorân — Qorân encourages study — The "seven readings" — Was Muhammed able to write?

Note I. — Islâm.

„ II. — The terms for Logos in the Qorân.

„ III. — Ibn Ḥazam on the transcendental character of the Qorân.

---

Ibn Khaldûn, one of the most intelligent and enlightened critics of the Moslim religion and history, defines the Qorân in the following words :—

"Know that the greatest, the most sublime and best accredited miracle is the noble Qorân which was revealed to our Prophet. Miracles, which are contrary to the laws of Nature, do not usually occur simultaneously with a prophet's inspirations, but, as is well known, follow in the wake of his annunciation. The Qorân, however, is inspiration given exclusively to Muhammed, and is at the same time a miracle, bringing its own credentials, and requiring no external verification as is the case with miracles performed by other prophets. No better guarantee can be given than the identity of the test itself with the thing tested, and it was this to which the Prophet alluded in the words : 'A prophet is only he who brings such signs as are believed in by men. The inspiration granted to me is of such character, and I therefore hope that the number of my followers will increase until the Day of Resurrection.'

"With these words the Prophet wished to convey, that a miracle of so manifest and convincing a character, while being revelation, must necessarily increase the number of True Believers, and this is what he terms 'Community of Followers.'

"All this will serve to show that the Qorân is of all divine books the only one communicated to a prophet by word of mouth, standing as it does with regard to its verbal endowment in contrast to the *Tôrâ*, the *Gospel* and other heavenly books, which their prophetic authors received in the form of ideas. Then when returning into the state of ordinary life, they expressed those ideas in common language, and could therefore not claim any superhuman power. Our Prophet, like others, received ideas from Allâh, as we may conclude from many traditions, but he alone rendered Allâh's words, when stating that the Qorân was communicated to him orally, in the following manner (Qor. lxxv. 16-17) : 'Do not move thy tongue thereby to hasten it,[1] it is for us to collect and discourse on it (the Qorân).'

"These two verses were revealed, because Muhammed used to hasten to imbibe the [new] revelations for fear of forgetting them, and because he was anxious to know them by heart. Allâh then spared him that trouble in the revelation (xv. 9): 'Verily, we have sent down the Reminder, and verily we will guard it.' This is what guarding[2] means, being one of the special characteristics of the Qorân, but not as the general public understands the term,[2] while distorting it from its true meaning.

"There are many verses which prove that the Qorân was communicated to Muhammed in the oral way, so that no one can imitate one *Sûra*. No greater miracle was vouchsafed to our Prophet than the Qorân and the manner in which it attracted the Arabs, and caused them to rally round it. If one were to spend all that is on earth, one could not unite their hearts, but Allâh has accomplished it, and thou wilt find unmistakeably what I wished to establish that the Qorân furnishes irresistible evidence of the superiority of our Prophet over others."[3]

---

[1] *Cf. Sûra* xx. 113.

[2] *Alḥafẓ* is commonly interpreted by "learning by heart," see below.

[3] *Prolegomena*, ed. Quatremère, *Notes et Extraits*, Vol. XVI. p. 171, *sqq*.

Briefly stated in Ibn Khaldûn's opinion the Qorân is the result of miraculous revelation accorded to Muhammed exclusively, and in such a manner that no other human being was or will ever be able to boast of a similar privilege. However orthodox such reasoning may sound, there is one important item missing which at once shows its author's standpoint with regard to the great question whether the Qorân is created or eternal. In the course of the following researches we shall have to consider this question which for long has stirred the Moslim world to its very depths.

About one-tenth of the human race style themselves Muhammedans, *i. e.*, followers of the creed that Allâh is a unique Being who sent Muhammed as the "Seal" or last of the prophets to invite the whole world to believe in Him. The believers in this creed have for many centuries not been confined to one people, but comprise children of many nations and races. The cradle of the Muhammedan religion which now bears so universal a character, stood in a small territory in the north-west of the Arabian peninsula, called the Hijâz, a province important from the earliest ages as one of the commercial high roads for the gold and incense trade between South Arabia and the northern countries.

Considered as a church the Muhammedan religion is called *Islâm*[4] which means "Perfect Submission," and the Believers are described as *Moslims*. An originally small number of the Moslims has, in the course of the thirteen centuries of the existence of the creed, grown to a multitude, and is, to all appearance, still growing. It requires, therefore, but little knowledge of universal history to perceive that the origin and development of Islâm must be of unusual significance, and that a movement productive of such gigantic results, must be more than accidental, particularly if we consider that it spread even more rapidly than Christianity.

A traveller in the east will probably obtain a false conception of the original nature of Islâm, because its present condition differs materially from that, owing to the many sects into which it has been divided, and also to customs and rites influenced by historical, geographical, and ethnographical circumstances. It will be easily understood that a religious system, in the course of many centuries, must have departed from its primary simplicity. It is therefore necessary for any one anxious to obtain a true idea of the tenets of the Moslim belief, to study the history of its origin, even though he have opportunities of watching the daily life and the performances of religious rites in Moslim countries. These tenets are laid down in a book styled the Qorân[5] which is written in the Arabic language. This book, although first revealed to a single individual for the use of a small community, now belongs to the world's literature and is translated into numerous other languages. It consists of one hundred and fourteen chapters called *Sûras*[6] which are so peculiarly arranged that the longest, although not the oldest, stands at the beginning and the shortest at the end. The Moslim church, at a very early epoch, adopted this arrangement for political reasons as the official one, and allowed the chronological order, as far as could then be ascertained, as well as variations of the text, to fall into oblivion. For historical research the chronological order is, of course, the only one to be taken into consideration. Attempts to restore the same were, indeed, initiated shortly after the compilation of the book had been completed both as regards whole Sûras and portions of such, and were continued until very recently. Many questions have been solved by the improved methods of Occidental criticism, but more remains obscure, and for many there is little hope of ever finding a satisfactory answer.

It is, however, evident that the Qorân represents the Bible of Islâm. Placing the Qorân side by side with the Bible for the sake of finding points of resemblance between both, we soon see that these are limited to the circumstance that they each form the Holy Writ for large masses of Believers.

---

[4] See Note I. at the end of this chapter.

[5] See below.

[6] As to the etymology of *sûra* the Arab authors have built up a number of theories none of which is, however, satisfactory (see *Itqân*, p. 121). This also applies to the suggestion made by Nöldeke (and universally adopted), that the word is identical with Hebr. *shûrâh*, "row" (*Gesch. d. Qor.* p. 24). Nöldeke has overlooked the fact that the term is already used in Meccan revelations, when Muhammed hardly expected to see any of them put down in a book. What could have induced him, then, to use such a term? Just as the meaning of *sûra* runs parallel to what the Jews call *sidrâh* of the Pentateuch, it is also a corruption based on misreading of the latter. More instances of the same kind will be given below. The question is therefore connected with the other, whether Muhammed was able to read.

With regard to the infinitely more complicated questions connected with the Old and New Testaments we should expect to be in a more favourable position as concerns the Qorân for reasons which at once indicate the vast differences between the latter and the Bible. Firstly, the Qorân was entirely composed in the first half of the seventh century of the present era, and is therefore many centuries younger than the latest portions of the New Testament. Secondly, it has but one author, and the whole period of the production of the material of which it was composed scarcely extends over twenty years. Thirdly, the collection and compilation of the sundry revelations were made by men who had witnessed the first delivery of most of them, and finally the book was hardly finished when it was covered with a mass of explanatory traditions and lengthy commentaries.[7]

The conflux of so many favourable circumstances should justify us in concluding that hardly any critical question dealing with the Qorân is left open. Unfortunately this is not the case. The assistance offered by the explanatory traditions just mentioned keeps within narrow bounds and does not even satisfy linguistic demands. A large number of them are quite untrustworthy. It is therefore safest to let the Qorân explain itself,[8] and this we will endeavour to do as much as possible in the following researches. References will, of course, be made occasionally to some of the most renowned historical, traditional, and exegetical works illustrative of incidents to which many revelations owe their existence, and also to the manner in which prominent Moslim theologians interpreted the principal doctrines laid down in the revelations.[9]

It is worthy of notice that the Arabs, taken as a people, were the last Semitic tribe to exchange paganism for the belief in One God. It is, however, not this circumstance which we have to discuss here, but rather the reason why this occurred so late. The fault certainly did not lie in the lack of acquaintance with the monotheistic belief. Arabs had not only for centuries previously been continually in contact with monotheists, but their country became in the course of time more and more narrowed in both by Jews and Christians.[10] A lively commercial intercourse existed with the Christian inhabitants of Africa, Syria, and even Byzantium. Sundry northern tribes had embraced Christianity (probably Nestorian), and fought under the banners of Greek Emperors against the Persians. In South Arabia Christians were to be found as early as in the sixth century, and Judaism had even made greater progress through the conversion of a royal house. Jews lived in the whole north-west of the peninsula as far as Medina, and the surroundings of this city were in the hands of the Jewish clans.[11] Jewish influence was so great in Medina that many Arab families not only accepted this faith but freely intermarried with Jews. Thus at the beginning of the seventh century in the Ḥijâz, which here chiefly comes into consideration, only the country around Mecca where no Jews and very few Christians existed — these few moreover living in very humble positions — was kept free from the influence of followers of monotheistic beliefs.

Meanwhile the reverence for the national deities was already on the wane everywhere in Arabia, Mecca included. In places with a settled population of agriculturists or growers of palm-trees one of the two monotheistic forms of belief was predominant. The spiritual tension produced in many minds by the decay of the old faith found in those places a solatium either in Judaism or Christianity which goes far to explain why Islâm was slow in taking root there. The state of things in Mecca was, however, different. Open intrusion of alien views of belief was not tolerated in this city for various reasons. Spontaneous restoration of the equilibrium was, therefore, not to be expected in a place which sheltered the ancient national sanctuary of the Ka'ba, which not only gave it a theocratic predominance over a large area, but was also a veritable source of material gain. For these reasons

[7] *Itq.* 908 *sqq.* gives a classification of the oldest commentators, beginning with Muhammed's own friends and their successors. *Ibid.* 918 to 954, see traditions on explanatory remarks handed down on behalf of Muhammed himself. In many cases Al Suyûti enters into a criticism of these annotations.

[8] See Sprenger, *Das Lebene u. d. Lehr d. Muh.*'s I. p. xiii.

[9] *Itq.* 893, *propædeutics* of the exegesis of the Qorân, which necessitates the acquaintance with fifteen different subjects.

[10] See the verses in *I. Hish.* p. 293; Wellhausen, *Reste*, 2nd ed. p. 238, rem. 1.

[11] See *Rev. Et. J.* vii, p. 169 *sqq.*

the crisis was bound to occur here. In other parts, as in Ṭâif and in the desert, religious matters were treated with so much indifference, that no excitement whatever was caused.

The Arabs all round had thus been familiar with Judaism and Christianity for a long time. Nevertheless, the progress made by these forms of belief was but slow and intermittent, and the reasons for this are obvious. Both creeds were anything but compatible with the condition of life in Arabia. For travelling merchants[12] and much more for starving Bedouins the Jewish dietary laws and Day of Rest were not acceptable, and the moral code of the Bible stood in sharp contrast to licentious habits against which there was no heathen prohibition.[13] For some of these reasons it proved difficult enough to gain many tribes even for Islâm. The Christian Church, on the other hand, was split up in so many sects, each stamping the other as heretics, that their quarrels were for an outsider as unattractive as their principles unintelligible. I doubt whether the converted Arab families and tribes mentioned above had ever become Jews or Christians from conviction. The proof is that it afterwards required but little inducement to make them forsake either faith for that of a national prophet who combined a simple creed with a plain ritual, and whilst taking into consideration the nature of the country and some of the sacred traditions of their forefathers, promised them tempting rewards in the life hereafter.

To gain a knowledge of Islâm, a study of the Qorân in the original or in a good translation should be sufficient, as all that is necessary for the comprehension of its fundamental principles is contained in that. Here, however, we encounter a great difficulty. Strictly speaking, the Qorân can only claim to be a child of Arabic literature through the language in which it is written. Although Arabic may be regarded as the most successfully investigated of all Semitic tongues, yet its substance and its poetic forms in particular in the Prophet's time present serious difficulties. If we omit northern and southern Arabic inscriptions, coherent pieces in prose dating from the pre-Islamic epoch do not exist. Other literary monuments, *viz.*, songs, lived in the mouths of the people. The Qorân is written neither in poetry — in which the prosody and standard practices assist the interpretation — nor in prose. The Prophet could neither detach himself wholely from the custom of speaking in chromatic verses,[14] nor did he at once succeed in discoursing in calm oratory. He chose a new theme. The Qorân does not praise love, woman, combat, sword, steed, or camel, but a stern and awful Being invisible and indescribable. Thus the Qorân appeared so foreign to everything with which Arabic thought was familiar, that the ordinary vernacular was inadequate to express all these new ideas. To study the Qorân, therefore, a totally different course must be pursued from that which would be taken for the comprehension of a poem. Dictionary and grammar will in most cases be of assistance in making a literal translation, but must fail to disclose the spirit which pervades the book. When discussing the very oldest revelation we shall have an opportunity of seeing how the first breath of Islâm has been misinterpreted by wrong translation. It is the knowledge of the original sources that can alone throw a light on what often appears at first obscure and meaningless. One of the principal difficulties before us is therefore to ascertain, whether an idea or an expression was Muhammed's spiritual property or borrowed from elsewhere, how he learnt it, and to what extent it was altered to suit his purposes.

There is no lack of translations of the Qorân, many of which have been made by very able scholars.[15] None, however, can claim anything like perfection, and if we must for ever abandon the

---

[12] Al Jâḥiz (died 255 H.) explains on this basis the name of the Qoreish (cod. Brit. Mus. Or. 3138, fol. 267) as "derived from trading and profiting (التجارة والتقريش); this is their grandest title and their noblest parentage which Allâh has extolled in His Book." See also Tabari, p. 1103 to 4. — Al Baihaqi (fol. 25) brings a tradition on behalf of Ibn Abbâs, according to which *Qoraish* is derived from a sea monster called *alqarsh*. See also Caussin de Perceval, *Essai*, I. p. 231 (I. Hish).

[13] See Nöldeke, *Beitraege Zur Kenntniss*, etc. p. 183 *sqq.* "*Die Beduinen als Betrüger ihrer Gläubiger.*"

[14] See below.

[15] I only mention the two latest translations which mark a great progress in this field. The best English one is E. H. Palmer's (*Sacred Books of the East*, Vols. VI. and IX.) with an excellent introduction. I have frequently followed this translation, but marked places in which I disagree with it. The palm, however, belongs to Fr. Rückert's (posthumous) German version: *Der Koran in Auswahl übersetzt* ed. A. Müller. This translation is hard to beat.

hope of obtaining a version in which all the mysteries of the book should be explained, the fault lies with the author alone. In the first place we are not able to gauge the real signification of many words in use at that time, and which have been embodied in the Qorân. Secondly, our knowledge of the language does not enable us to grasp all the idioms of an orator who purposely used uncommon as well as foreign words, and who also changed the meanings of Arabic words or of such differing in dialect.

Under these circumstances it is not astonishing that the manifold difficulties repel rather than encourage the study of the Qorân, especially as it is monotonous to read in spite of its bombastic rhetoric. The later and longer chapters in particular are indescribably tedious, and offer a hard task even to the most enthusiastic student. This is no doubt the reason why researches into the Qorân are at present more than duly supplanted by other branches of Arabic literature. Yet there is much to be done in this field. The sources, in particular, from which Muhammed drew, have not yet all been discovered. Only by investigation will it be possible to understand, how an intelligent man with a training gained autodidactically and by stealth, was able to create from the fragments of older creeds not only a new one, but also to endow it with many features of a universal religion. It is the monotheistic basis which secures a prolonged existence to the frail building in spite of many prophecies to the contrary. Never has a people been led more rapidly to civilization, such as it was, than were the Arabs through Islâm. We are not a little indebted to them for the preservation and interpretation of some of the treasures of Hellenic wisdom, but it is very doubtful, whether the Arabs would ever have trodden the paths of science, had they not been forced to do so by the Qorân.

Although Muhammed is the author of the Qorân he did not leave it to his disciples in the form of a book, but in fragments of various lengths on all kinds of writing material. Now the question arises whether he was prevented by death from compiling the revelations into a book, or whether he purposely omitted to do so, preferring to entrust them to the piety and memory of the faithful. The latter appears more probable for several reasons. The amount of the revelations themselves are so frequently styled "Book" in the Qorân that Muhammed seems to have deemed any special arrangement superfluous, and he took no steps to ensure such being made when he felt his death approaching.[16] A more important reason was Muhammed's wish to leave himself freedom to alter or suppress verses which became unsuited to changing circumstances. The advisability of such procedure must — and this is a most striking proof of the systematic manner in which Muhammed acted from the outset — have dawned upon him at a very early epoch, as even in one of the first revelations he inserted a clause alluding to words which Allâh might have caused him to forget.[17] Now this may appear mere cant, if nothing worse, particularly as Muhammed on two other occasions endeavoured to justify his action by special revelations (Q. xvi. 103; ii. 100). Yet if looked at more closely, the liberty which the Prophet reserved to himself of abrogating some revelations in favour of others is so closely connected with one of the fundamental principles of Islâm, that Believers must regard it as a divine institution. The ritual of the Moslim church, following the example of the Christians (*e. g.*, S. Matth. xv. 11), is built upon the rules of *abrogating* and reforming such laws and customs practised by Jews, Christians, and pagan Arabs, as either favoured pagan interests, or were incompatible with the life in Arabia. Of those primarily retained to assist in forming a ritual, many were also eventually abrogated and, from political motives, replaced by others, Muhammed being ignorant of the differences between Biblical precepts and rites, or customs of Rabbinical origin. The explanations Moslim theologians offer for such measures is simply this, that Allâh, when giving precepts to

because it gives everything the general reader requires, and in the most attractive form. The notes attached to it form a valuable appendix. For more critical purposes the Qorân will always have to be read in the original.

[16] See the well known tradition *Shahrast*, p. 11.

[17] *S.* lxxxvii. 6 (see below Ch. III.); xvi. 103; ii. 100. The commentators (Al Baghawi) on the last quoted passage admit that the heathens (Al Beidh. adds: and the Jews) had said that Muhammed one day commanded a thing which he forbade the next day, and commanded the opposite. Sprenger, III. p. xxxvi., only makes weakness of memory and negligence on the part of Muhammed's followers responsible for occasional omissions, but the three verses quoted leave no doubt, that it was done on purpose. See also Bokh. X. 46.

certain peoples, had already made up his mind to abrogate the same after a certain period.[18] The alleviation of the ancient *vendetta*[19] by allowing a fine, the abolishment of the sanctity of the Sabebath, the re-direction of the *Qibla* from Jerusalem to Mecca,[20] the adoption and subsequent revocation of the fast of *Ashûrâ*,[21] are statutes entirely different in origin and gravity, but thus placed on the same level. Of the attitude of the Christians towards such theories no account is to be found, but the objections of the Jews were set at naught by the contention that they had themselves made alterations in the law. The substitution of certain Qoranic verses for others better suited to the circumstances was therefore warranted to some extent by precedent. When reproaching the Jews for altering their law, Muhammed overlooked the fact that this had been done on the basis of tradition with a tendency to make the ritual, if anything, more strict rather than otherwise, while his own *naskh* was chiefly dictated by reasons of policy or unforeseen events. At any rate an acquaintance with the rules of abrogation is incumbent on every Moslim, as it forms a special branch of Qoranic lore.

When the Prophet died the possibility of change in the revelations ceased, and the Moslims were confronted with the necessity of uniting in one volume all they could collect either from the fragments mentioned above. or from their own recollections. When they had accomplished this they found themselves in possession of a tangible Testament — a guide for future generations. The Qorân was the Palladium which accompanied the armies, and it is only necessary to recall the role it played in the battle of Siffin (A. H. 37) between the Khalif Aliy and Muâwiya, the governor of Syria, to recognize its importance. Although the appeal of the latter to the sacred book was vague, and contributed but little to the settlement of the quarrel between the Commander of the Faithful and his lieutenant, which was personal rather than religious, the mere aspect of the Book was sufficient to compel submission even from the head of the state.[22]

The difficulty of interpreting many essential parts of the Qorân was soon apparent. It was written in the vernacular, and frequently styled by the author "Plain Arabic Qorân."[23] This assurance should have been superfluous, if the book had been composed in plain Arabic; yet it is repeated three times. In reality much that is in it is not Arabic[24] at all, and this does not apply to the vocabulary alone.

---

[18] Ibn alNaḥḥâs (died 338 H.), كتاب الناسخ والمنسوخ fol. 1, introduces his work thus: The differences between abrogation (النسخ) and innovation (البدا) consists in the circumstance, that the former restricts people from things that had been lawful before, and permits what had been unlawful, with a view to benefit mankind. It was known to Allâh already at the time of command that He would abrogate it after a certain period. Such was the case with the alteration of the Qibla from Jerusalem to Mecca, further with Qor. lviii, 13, with the law of Sabbath, which was not binding for other nations. — Very minutely and (as Nöldeke has already remarked), in an exaggerating manner, the subject of *naskh* is discussed in *Itqân* (pp. 514 to 527). Al Suyûti distinguishes five questions with several subdivisons, and also mentions the protest of the Jews against it on the ground of its being a *badâ* (p. 515). Similar are the remarks of Ibn Ḥazm on the same subject كتاب الناسخ (ed. Bulaq 1301 together with the تفسير of Jalâlain) II. p. 169: "The *naskh* assumed the character of divine law, as among some branches of Adam's descendants it was considered lawful for a man to marry his sister, and besides this, working on Sabbath was forbidden, but this law is now abrogated by Islâm."

[19] Qor. ii. 173-175.

[20] Qor. ii. 138-9; v. 98.

[21] *Itqân*, 515; 523; Muslim, I. p. 310 *sq*. Urwa describes the *Ashûrâ* as having been observed by the Qoreish, but see Sprenger, III. 53 rem. Muslim, *ibid*. corrects the statement just mentioned saying that the Ashûrâ was a day reverentially kept by the Jews (with another Isnâd see Bokh. ed. Krehl I. 472). According to Ṭabari p. 1287, who mentions no authorities, the Jews celebrated it "in remembrance of the exodus from Egypt." Another instance of *abrogation* with regard to fasting see Qor. ii. 180 *sq*., and Muslim, *ibid*. p. 315.

[22] See Weil, *Geschichte der Chalifen*, I. p. 227.

[23] Not until the narrative period (see ch. V.), but then rather frequently. The oldest passage is xxvi. 195. The phrase occurs particularly often at the beginning of *Sûrâs*, *e. g.*, xliii. 1; xli. 2, 44; xii. 2; xlii. 5, etc. S. xiii. 37 حكما عربيًّا. The definition of Al Ashari (Kit. al Luma'. *Cf.* Spitta, *Al Ashari*, p. 86) p. 126 with regard to Qor. xxxix. 29. قرانًا عربيًّا غير ذي عوج بلسان العرب الأمّيّين "in the undistorted language of the unlearned mass" is orthodox rather than critical. See also *Itq.* pp. 281, 315. The commentaries furnish innumerable cases of the contrary.

[24] *Itq.* p. 315.

If the revelations were delivered in "plain Arabic,"[25] and yet many of them remained unintelligible, this was evidently designed as a further proof of their divine origin. The dogmatic portions in particular continued obscure, owing chiefly to the large number of foreign words and new meanings pressed into service. In many cases sayings, actions, customs, decisions, and even the silence of Muhammed were quoted to suit emergencies, and in this way arose the traditional supplement of the Qorân which is called Sunna, and which is regarded as authoritative by the majority of the Moslim world. Political differences, combined with the formation of religious sects, were productive of views which disagreed even on fundamental doctrines. The following will serve as an instance. In one of the earliest revelations (lxxxv. 21) Muhammed speaks of the "Noble Qorân on a well preserved tablet." Theological controversies arose in connection with this sentence, and one of the most important dealt with the question: was the Qorân created, or was it [an] eternal [attribute]? The orthodox school maintained the latter theory, whilst a class of men with philosophical training — the Mu'tazilites — came to the conclusion that besides Allâh no other eternal Being could exist. They therefore declared the Qorân to be created. This, of course, caused a great stir among those who held that the divine character of the Qorân was impaired by such a theory, and with the aid of the official authorities the latter party ultimately remained victorious. How the supporters of the dogma of the non-creation of the Qorân came to form their theory is well illustrated by an abstract from one of the most popular manuals of Sunnite beliefs, and is as follows[26]: And He whose Highness is great speaks with *one Speech*[27]; this is an attribute [to Him] from eternity; it has nothing to do with letters and sounds. It is [further] an attribute which repudiates silence and bane whilst Allâh the most High speaks with it commanding, prohibiting and narrating; and the Qorân is the *Speech of Allâh not created*,[28] whilst written in our copies, preserved in our hearts,[29] and recited[30] with our tongues, heard with our ears, and is not a [transient] state in this [attribute]." — It is easy to perceive the difficulty experienced in trying to demonstrate philosophically what had already been laid down dogmatically. The Qorân is the *Speech of Allâh*, and this *Speech* is so closely connected with His nature that to declare it an item of creation and consequently perishable seemed to the orthodox school to clash with very essential doctrines of the Qorân which repeatedly asserts the "truth" and "perfection" of the Speech of Allâh.[31]

What makes the dogma of the eternity of the Qorân remarkable is that Abul Ḥasan Al Ash'ari, the man who may be called its father (died 324 H. in Baghdâd), after having been an ardent follower of the Mu'tazilite school, suddenly changed his attitude, and adopted the opposite view.[32] This circumstance as well as the general victory this theory subsequently gained through Al Ghazâli,[33] the greatest genius of Moslim scholastics, shows that it would be rash to stamp the dogma of the non-creation of the Qorân as a mere fad of orthodoxy. In reality there is very little religious feeling

---

[25] مبين *cf.* Sprenger, II. p. 352, *rem.* 2.

[26] Najm'uddin Abu Ḥafs Omar b. Muhammed al Nasafi (1068-1142) ed. W. Cureton, London, 1842, p. 2. The treatise has been translated into English by Prof. Macdonald in the *American Journ. of Semit. Languages and Lit.* Vol. XII. p. 111 *sqq.*

[27] Not "word" as generally translated, which is rather Biblical. *Cf.* Is. xl. 8. See also note II. Al Nasafi's follows here the Asharite doctrine which is vigorously combated by Ibn Ḥazm, Al Milal, f. 151vo.

[28] In order to prevent misunderstandings Sa'd alDin Al Taftazâni (died 721 H.), the commentator of Al Nasafi's work, explains this as follows (fol. 25vo): According to the teachings of the Doctors the Qorân follows the Speech of Allâh. It is to be said 'the Qorân is the Speech of Allâh which (the latter) is not created,' but it must not be said 'the Qorân (itself) is not created,' lest some one might too hastily think that the transport of the Qorân into sounds and letters is without beginning, as the school of Ḥanbal (founder of the most reactionary of the four high schools) assumes . . . . He who says that the Speech (of Allâh) is created, negatives Allâh the Almighty.

[29] With this the words of Ibn Khaldûn (p. 2) must be contrasted. Al Ispahâni in his *Kitâb Muḥâḍarat al'adbâr* (fol. 315ro) says that Omar gave hundred Dinârs to every one who knew the Qorân by heart.

[30] Prof. Macdonald translates: "repeated" which would be مكرر in Arabic; Al Taftazâni has, however, مقروا "read," which is not only much more appropriate, but belongs to the root of قرآن. Still better would be مقرا "confessed."

[31] Qor. vii. 133; xi. 120; x. 36; xl. 6.

[32] See Kremer, *Geschichte der herrsch. Id.* pp. 35 and 128.

[33] *Ibid.* p. 45, Al Ghazali Aqida; *cf.* Iljâm, p. 43.

in it at all, but it is the result of so one-sided and exaggerated a development of the monotheistic idea, that it all but touches the other extreme. Neither is the identification — according to the Asharite doctrine the *juxtaposition* — of the Speech of Allâh the spontaneous outgrowth of Islâm. On the contrary it actually departs from the pure monotheism as preached by Muhammed, and is indeed nothing more or less than the transplantation of the idea of the Logos, which in the earlier centuries of the Christian era caused so much bitter strife within the Church, on Islamic soil. It is quite within the bounds of possibility that Muhammed should have become acquainted with it both in the Jewish and Christian interpretations. By introducing it in the Qorân under not less than *three* names[34] he has shown distinctly how to deal with a hypostasis of the divinity which appeared desirable enough to be introduced as a spiritual constituent of his theology whilst, being but a tool in the hand of Allâh, it could be accorded the rank of a created being.

As a consequence of the exalted origin of the Qorân, Moslim theology has developed the theory of the I'jâz, *viz.*, the esoteric quality of the Qorân to exclude any other being beside Muhammed from being favoured with the power of producing a similar book or even part of it. The theory rests on a series of revelations in which unbelievers both in Mecca and Medina are challenged to show ten or even one *Sûra* like Muhammed's. Since the *I'jâz* of the Qorân is not dependant on the question of its being created or not, all classes of believers hold it as an inviolable dogma, only differing in minor points.[35] Muhammed could safely defy Arabs all round as well as Jews and Christians in Medina and elsewhere to try and preach in exactly the same manner as he, because every would-be imitator was bound to lack either the knowledge or the faculty, or the audacity of mixing up truth with fiction, or the pathos, or was unwilling to acknowledge the conditions upon which the inspiration was based. The Qorân could as little be imitated as Muhammed's individuality which gave it its stamp. He was so conscious of this fact that he could boast (*S.* xvii. 90): "Say, if mankind and *jinn* united together to bring the like of this Qorân, they could not bring the like, though they should back each other up." The more of the Qorân existed, the less fear there was of its being copied, and Muhammed dared therefore, when in Medina, to taunt the Jews with their inability to produce anything similar.[36] The Qorân is unapproachable as regards convincing power, eloquence, and even composition,[37] and this is in so far of great importance for Islâm in general, as it afforded Muhammed the means of pluming himself with a miracle which otherwise was denied to him. A miracle was the one great desire of his life, and the assurance that the Qorân *is* a miracle, is repeated *ad nauseam* through nearly the whole book. Tradition has, it is true, collected a large number of other miracles[38] performed by Muhammed, but none equals the greatest which is the Qorân itself.

The exalted character of the Qorân — very minutely described in the great collections of traditions as well as in other works under the special title "High Qualities of the Qorân" — received its ecclesiastical interpretation in various practical regulations, which not only embrace the manner in which the book is to be treated for liturgical purposes, but extend also over the handling of the copies. A tangible basis for such regulations was given by the Prophet himself in the words (*S.* lvi. 76): "Behold it is a noble Qorân (77) on a well preserved tablet (78), none but the pure may touch it." — Although Muhammed only used these expressions metaphorically, the doctrine of the church took them literally and prohibited persons from touching a copy of the Qorân otherwise than in a state of

[34] See Note II.

[35] See Note III. and above the concluding paragraph in the abstract from Ibn Khaldûn's *Prolegomena*. The various theories on the nature and branches of the Î'jâz are broadly discussed *Itq.* pp. 628 and 744 *sqq.*

[36] Nöldeke, Q. p. 44, overlooks the fact that Muhammed addressed himself also to the Jews who ridiculed the Qorân from other points of view than the pagan Arabs did.

[37] Note Al Ash'ari's, *cf. Shahrast*, p. 75, and Ibn Ḥazm, *l. c.*

[38] Mosl. ii. 204 *sq.* Ibn Ḥ. fol. 122vo; of I. Khald. *ibid.* p. 169, on the nature of the miracle. The Arabic term for the same (المعجزة) is a participle active fem. of the same root and conjugation, of which اعجاز is the infinitive. The word does not occur, however, in the Qorân. To what extent نسخ and اعجاز appeared to outsiders as chief dogmas of Islâm, is shown in Jehûda Hallêvi's *Kit. Alkhazari*, I. par. 5. The Moslim Doctor who speaks there, expounds his faith from the Mu'tazilite point of view (see ed. Hirschfeld, p. 12).

ritual purity.[39] The writing[40] and reading of the Qorân are likewise regulated by strict rules.— According to the Qorân (lxxiii. 4) the reading is to be performed in a chanting manner[41] and a tradition which is, however, not well founded, gives Muhammed's advice to read it with the *I'râb* (*i.e.*, grammatical terminations[42]). To carry the Qorân into an enemy's country,[43] is strictly forbidden; likewise to sell it to an infidel.[44]

We must not be surprised to find the Qorân regarded as the fountain-head of all the sciences.[45] Every subject connected with heaven or earth, human life, commerce and various trades are occasionally touched upon,[46] and this gave rise to the production of numerous monographs forming commentaries on parts of the holy book. In this way the Qorân was responsible for great discussions, and to it was also indirectly due the marvellous development of all branches of science in the Moslim world.—This again not only affected the Arabs but also induced Jewish philosophers[47] to treat metaphysical and religious questions after Arab methods. Finally, the way in which Christian· scholasticism was fertilised by Arabian theosophy need not be further discussed.

Spiritual activity once aroused within the Islamic bounds, was not confined to theological speculations alone. Acquaintance with the philosophical, mathematical,[48] astronomical and medical writings of the Greeks, led to the pursuance of these studies. In the descriptive revelations[49] Muhammed repeatedly calls attention to the movements of the heavenly bodies, as parts of the miracles of Allâh[50] forced into the service of man[51] and therefore *not* to be worshipped.[52] How successfully Moslem peoples of all races pursued the study of astronomy is shown by the fact that for centuries they were its principal supporters. Even now many Arabic names of stars and technical terms are in use. Mediæval astronomers in Europe were pupils of the Arabs, and the last Muhammedan astronomer, who was at the same time one of the greatest,[53] only died about twenty years before the birth of Copernicus.

In the same manner the Qorân gave an impetus to medical studies[54] and recommended the contemplation and study of Nature in general.[55] The very necessity for a better understanding of the Qorân itself impelled Moslems and particularly those who were not natives of Arabia to study its language.[56] Renan[57] has shown that the beginning of linguistic research among the Arabs was

---

39 Mu'aṭṭâ, p. 67. *Cf.* Goldziher, *Zahiriten*, p. 52. 40 Al Nawawi, *Tibyân*, p. 272. 41 *Ibid.* 112.

42 Al Baihaqi from Abu Hureira in منار الحق by Al Ushmûni, p. 15; *Itq.* pp. 266, 879; according to Al Isfahâni, fol. 313ʳᵒ. Abu Bakr recommended the same.

43 Mu'aṭṭâ, p. 153; I. Hzm, fol. 182ʳᵒ, Tibyân, p. 274. 44 Tibyân, *ibid.*

45 *Itq.* 762; *cf.* 769 *sq.* The three chief sciences are احكام, تذكير, توحيد 46 *Itq.* 768.

47 A reflex of the dogma of the اعجاز is also visible in mediæval Jewish poetry. It seems to be a kind of protest against the same, though deprived of its ecclesiastical character, if Jewish poets in Moslim Spain, whilst adopting Arab forms, boast of their ability to imitate the same in Hebrew; see Ḥarîzî, *Taḥkemôni*, Introduction.

48 *Itq.* 767. 49 See Ch. VI.

50 *E. g.*, *S.* xli. 37. Muhammed denounced those who studied astronomy for other than sacred purposes. *Cf. Mishk.* xxi. ch. 3, pt. 4.

51 *Ibid.*

52 *Itq.* 763. *Cf.* Sprenger, III. 531. To judge from the Qorân, Muhammed's ideas of astronomy were those which were current in Arabia at his time, and show at any rate that he did not belong to the unlearned mass. He was acquainted with the retrograde movement of the planets (lxxxi. 5-16). He speaks of the zodiac which he calls by its Greek name *burûj* (πύργοι), *S.* xv. 16; xxv. 62. Of constellations he mentions the Scales (lv. 7): of single stars the Sirius ("the hairy one"), liii 50. This word is an interesting specimen of popular etymology, but see Hommel in *Z. D. M. G.* XLV. p. 597. If the name occurs in pre-Islamic poems, this does not warrant its being "*uralt.*" Muhammed further speaks of the stations of the moon (x. 5; xxxvi. 39), arranged for the calculation of the seasons. The sun runs in a sphere prescribed for him, and is occasionally eclipsed (*ibid.*). According to a tradition related by Bokh. III. 305, Muhammed on the occasion of a total solar eclipse, said that it did not cause the death of any man; yet he recited special prayers during the eclipse, Muslim, i. 246; Tirmidi. (ed. Cairo, 1292) i. 110; *Mishk.* iv. ch. 51. Tradition, of course, makes him a great astronomer. According to Al Baihaqi (*Itq.* 932) Muhammed knew by the aid of Gabriel the names of the stars which Joseph saw in his dream. *Cf. J. Q. R.* X. p. 108.—As to his medical learning see Ch. VIII.

53 Ulugh Beg. 54 *Itq.* 767 with reference to Q. xvi. 71, where honey is mentioned as a medicament.

55 See Ch. VI. 56 *Itq.* 764 *sq.* 57 *Histoire des langues Sémitiques*, Vol. I. p. 378.

due neither to Greek influence nor to that of Syrian Christians. These studies resulted in the production of an unrivalled grammatical and lexicographical literature as immense as it is minutely worked out, and upon which our knowledge of the Arabic language is based. Linguistic pursuits were followed by literary pursuits. — Moslim scholars had the good sense not to allow the treasure of songs which had come down from pre-Islamic times to fall into oblivion, but collected them reverently and accompanied compilations with annotations, most welcome to readers of old poems. Not less important were these endeavours to settle questions connected with the forms from which the poems were composed, and they thus produced a most extensive literature on prosody.[58] For many centuries after, Arabic prosody furnished the forms in which the best productions of mediæval Jewish poetry both in Hebrew and Arabic[59] were written. Even in the development of Arabic poetry itself the Qorân marks a very important phase. In pre-Islamic Arabic short ditties were the recognised medium for conveying public opinion from mouth to mouth. The forms of poetry had become so firmly established in the minds of the people, that even Islâm could not alter them, though it succeeded in revolutionising all else. As regards the theme of the poems, however, the effect was different.

When entering upon his mission, Muhammed could not incline favorably towards poetry. Although conscious of its beauties, its fictitious character and low moral standard clashed with the stern truth in the revelations of Allâh. He also feared the effect of a smart epigram on his cause, and this fear was eventually justified.

We can well believe him, when, on behalf of Allâh, he says that he was not gifted with poetic skill, neither was such talent proper for him.[60] So little, however, could he detach himself from traditional forms,[61] that when he first commenced his addresses, he scarcely did more than drop the metre, whilst observing various standard rules and above all retaining the rhyme. This last habit in particular[62] eventually caused some dogmatic disquietude, as it did not harmonise with the character of the Qorân as an eternal attribute. Ash'arite opinion declared it unlawful to recognise in the Qorân, rhymes in an æsthetic sense, or the so-termed *saj'*.[63] This gave rise to a discussion as to which *saj'* stood for its own sake and which did not, but non-Ash'arites only saw an embellishment of the language. Yet Muhammed did introduce poetic features into the Qorân in the form of comparisons, aphorisms, figures of speech, and parables,[64] but this passed unnoticed, whilst the attention of the faithful was concentrated on the above mentioned theological quibbles. They only noticed the *saj'*, because it was easily seen and very familiar to them. Some anxious ones feared that it might impair the *i'jáz*, since it could be imitated. The *saj'*, moreover, was the form in which the pagan augurs rendered their oracles.[65] Muhammed himself is said to have deprecated the practice in the maxim: "(This is) more *saj'*-like than the *saj'* of the augurs" (or some poetry is like magic).[66] It is not in the least surprising, therefore, that when the Meccans heard him make use of the same form of speech, they took him for an ordinary augur or a poet endowed with little talent and a peculiar madness of his own. He was naturally incensed at being styled a poet, and thus placed on a level with augurs and bards, who sang of foolish and profane things. He protested energetically against these insinuations, declaring that he was neither a poet nor mad.[67] When

[58] See Brockelmann, *Geschichte dar Arab. Literatur*, p. 100 *sqq*.

[59] Apart from the poems composed by Arab Jews before and at the period of Islâm, many were written in Arabic by later Jewish poets. The Jews in all Arabic speaking countries have composed innumerable liturgical poems in the vernacular as late as the 17th century.

[60] See Qor. xxxvi. 69 and the commentaries, and Nöldeke, *ibid.* p. 28 *sqq*. Tradition attributes two verses to Muhammed which he is said to have composed in a battle when his toe was slightly wounded, as follows:—

Thou art but a toe that bleeds
And thou didst suffer in the fight of Allâh. — *Mishk.* ii. p. 401.

According to other traditions he praised the poems of Labîd, whom he nevertheless condemned to hell. He is said to have been very partial to the verses of Omayya b. abi-l Ṣalt. Traditions on the subject are collected by Sprenger, I. 110 *sqq*.

[61] *E.g.*, ذرني "let me." *S.* lxxiii. 11; lxxiv. 11; lxviii. 44. See Ch. III.

[62] On the influence of the rhyme on the composition of revelations see Nöldeke, *ib.* p. 30.

[63] *Itq.* 695 *sq.* [64] See Ch. VIII. [65] *Itq.* 697.

[66] *Mishk.* ii. 422. [67] See Ch. III.

he had acquired some secular power, however, and could count among the believers a poet although not an eminent one, he was wise enough not only to abstain from reviling such bards, but to employ their talents on his own behalf. He provided new themes for them, which by their novelty contrasted favorably with the worn out burdens of the heathen songs, although lacking their grace and charm. They impressed many by their moral sentiments, rather than by their artistic merits, but as they appeared at an opportune moment, the effect was considerable. Moslim traditionists relate a good deal about poetic competitions which took place, and from which, of course, the Muhammedan bards emerged victorious. Although discretion must be used in dealing with these reports, yet it is quite intelligible that elegant verses on hackneyed themes might be supplanted by others less graceful, but composed for the glorification of Allâh, and real or imaginary self-sacrifice in the service of his prophet. Their strength lay in their idealism, though the proportion of this may have been but small.

Muhammed thus inaugurated a new era in the songs of the Arabs, and became indirectly the father of Arabic sacred poetry, which boasts of more than a few fine compositions. Great and small events, which concerned the Moslim community, were immortalised in verse, and although not all of these are authentic or of great poetic value, they have no slight claim on our interest. Entire phrases are borrowed from the Qorân. This being the case not only in the verses of Ka'b b. Zuheir[68] and the Medinian Ḥassân b. Thâbit[69] and many others[70] but even in the celebrated and glowing panegyric the "Burda" of AlBuṣîri,[71] written six hundred years afterwards. The following few quotations from this poem show how thoroughly it is impregnated with the spirit as well as with the language of the Qorân:

> "How many an impetuous opponent in dispute about Muhammed have the words of Allâh overpowered, and how many an ardent litigant has been convinced by his evidence.
>
> Regard as satisfactory signs[72] that the Ignorant at the time of universal nescience[73] possessed knowledge, and also that he acquired education in the desolate age.
>
> I have devoted to him this poem of praise in the hope of obtaining forgiveness for the sins of a life spent in writing songs and courting the great."

Although the Moslim liturgy, in contradistinction to the Jewish and Christian prayers, did not lend itself to the chanting of songs during service,[74] the Burda is looked upon as inspired by the

---

[68] The famous poem styled after its beginning بانت سعاد has frequently been printed, lastly in Nöldeke-Müller, *Delectus*, p. 110. *Cf.* Brockelmann, *l. c.* p. 39.

[69] The best part of the polemical poetry of early Islâm was attributed to Ḥassân, who was made its chief representative, although many poems handed down under his name are of doubtful authenticity. I reproduce one of these poems in translation, because its language is in such close touch with the diction of the later portions of the Qorân, that Ḥassân, provided he is the author, could only have composed it in his declining years. The song runs as follows (Diwân, ed. Tunis, p. 23):—

> He (Allâh) has crowned him with glory in order to exalt him; yea, the *Occupant of the Throne* is praised, but this one is extolled (*Muhammed*).
>
> A *prophet* is come to us after we had lost hope in the long absence of messengers, whilst idols were worshipped on earth.
>
> He is a brilliant, guiding light, and shines like a polished sword from India.
>
> He has *warned* us against the *fire of hell*, and has *promised paradise*, and taught us [the doctrines of] *Islâm* now we praise Allâh.
>
> And thou art the God of creation, *my Lord and Creator*; this I will declare as long as I live among men.
>
> Thou art extolled, Lord of mankind, above the praise of those who worship other gods beside thee; thou art the highest and most revered.
>
> Thy nature is benevolence, and omnipotence, to thee we pray for *guidance and thee we serve.*
>
> For Allâh's recompense, for every one who adores Him alone, is the shelter of Paradise where he shall live eternally.

The last verse but one contains an almost literal quotation from Q. i. 4. — A versification of the tenets of Islâm by Muh. b. Al Ḥasan Al Shaibâni (died 189 H.) is without poetic value. The work exists in numerous MSS. and has been printed, Cairo, 1863.

[70] See *Delectus*, pp. 3, 4, 18 *sq.*, 51 *sq.*, etc.

[71] Ed. Rahlfs, Vienna, 1860, vv. 138-140 (p. 16-17).

[72] *Cf.* chapters IV. to VI.

[73] On the term *jâhiliyya* see Goldziher, *Muhammadan. Studien*, p. 219 *sq.*

[74] See *Salâḥ Al Mu'min* by Al Ḥâfiz Taqî aldîn Muḥ b. Tâj aldîn fol. 2ro: "What is told of the Prophet's objection to rhymed prayers." As to the prohibition to regard the Qorân as work of poetry even with respect to *saj'*, see *Itq.* 195 *sq.*

Prophet himself, and the reading of it is recommended as a means of salvation. This naturally applies with even more force to the study of the Qorân itself, whilst to copy it or to write a commentary on it, is, according to orthodox tradition, a sure passport to Paradise. The religious motive coupled with the necessity of clearly understanding the Qorân proved an important factor in the development of an immense literature treating of every imaginable point connected with it. Besides commentaries on the whole book or portions of it, representing every shade of theological or sectarian doctrine, there exist glossaries, works on orthography, and on the art of writing and reading the Qorân. In one of the earliest revelations,[75] Muhammed is told that *ease* should be granted to him.[76] From the expression used for this word *(nuyassiruka)* the title of a work is derived, which is styled "Book of facilitating the cognizance of the seven fashions of reading the Qorân" by Abû Omar Othmân Al Dâni.[77] The Qorân was supposed to have been revealed in the dialect of the clan of the Qoreish of which Muhammed was a member; yet believers of other tribes allowed idioms to creep in, which subsequently led to friction. To rectify this Muhammed is said to have declared that the Qorân was revealed to him in seven readings,[78] and the believers were to recite it in the easiest manner. It need hardly be mentioned that there is nothing real in the number seven, whilst it is intelligible that the various Moslim tribes differed as to the pronunciation of many words or changed expressions used by Muhammed for idioms of their own.

It was, however, necessary to dogmatise the "seven readings" in order to bring them into harmony with the nature of the Qorân as the "Speech of Allâh." From the linguistic point of view it is regrettable that the practice of reading the Qorân in sundry dialects had to be abandoned. The Khalifa Othmân was obliged to settle this question in so radical a manner, that by cancelling all other readings, except the Qoreishite, the difficulties of dialect were abolished for ever; but whilst promoting religious unity he did away with a most important medium for our enlightenment on the problem of old Arabic dialects.

To the Qorân we also indirectly owe an immense literature of biographies of Muhammed, as well as of his contemporaries, but many of these works are distinguished by religious zeal rather than by trustworthiness. The same may be said of numerous works of tradition (Ḥadîth), and evolving from the latter, Muhammedan history in general.

It need hardly be demonstrated that the spread of the art of writing throughout the Moslim world is also greatly due to the Qorân. Though writing was not unknown in Mecca before Islâm, it was only practised by a few of the more enlightened, such as Waraqa, the cousin of Muhammed, who had embraced Christianity, and had copied parts of the New Testament in Hebrew square characters.[79] Among modern authors on Muhammed the opinions as to his ability to write are divided. Within the Moslim world it is regarded as heresy to assert that he was able to write. This rests on a late Meccan revelation which refutes a charge made by unbelievers that Muhammed preached from notes dictated to him every day.[80] His reply was that the revelations were miracles, but a little later he added that he was "not able to read *before*, nor to write." This is as good as an admission, and from the same we may safely conclude that he *could* read and write. To learn the Hebrew characters was not very difficult, and it is highly probable that he made himself acquainted with them when travelling in Syria. It is, however, an established fact that Muhammed was able to write in Medina, though not very fluently, but it is hardly credible that he should

[75] lxxxvii. 8. [76] Repeated liv. 17, 32, 40, v. (16 and) 17 omitted in Palmer's translation.

[77] Died 444 H., see de Sacy, *Not. et Extr.* Vol. VIII. p. 292 *sqq.* On *taisîr* see *Itq.* 515, as subdivision of *naskh*

[78] See Bokh. III. 394 *sq.*, tradition according to two different authorities. — *Cf.* Nöldeke, Q. p. 39. Lane translates "dialects." *Itq.* p. 113 enumerates thirty-five methods of explaining them.

[79] Bokh. III. 5, 380. Sprenger, I. 128, is to be corrected into *bil'ibrâniyyati*. I. I. 121 only says that Waraqa *read* books (قد تتبع الكتب).

[80] Q. xxv. 6; xxix. 47. Both passages belong to the latest Meccan revelations (legislative period). *Cf.* Sprenger, II. 377 rem., *Ibid.* pp. 398-402, the question whether Muhammed was able to write is discussed with the assistance of traditions bearing on the question. Sprenger is convinced that Muhammed was an expert penman, but he is surely mistaken that the initials of *S.* xix. — or any others — belong to Muhammed (see ch. XIII.).

only have learnt it when over fifty years old. Apart from the traditions dealing with the matter it appears to me that the disfigurement of many Biblical names and words mentioned in the Qorân is due to misreadings in his own notes made with unskilful hand.[61] Finally he encouraged the art of writing by decreeing that I. O. Us. and bills of sale should be given in writing, according to what "Allâh has taught."[62] Muhammed himself appointed Zeid I. Thâbit to act as his secretary, and controlled all revelations and letters which Zeid wrote down on his behalf. The oldest ("Cufic") copies of the Qorân which we possess are indeed written in characters of very primitive shape so that they are difficult to read without practice. Arabic penmanship, however, speedily improved and there are now few alphabets which rival Arabic in elegance and neatness. Now the settling of the Mâsôrâ of the official text (the language of which was considered classical in every respect) was another and a very strong inducement to make linguistic investigations, and thus, from whichever point of view we look at the book, we see how irresistibly it has drawn an intelligent nation along the channels of civilization. Arab culture and learning represent the bright side of the Middle Ages. On the other hand it must be said that there is so much conservatism in the teachings of the Qorân, and it is besides so clearly stamped with the individuality of its author, that it must necessarily deter Moslims from reaping the full benefit of modern European education. This is, however, beyond the sphere of the present observations which only endeavour to sketch in outline the significance of the Qorân in the world's literature. Everything connected with it causes it to outstep the limits of a religious Testament of one nation or creed, and the interests we have to follow in dealing with it critically, are as manifold as are the ties which link us directly or indirectly with the Islâmic world. Our sciences, our languages, certain terms used in daily life show more Arabic and also Qoranic words than the world at large is aware of. The person of Muhammed himself forms the focus of several universal proverbs.

There is yet another reason which makes the Qorân appear familiar to its readers, *viz.*, its close relationship to the Bible. It is that ancient book which speaks through the mouth of the "Seal of the Prophets." With all his shortcomings he has *mutatis mutandis* something of the self-abnegation and enthusiasm of the Prophets of the Old Testament. If one reads the addresses of the Qorân, particularly those of the later *Sûras*, at every word one is tempted to say: this is Biblical. Still one must be careful not to make such a statement indiscriminately. Thus much is certain that, before entering upon his first ministry, Muhammed had undergone what I should like to call a course of Biblical training. This, of course, did not consist of systematic study nor regular instruction from teachers, but was much rather from gathering here and there sayings, tales, prescriptions, warnings, laws, morals, and parables, and supported by occasional notes gleaned by stealth and learned in seclusion. Clothed, then, in Arabic speech, adapted to the views, customs, and wants of the country the originals of the revelations are frequently hidden beyond recognition. This autodidactical method of studying accounts for nearly all the peculiarities of the Qorân. It influenced Muhammed's ideas and affected his style. The Qorân thus betrays Biblical colouring even in those portions, in which Muhammed expressed views which were undoubtedly original, or when he promulgated laws, which grew out of the incidents of the day.

In dealing with so delicate a subject it is not easy always to find the narrow path of truth, and to keep from attributing too much or too little to the man who was one of the greatest reformers of all ages.

## APPENDIX TO CHAPTER I.

### Note I. — Islâm.

Sprenger (*Leben M.'s* I. p. 69; III. p. 500) endeavours to identify the term *Islâm* with the faith of the *Ḥanîfs*, although a sect bearing this name, and possessing a holy book styled *Suḥuf* never

[61] See above rem. 6. Sûra written in square characters סורה could easily be misread from סדרה. The name of Kôrah is in the Qorân *Qârûn* קרון misread from קרח which is all the more possible as ח was written ר"ר (see Mishna Sabbath xii. 5); פרשן in a similar way misread from פרשה; גלות for גלית. See Al Tha'alibi, Cod. Brit. Mus. Add. 9558, fol. 63[vo]. راس الجالوت الجالوت راس اليهود

[62] Q. ii. 282-283, the art of writing thus emanating from Allâh, *cf.* xcvi. 4; xxiv. 33.

existed. Some modern Muhammedan authors, imbued with Western ideas, seem to dislike the time-honoured explanation of *Islâm*. Thus Syed Ameer Ali (*Life and Teachings of M.* p. 226) renders *Islâm* by "striving after righteousness." This translation is seemingly well founded, since it is supported by a rather old passage in the Qorân (*S.* lxxii. 14): "And that[83] of us are some who are Moslims, and of us are some who transgress, but those who are Moslims[84] (*faman 'aslama*), they strive after righteousness."

The learned author's definition, however, only reflects the theoretical and moral side of the question, which is limited to the initial stage of Islâm. If we follow up the development of the term Islâm in the Qorân, we find that it gradually assumed a practical meaning which was eventually retained by the Moslim church. In Meccan revelations *Islâm* only occurs once, *viz.*, xxxix. 23: "He whose breast Allâh has expanded for *Islâm*, is in a light [issuing] from his Lord, but woe unto those who harden their hearts, etc." Again in connection with "expanding the breast" *Islâm* appears for the second time in the Medinian revelation, vi. 125, but it gradually becomes more and more exacting. In *S.* iii. 17 (*cf.* v. 79) *Islâm* is identified with *dîn* (*cf.* lxi. 7-9), and the relation between these two synonyms is broadly discussed by Al Shahrastâni, *Milal*, pp. 25-27, and is stated to embrace the five duties, *viz.*, of testifying to the Unity of God and the divine inspiration of Muhammed, the duties of reciting prayers, giving alms, fasting in the Ramadhân, and performing the pilgrimage to Mecca. — It is quite natural that during Muhammed's life-time *Islâm* already comprised the whole of the theoretical and practical constitution of the faith, since the violation of one of its branches implied disobedience which the Prophet himself denounced as tantamount to disbelief. His own final definition of *Islâm* is laid down in one of the deuteronomic revelations (*Sûra* v. 5, "the verse of the *dîn*") as follows: "To-day I have perfected for you your *dîn* and fulfilled upon you my favour, and am pleased for you to have *Islâm* for religion (*dîn*)." — It would be preposterous to limit *Islâm* here solely to the moral code, standing as it does surrounded by ritual precepts. The official interpretation given to the term by the orthodox church is unmistakeably laid down in the following exposition by Al Ghazâli (*Iḥyâ 'ulûm aldîn*, I. p. 104): *Islâm* is an expression for *submission* and unquestioning obedience, abandonment of insubordination, defiance and opposition. The special seat of firm belief (*taṣdîq*) is in the heart, the tongue being its interpreter. In contradistinction to this *taslîm* engages heart, tongue and limbs in general, so that every *taṣdîq* with the heart becomes *taslîm*, connected with abandonment of defiance and denial. The same applies to the acknowledgment [of Allâh and His Prophet] by the tongue, or unconditional obedience of the different parts of the body. When compared as synonyms, *Islâm* is in general what *Îmân* (belief) is in particular. *Îmân* expresses the loftier components of *Islâm*, consequently every *taṣdîq* is *taslîm*, but not *vice versâ*." Al Shahrastâni (see above) constructs the following climax: *Islâm*, *Îmân*, *Iḥsân* ("Serve Allâh in such a manner, as if thou see Him, but although thou do not see Him, He sees thee, *ibid.*)."

The difference prevailing between religious observance (*Islâm*) and theoretical faith (*Îmân*) has been very clearly expressed by Muhammed himself, who placed the former above the latter, although theologians declared that *Islâm* only led up to Faith. Muhammed, however, was a man of the world, and knew human nature better than these theorists. He insisted on practice and said (xlix. 14): The Bedouins say: We believe! speak: you shall not "believe [only]," but say: we practice *Islâm* (*aslamnâ*); the *Îmân* has not entered yet into your hearts, but if you obey Allâh and His Messenger, He will not defraud you of your works at all, etc. (15) The Believers (*almûminûn*) are only those who believe in Allâh and His Messengers; they are free from doubt, and fight vigorously by [offering] their wealth and persons for the [war] path of Allâh, these are the truth tellers.

In thus emphasizing the practice of the law in contrast to the expressions of faith pure and simple, Muhammed followed a Rabbinic principle which is very tersely given in Abôth, I. 16: It is not the

83 Palmer translates "and verily," which is, however, inaccurate, because the text has *anna*, but not *inna*.

84 "Moslims" are opposed to "sinners" in the still older passage, lxviii. 35.

study [of the law] which is most important, but the practice thereof (*cf.* iii. 9). — Finally see the articles in the *Dictionary of Technical Terms*, ed. Sprenger, I. p. 64 *(îmân)*, p. 696 *(islâm)*.

### Note II. — The Terms for Logos in the Qorân.

On examination of Muhammed's conception of the Logos (*cf. Sûra* v. 19 ; 76-77), it will be found that his interpretation of the term came much nearer the Philonian idea that the Logos was an intermediary between God and the world than to any other. In this character the Logos appears in the Jewish Targûms as well as in the Talmud under the two expressions *mêmrâ* and *dibbûr*[*â*].[85] The former is frequently met with already in Onqelos, *e. g.*, Gen. iii. 8, *qâl mêmrâ* ; *ibid.* xv. 1, as translation of *ânôkhî*, and is radically cognate to *amr* which represents the oldest form of the Logos in the Qorân. In earlier *Sûras* (lxxix. 5 ; lxxxii. 19, etc.) *amr* occurs in its original meanings of command, and affair respectively. This meaning it retains without any reference to God at all (xxvi. 151), even after it had assumed the individual character of Logos. This, however, did not take place until the narrative period. Thus in *S.* li. 44 ; xvii. 87 ; xviii. 48, *amru rabbî* forms the exact translation of *mêmrâ d'adônay*.

As to *dibbûr*[*â*] it is according to Talmudic view that of which angels were created, *e.g.*, Ḥagîgâ 14ʳᵒ : "From every *dibbûr* which came out of the mouth of God an angel was created." — In the so-called Fragmentary Targûm *dibbûr* frequently represents the Logos, *e. g.*, Gen. xxviii. 10 ; Numb. v. 89, etc. With this we have to compare a definition of *amr* given in the Qorân (xvii. 87) : They shall ask thee about the *rûḥ* : Say, the Spirit *(arrûḥ)* is part of the *amr* of my Lord.[86] Further (*S.* xvi. 2) : He sends down the *angels* with the Spirit [which is part] of His *amr* (*cf.* xl. 15 ; xcvii. 4-5). In later *Sûras* Muhammed endeavoured to counteract any foreign influence on the question of the Logos, and tried to reduce the *amr* to the rank of a created being, *e.g.*, *Sûra* liv. 49 : Verily everything have we created by appointment *(qadr)*, so our *amr* is but due like the twinkling of an eye (*cf.* ch. VIII.).

Of particular significance is a passage in *Sûra* xix. in which the *rûḥ* (v. 17) is dispatched to Mary to announce the birth of a son. He allays her anxiety with the assurance that the boy shall be (v. 21) "a Sign unto man, and a mercy from us (Allâh), and it is an ordained *amr*" (*cf.* v. 36). In other passages the *amr* of Allâh is "done" (viii. 43 ; xxxiii. 37) or "measured" (*ibid.* v. 38). The more familiar Muhammed became with the *amr*, the more he made use of it for his private ends. So in the last named passage it is merely a permission given by Allâh to Muhammed to marry the divorced wife of his adopted son, and to abolish an ancient heathen custom which forbade such marriage. A complete lecture on the *amr* is *Sûra* lxv., in which the term occurs not less than eight times. Man has no influence on the *amr* (iii. 123),[87] because it is entirely under the control of Allâh (*ibid.* v. 148).

On the ground of these and other revelations (see also x. 3, 32 ; xii. 21 ; lxv. 1, 3) the Zahirite school taught that the *amr* was created (Ibn Ḥazm, *Kitâb almilal wal niḥal*, Cod. Brit. Mus. Or. 842, fol. 166ʳᵒ) in contradistinction to the Asharite doctrine which inculcated the belief in its eternity (Ibn Ḥazm, *ibid.*, Al Shahrastâni, *l. c.* p. 67). Otherwise the Spirit which is part of the *amr* (see above) must also be eternal, an axiom with which no Móslim would agree. According to later eschatological views the *amr* dwells *on* the throne of (or next to) Allâh, whilst the *'ilm*[88] *(i. e., dîn)* has its place beneath it. See the pseudonymous book *Kitâb masâil alnabiy* attributed to Abd Allâhb. Salâm, p. 11. See also Sprenger, *Dictionary*, etc., p. 68. The Sûfi conception of *amr* does not concern us here.

---

[85] *Cf.* Grimme, *Muhammed*, II. p. 51.

[86] See Lactantius, Div. Inst. (ed. Brandt, p. 226) : *Nam sermo est spiritus cum voce aliquid significante prolatus.* — *Cf.* Baur, *Christl. Lehre von der Dreieinigkeit*, I, 92 : "*Der πνεῦμα ist dem Logos untergeordnet.*"

[87] The verse is said to have been written when Muhammed lay wounded on the battle field of Uḥud. *Cf.* I. I: p. 571.

[88] Γνῶσις. *Cf.* Epiphanius Haer. ed. Dindorf, II. p. 49. (Anz, *Urspr. d. Gnosticism.* p. 20 *sq.*) On the various interpretations of *'ilm* by Moslim theologians see Ibn Ḥazm, *l. c.* fol. 143 *sqq.*

Another rendering of *dibbûr* (or *dibb'râh*) in the Qorân is *kalima*. It is used in the same combination as *amr*, *viz.*, "the *kalima* of thy Lord has been fulfilled (*Sûra* vi. 115; vii. 133; xi. 133; xxix. 20, 71; xl. 6, etc.), or "the *kalima* of Allâh," the "*kalima* of punishment" is fulfilled (x. 34, 96; xxxix. 20, 71). "Were the trees that are on the earth pens, and the sea [ink, *cf. Sûra* xviii. 109] with seven more seas to swell its tide, the *kalimas* of Allâh would not be spent (*Sûra* xxxi. 26)." "Abraham made it a lasting *kalima* among his posterity (*Sûra* xliii. 27) and was tried with *kalimas* (*Sûra* ii. 118)." — Whether these verses stand in some connection with Gen. xv. 1 or not, is difficult to say. Of greater importance is the statement that the *kalima* of Allâh cannot be altered (*Sûra* vi. 34, 115; x. 65; xviii. 26; xli. 45), because this refers to one of the chief reproaches made to the Jews, *viz.*, that they altered the law. If the "illiterate Prophet believes in Allâh and His *kalimas*," this should be a stimulus for others to do likewise (*Sûra* vii. 158). The following (Medinian) passage (xlviii. 26, *cf.* ix. 40) has a strong Jewish colouring: Allâh has set down His *sakîna* upon this Messenger and upon the Faithful, and enjoined them the *kalima* of piety. *Kalima* has here the meaning of Hebr. *dib'brâ* as also in the (likewise Medinian) passage iii. 57, where a brief abstract of the Decalogue (Exod. xxxiv. 28, *assêreth hadd'bârîm*) is given. — The *kalima* goes forth from Allâh as a judgment in *Sûra* x. 20; xi. 120; xx. 129; xxxvii. 171; xli. 45, xlii. 13. (*Cf.* v. 20.)

Muhammed was well aware that the term Logos was applied to Jesus. In the Medinian repetition of the tale of Jesus' birth he therefore says *kalima* instead of "ordained *amr*" (see above) but allows angels (here plural) to announce to Mary from Allâh a *kalima*, whose name is the Messiah Jesus (*Sûra* iii. 40). Perhaps Muhammed was now less apprehensive of evil resulting from such a statement, or else he desired to exhibit his learning. He, however, cautiously repeated that Jesus is "the Messenger of Allâh and His *kalima* which He has thrown upon Mary, and the *rûḥ* is part of it," thus manifesting the identity of *kalima* and *amr* (see above and *Sûra* iii. 34; lxvi. 12).

In order to avoid misunderstanding Ibn Ḥazm here again points out that the *kalima* is a created being, and that Jesus is a *kalima* in this sense only (fol. 183vo). To discuss all passages in which the *kalima* is used in the Qorân, would lead us too far, especially as the word is also employed in the quite usual sense of "word" (*Sûra* xiv. 29, 31; xxxv. 11).

*Kalâm* differs from *kalima* in so far as it occurs in Meccan revelations but once (vii. 141) in the signification of "speech," and represents the distinction conferred upon Moses (Exod. xxx. 11). The *kalâm* is *heard*, and on several occasions persons endeavoured to "alter" it (*Sûra* ii. 70; ix. 6; xlviii. 15, *cf.* iv. 48). In Moslim theology it is not the *kalima*, but the *kalâm* which forms the object of discussion between those who declare it to be created or the contrary. This is in so far correct as *kalâm* (speech) includes the *kalima* (word). See also Sprenger, *Dict.* pp. 1267-8.

Still more frequently than any of the terms for Word or Speech mentioned occurs *almilla*, which is, as has long been known, derived from the Aramaic *meltâ*. The manner in which Muhammed treated this word is very significant. He owed his knowledge of the same solely to Christian sources, since the Jews did not employ it for Logos, but only for "word" or "thing." As we shall presently see, however, Muhammed seems to have heard a similarly sounding term from the Jews, and mixed the two up. There is a marked difference in the Qorân between *milla* on one side, and *amr* and *kalima* on the other, since the former is generalized to signify "religion" which is never the case with the latter. The term was so common in Arabia, that even the pagan Arabs styled their religion *milla* (*Sûra* xxxviii. 6[89]; vii. 86, 87; xiv. 16; xviii. 19), and was, probably through Christian Arabs, also brought into Mecca prior to the birth of Islâm. In the majority of cases *milla* stands in connection with Abraham, both in Meccan and (still more) in Medinian revelations, in order to express the monotheistic belief of the Patriarch. This is to be explained either by means of Gen. xv. 1, 4 (see above) or possibly with the help of the ordination of circumcision (ch. xvii.), for which the Rabbinic term is *milâh*, whilst the Arabs used quite a different

[89] "The last religion," *viz.*, that of the pagan Arabs. Palmer translates wrongly: "any other creed."

word for it. Now the orthographies *milâh* and *milla*, when written in Hebrew square characters, so closely approach each other, that an interchange is quite easy. This was still furthered by the circumstance, that in unvocalized texts *millâ* is frequently spelled *plene*, and probably this was the case in the oldest copies of the Mishnâ and Talmûd. I give this all, however, as a mere suggestion with due reserve. — As is well known *milla* is used later on in various titles of famous works on the history of religions in the same sense ; see also Sprenger, *l. c.* p. 1346.

## Note III. — Ibn Ḥazm on the I'jâz of the Qorân (Milal, fol. 187vo. *sqq.*).

The following is an abstract from the chapter on the *I'jâz* (miraculous character) of the Qorân in Ibn Ḥazm's work on "Religious and philosophical sects." He sets down *five* points of controversy.

1. Asharite doctrine teaches that the divinity of the Qorân — on the level of which men strive to place something similar — is to all eternity with Allâh. It is inseparable from him, has never been revealed to us, nor have we ever heard it (*cf.* Al Shahrastâni, p. 75, Ibn Khaldûn, *Prolegom.* p. 169 on *taḥaddi*). — To this Ibn Ḥazm opposes that according to Asharite theory the Qorân, when being recited, is not *mu'jiz* (transcendent), and can only be qualified by itself. This view is entirely heterodox, because it stands in contrast to Qor. x. 39 ; xi. 16. What Al Asharî defines as *mu'jiz* in the Speech of Allâh, is not expressed in *Sûras*, but it is a unity which Ibn Ḥazm has endeavoured to disprove prior to this chapter.[90]

2. The question whether the *i'jâz* is eternal or terminated after its existence had been established through the life of Muhammed is answered by Ibn Ḥazm who refers the readers to Qor. xvii. 90. It is there laid down that neither mortals nor spirits shall ever be able to produce anything similar to it.

3. Some scholastics *(ahlu-l-kalâm)* maintain the transcendent character of the *contents* of the Qorân only, but deny this quality to its composition. Ibn Ḥazm upholds the view of those who consider the one as transcendent as the other. Qor. ii. 21 speaks of such revelations [which infidels are challenged to bring] in which no allusion is made to things unseen [and which therefore must be taken for granted, *cf.* Qor. ii. 2]. Nothing must be declared miraculous in opposition to what Allâh has decreed to be so.

4. The manner of the *i'jâz* represents according to one opinion the highest degree of impressiveness. Others see in it the inability of mortals to produce anything similar to the Qorân. This the latter class endeavours to demonstrate to the former with the aid of Qor. ii. 175.

Ibn Ḥazm argues on this point as follows: *(a)* If the *I'jâz* were based on nothing but its impressiveness, it would be on a par with other human productions which occupy the same rank, but the "Signs" of Allâh go beyond the common. — *(b)* Allâh cannot be asked what He does nor why He does a thing. He can therefore not be asked why He has rendered only *this* composition of the Qorân transcendent, and has sent *this* prophet and no other person. *(c)* It is absurd to say that if the *i'jâz* included all languages, there would be no difference between Arabs and [Moslims of] foreign nations as to the knowledge of the same. Foreigners, in fact, only learn of the *i'jâz* through communication made to them by Arabs. To say that Qor. ii. 175 and other verses of the same kind have no demonstrative power is heresy. By picking out such verses and omitting others the opponents endeavour to shew that the Qorân is transcendent only in part. One must, in reply to this, put to them the question, whether the [other] revealed books, of which the Qorân speaks (iv. 161) are likewise transcendent [and warning] against evil and wickedness. If they admit this, they speak the truth, but they must not confuse up elegance of style with warnings against evil and wickedness. Furthermore, if the miraculous character of the Qorân consisted merely in its impressive diction,[91] it would be on the same level as Al Ḥasan, Sahl b. Hârûn, Al Jâḥiz, Ibn al Muqni' and the poetry of Imru'ulqeis. Were the *i'jâz* dependent on loftiness of style [alone], this must also become visible in any portion of a verse which [is only the case with the Qorân, and therefore] is sufficient to upset their opinion, that there are

[90] Fol. 131vo. The Asharite doctrine that the Speech of Allâh is a unity, *cf.* Goldziher, *die Zahiriten*, p. 140.
[91] *Cf.* Qor. xxiv. 53, *albalâgh almubîn*.

at least three verses required in order to be miraculous. If verses like xvii. 94-95 were spoken by a mortal being, no Moslim would take them as miraculous, whilst Allâh has made them so by rendering them part of his own Speech.

5. As regards the compress of the *i'jâz*, the Asharites have fixed it to be like unto the smallest *Sûra*, *viz.*, cviii. (3 verses), below which, according to Qor. ii. 21, no *i'jâz* takes place. All other Moslims believe that even the smallest particle of the Qorân is miraculous, because the verse ii. 21 does not refer to quantity, but to kind. Since every part of the Qorân is Qorân, it shares its miraculous nature.

Ibn Ḥazm concludes his remarks on the subject as follows: The truth of the matter is expressed in Qor. xvii. 90, from which we must gather that every sentence in the Qorân which conveys a meaning, is miraculous, and cannot be imitated in all eternity. For the last *four hundred and forty years* men have been unable to imitate the Qorân. An instance of double interpretation of a passage is given in *Sûra* xix. 65-66.[92] The purport of these verses is out of connection both with the preceding and following passages, each having a separate meaning. To this the various degrees of ordinary human eloquence cannot be applied. The style of the Qorân is neither that of orators, nor writers, preachers, or authors. Passages of the same character (as the just mentioned) are in the Qorân many, and make it convincingly clear that it is utterly unwarrantable to measure the Qorân by way of human eloquence.

## CHAPTER II.

### The First Proclamation.

Text and origin of the same — Legends on the *iqra*-verse — Muhammed's mental condition — [Swedenborg and Kant] — Metaphysical elements in the Qorân — Muhammed's methodical manner — The alleged Mentor — The Baḥîra legend analysed — Period of preparation — Parable of the lamp — Development of the formulas of Unification — Exegesis of the *iqra*-verse.

Note.—The legend of the cleansing of the heart.

In the summer of the year 612 of our era — Moslim tradition relates — a man was frequently to be seen roaming restlessly through the deserted environs of Mecca, a prey to mental disquietude. This figure still remains shrouded in mystery because of the mass of legends surrounding it. We do not know his name, although we are acquainted with those of his parents, his wife, and relatives, but we call him Muhammed, which is only anticipating an appellation adopted by him many years later. Nor are we able to state with certainty, why he left his home and family, and spent his time in the solitude of the desert. A day came when he ended his musings and uttered the following words:—

*Sûra* xcvi., v. 1. *Proclaim* the name of thy Lord who has created,
2. Has created man from congealed blood,
3. *Proclaim*, while thy Lord is the Most High,
4. Who has taught the use of the pen,[93]
5. Taught man that which he knew not.

These verses form the first part of a chapter of the Qorân which, according to the unanimous verdict of the traditionists, is the first prophetic utterance of Muhammed. No real historic proof, however, exists for it, and the truth is only vouched for by the Prophet himself, and, on his authority, by Âisha, his second wife, who was not born at that time. From their narrative which was written down many years afterwards, we must assume that no other person was present, when Muhammed proclaimed his first revelation. As the account of the incident, on which it is based, has been frequently printed, a very brief abstract of the same will here suffice.

[92] See the *Commentaries* and *Sûra* lxv. 12.

[93] May also be translated: *by means of the pen*. The phrase is, however, explained in *S.* ii. 282, that Allâh has taught man to write, see Ch. I.

"During my sojourn on mount Ḥira, said the Prophet, the archangel Gabriel appeared to me, seized me, and said: *Iqra* (proclaim!). I replied: I am no proclaimer (reader).[94] The angel seized me again and repeated: *Iqra*. I said: I am no proclaimer. Finally he forced me to say: *Iqra' bismi rabbika*."

The authenticity of this tradition has not been questioned even by many modern scholars, though it evidently referred to a dream.[95] This view, however, although shared by the late E. H. Palmer, in his otherwise excellent translation of the Qorân, and by Sir William Muir, one of the latest and best of Muḥammed's biographers, requires some modification even according to the interpretation of the last named two scholars. The name of the angel Gabriel is not mentioned in any Meccan revelation at all, and was, at that period, apparently unknown to Muḥammed. The composition of the miraculous tale could, therefore, not have been made till more than ten years later in Medina, when the author's recollection of the circumstances under which he made his first proclamation was largely supplemented by his imagination.

I did not translate the word *iqra'* in my rendering of the legend, although I translated it in the verse by *proclaim*, my object being to call attention to the early misunderstanding of the word by traditionists and interpreters of the Qorân as well, as by modern translators and biographers[96] of the Prophet. For the sentence in question is nothing but an Arabic version of the phrase in the Pentateuch (Gen. xii. 8 in connection with iv. 26), "He proclaimed the name of the Lord."[97]

The reduction of the first verse in the Qorân to a phrase frequently occurring in the Pentateuch[98] makes matters more simple at once. When Muhammed uttered these words, he had already broken with the past, because revocation was impossible without for ever forfeiting prophetic claims. They also throw a light on his mysterious conduct prior to the first proclamation. The view was, and is still generally held that the time spent by Muhammed on mount Ḥira was chiefly passed in mental anguish caused by his contrasting monotheistic with polytheistic dogmas, and striving to find the truth. He is represented as a nervous and excitable man, suffering from hallucinations and epileptic fits.[99] Sprenger in particular, who will always be considered one of the most important and comprehensive

---

[94] The term قارئ can only be translated by *reader*, which is sufficient evidence for the lateness of the tradition, as well as the ignorance of the real meaning of *iqra'*. Muhammed evidently only gave the nucleus of the tale, which was handed down in the form given to it by 'Âisha or 'Urwa. In order to justify the alleged "reading," already I. Isḥ. p. 151, speaks of a silk scarf which was brought by Gabriel, and on which the words of the first proclamation were embroidered In the account given by Bokh. I. 4, Muhammed is not named as authority of the tradition at all. Instead of Gabriel, 'Âisha only mentions "an angel." This version seems to represent the oldest form of the tradition, although in the older work of I. Isḥ. a younger one is recorded. Much more elaborate is the version of Tabari, 1449 *sq*. Here Gabriel addresses the Prophet by the name *Muhammed*. The kernel of the tale: *he pressed me*, varies in the sundry traditions, *viz*., Bokh. فغطني, I. Isḥ. and Tabari, فغتني, and in the version on Abd Allâh b. Shaddâd we find فغمني. Other expressions are quoted by Sprenger, I. p. 298; the traditions are to be found *ibid*. p. 330 *sqq*.—When relating the adventure to his friends, Muhammed used the word *taḥannuth* to describe the condition in which he was, when the angel appeared to him. The term has caused the traditionists some embarrassment. I. Isḥ. explains it by *taḥannuf* (to profess to be a Ḥanîf), and adds a remark which is interesting from a linguistic point of view, *viz*., that *th* and *f* interchange in Arabic. This remark is welcomed with satisfaction by Sprenger, who finds it a support of his *Hanyferei*. I believe, however, that *taḥannuth* is nothing but the Hebrew pluralis *t'ḥinnôth*, "prayers," a word very common among Jews to express voluntary devotions apart from the official liturgy. There is little doubt, that Muhammed heard this word often in Medina before he framed his report of the affair, and employed it readily on account of its strange and sacred character. Nöldeke, *Qor*. p. 67, seems inclined to give to the root حنث the meaning of "leading a solitary life" (see also Lane, *s. v.*), but if this were so, the traditionists would have little difficulty in explaining the word, whilst the signification they give it is derived from the spirit of the tradition to which it belongs.

[95] Unanimously characterized as such by I. Isḥ., Baghawi, Beidh., Tab., etc.

[96] Weil, Sprenger, Muir, Palmer, Krehl, Rückert, and all modern translators except Nöldeke, *l. c.* p. 65, who rightly translates: *Predige!*

[97] See my *Beiträge zur Erkl. des Q.* p. 6.

[98] Gen. iv. 26; xiii. 4; xxi. 33; xxvi. 25, and altogether frequent in the O. T.

[99] Weil, Sprenger, Muir, Palmer, etc.

biographers of the Prophet, endeavours to explain the prophetic mission of the latter from the point of view of mental sanity, and this theory he repeats in his last contribution on the subject.[100] He is inclined to identify religious mania with prophetism, especially in reference to Muhammed. The term "enthusiast," indeed, describes a man possessed by a divine spirit, and in this sense it is applied to the Biblical prophets. An enthusiast may at times perform extraordinary deeds, and by his example, rouse others to similar actions, but only under given conditions, and when carried away by strong feelings. All Biblical prophets, Moses not excepted, took their stand on ancient monotheistic traditions, and gave forth teachings as well as warnings against wickedness, immorality, and especially against relapse into idolatry. It is impossible to create a new faith out of nothing, and least of all could a mere fanatic accomplish such a task. Sprenger's description of Muhammed's behaviour during the time of his mental struggle is pathological rather than historical, but he is surely mistaken in attributing a larger share in the creation of Islâm to the state of his nerves than was really due to them. Hallucinations and hysterical frenzy are not factors strong enough to produce so general an upheaval as was caused by this new faith. The examples cited by Sprenger[1] only demonstrate the experiences of a few hysterical women who made insignificant statements concerning their persons alone, but this cannot be compared with the gigantic results of Muhammed's religious revelations. Sprenger further refers at great length to Swedenborg,[2] who, as is well known, asserted that he was favoured by God, and endowed with the faculty of conversing with angels and spirits. We will not enter here into details of Swedenborg's mission, but we cannot refrain from asking what he has really produced with the exception of various societies bearing his name, and which certainly count but little in the general enlightenment of the world. The principal outcome of his intercourse with the spiritual world is his *Arcana cœlestia*, which Kant describes as *Acht Quartbände voll Unsinn*, and which was also the origin of the same philosopher's famous treatise *Träume eines Geistersehers*, the perusal of which is to be recommended to every student of Muhammed's career.

To those dissatisfied with Kant's evidence I offer the experiences of another sufferer from hallucinations and visions, *viz.*, the literary bookseller, Friedrich Nicolai, in Berlin. This man, whom no one will charge with having created either a spiritual or a religious revolution, read before the Academy of Sciences in Berlin an essay styled *Beispiel einer Erscheinung mehrerer Phantasmen.*[3] The description he gave of the way in which absent persons appeared to him greatly resembles those of Swedenborg. Defunct persons appeared to him, he became exhausted, and after some time fell asleep (p. 12). Several weeks after the first apparition he heard those persons speak (p. 18). Whilst undergoing medical treatment the room seemed full of human forms of all kinds moving about, and these became more and more indistinct, till they disappeared entirely (p. 19). But Nicolai was "*von Geistern wie vom Geist curirt*" by so trivial a method, that to make any comparison between his case and Muhammed's, as Sprenger undertakes,[4] impossible. Islâm is not built on phantasmagoria, otherwise a simple but utterly prosaic remedy[5] might have deprived the world of one of the greatest spiritual and social revolutions on record.

No, Muhammed's case is quite different. The first revelation possesses too much of the metaphysical element to be the mere outpouring of a troubled mind and an hysterical constitution. On the other hand no one will assert that Islâm was brought into existence by the aid of metaphysical speculation. Whence came this idea? "He who has created" is nothing more or less than the Creator referred to in Genesis. Here as well as in the Qorân the existence of God is a postulate, as it must be in a revealed religion, and a demonstration to this effect would have been as injurious as it was beyond Muhammed's power. The belief in Allâh existed in Arabia long before Islâm, but side by side with the belief in other deities. It was, however, necessary to demonstrate his Unity, and this Muhammed endeavoured to do twice with a certain amount of logic, although not until some years later (*S.* xxiii. 93): Allâh neither had a son nor was there any god with Him; if this were so

[100] *Mohammed u. der Korân, eine psychologische Studie*, Hamburg, 1889, p. 8 *sq.* [1] I. p. 215 *sqq.*

[2] *Ibid.* 275 *sqq.* Sprenger even considers the profuse perspiration, from which Swedenborg used to suffer after a nervous attack as a parallel to Muhammed's condition.

[3] Berlin, 1799. [4] *Ibid.* p. 215. [5] See the *Walpurgisnacht* in Goethe's *Faust*.

*each god would go off with what he had created, and some would have exalted themselves above others, etc.*" When concluding the same speech he repeated (v. 117), "Who worships another god beside Allâh has no proof for doing so."[6] And finally he says (*S.* xxi. 22): "Were there in both (heaven and earth) gods beside Allâh they would do mischief."[7]

We thus see that the first proclamation speaking of the "Lord" and "Creator" contains a complete theological system. The imperative form in which the revelations is expressed tends to convince the hearers that the tenet of the proclamation is not the result of speculation, but of divine inspiration granted to Muhammed to the exclusion of other individuals. With regard to simplicity he even outrivals the Bible, commencing as he does with the creation of man, whilst the formation of the rest of Nature, which was more complicated to describe, was left for later occasions.[8] This was certainly a methodical way of proceeding. Muhammed would, however, have been unable to act in such a manner, had he not been far beyond the elements of learning.

Now we have still to collate the foregoing remarks with the traditions that Muhammed was subject to nervous fits. There is no need to deny this fact, but it chiefly applies to his younger years When the Prophet promulgated the first revelation, he had more than attained the ripe age of forty years, an age when the nerves generally become calmer. On the other hand he was a man of great self-control. The mental struggle which marked the period immediately preceding Islâm, and is described by all writers on the subject as a series of epileptic fits, was not a cause but a consequence which will be fully explained if we examine the circumstances with attention. His mind being far above those of his countrymen, is it possible that he could have rushed blindly into an adventurous life? There were many things to be taken into account, each in itself sufficient to arouse him to excitement. He was of the family of the Qoreish, who not only represented the nobility of Mecca, but were also guardians of the national sanctuary of the Ka'ba. Would they, he must have debated, suffer the shrine to be attacked, damaging alike their authority and material interest? Even if he succeeded in overcoming this difficulty, would the rest of tribes submit to the demolition of their time-honoured deities? Such misgivings were sufficient to fill him with no small anxiety, and these were not all. Whoever seemed willing to acknowledge the new mission had to be made welcome, and no difference could be made between high or low, or between freeborn or slaves. It is quite possible that Muhammed himself did not immediately realise all the consequences, which the racial revolution he was about to create, might have, but he must have expected to win his first followers from the ranks of those who had nothing to lose. The benefit of salvation could not be denied even to the poorest. As an example of the levelling power of Islâm I repeat the well known anecdote connected with one of the oldest addresses of the Qorân. While one day conversing with some of the Qoreish chieftains, the Prophet was accosted by a poor blind man,[9] who, the tradition says, asked for religious guidance. Muhammed turned angrily away, refusing to be disturbed. Although the man was evidently only a beggar, Muhammed not only saw the blunder he had made, but also that this was a good opportunity of advertising the new faith. He, therefore, on the spot extemporized an address (*S.* lxxx.) in which he reprimanded himself for being harsh to a blind man who might perhaps have wished to become a believer. The ad dress teaches the equality of mankind. Man is born, consumes food, and dies; the believers are happy, the infidels go to hell. Since, however, the social institutions of Mecca

[6] There is nothing to deprive Muhammed of the ownership of this argument, but it appears that he had learnt it from some Christian source. His protest against the dogma of the Trinity speaks in favour rather than against the probability of his having borrowed the argument, as he regarded the beliefs in Allâh side by side with belief in the Hypostatic Union as illogical, and endeavoured to correct it. As to a somewhat similar Christian proof of the Unity see Lactantius (ed. Brandt.) Inst. Div. I. 3 (p. 8): *At si plures partiantur orbem, minus certe opum, minus virium singuli habebunt; cum intra praescriptam portionem se quisque contineat. Eodem etiam modo Dii, si plures sint, minus valebunt, aliis tantumdem in se habentibus.*

[7] *Itq.* 765 quotes this verse as a proof that the Qorân contains the principles of Moslim scholasticism.

[8] See Ch. VI.

[9] Tradition calls him Ibn Umm Maktûm of Fihr, but Nöldeke, *Q.* p. 76, has already rightly suggested that this name stands for the traditional Moslim pauper in general. If the person alluded to in the revelation was really a member of the Fihr family, Muhammed had an additional reason to appease him. Ibn Ḥazm, fol. 335[vo], takes pain o defend Muhammed's conduct in this affair.

were anything but democratic, the idea of having to proclaim theories so distasteful to the haughty Qoreish must have filled Muhammed with grave apprehensions.

Various biographers of Muhammed, principally Weil and Sprenger, provide him with a mentor, who secretly instructed and encouraged him in hours of despondency. Sprenger in particular believes this mentor to have been an Abyssinian Presbyter of Jewish descent, but Christian persuasion and an adherent of celibacy.[10] In spite of the various characteristics with which Sprenger endows this individual, he seems rather uncertain on the matter. At one time he regards him as a believer in Muhammed's mission, whilst professing theological tenets of his own,[11] another time he and the Prophet are like "the two augurs" who unite to form in honour of Allâh a regular *Gründercomplott.*[12]

Sprenger also furnishes us with the name of this mentor whom he believes to be no other than Baḥira the monk, author of the *Ṣuḥuf*, by which he endeavoured to make proselytes to his views in the Ḥijâz.[13]

We can at once dismiss the idea that Baḥirâ is the author of the *Ṣuḥuf*, because such a book did not exist, save in the imagination of Muhammed, who employed the term to describe the Pentateuch at times, and at others the heavenly book in which the fates of men are inscribed. On the other hand Baḥirâ forms the centre of a circle of legends of which Sprenger has given a complete compilation,[14] but they allow no conclusion to be drawn that this person acted as Muhammed's tutor, as the following analysis will show.

Three strata are to be distinguished in these legends. In the *first*, told by Ibn Isḥâq (p. 115) Muhammed, when twelve years old, is taken to Boṣrâ in Syria. There the caravan meets the hermit Baḥira, who — against his former custom — prepares a meal for the travellers. They all partake of it, excepting the young Muhammed *who is left with the luggage.* On missing him, Baḥira insists on his being fetched, recognises in him a prophet, and discovers a *seal of prophecy, between his shoulders.* In the *second* version, given by Ibn Sa'd, Muhammed was twenty-five years old when the journey was undertaken. He rests with a companion under a tree in the neighbourhood of the cell of a hermit of the name of Nestor, who asks the companion after "the young man *under the tree*," and enquires whether he has a certain *redness in his eyes.* The question being answered in the affirmative, the hermit cries out: "This is the last of the prophets." — The *third* version which does not refer to any particular age of Muhammed, describes the journey to Syria, during which the travellers meet the hermit, whose name is not disclosed. Trees and stones bow to Muhammed, and the *Râhib* (monk) exclaims that he recognises *the seal of prophecy between his shoulders in the shape of an apple.*[15]

The elements from which the legends have been developed can now be traced with certainty. To be brief, they represent homilies on several Biblical passages which have become mixed up. Both the first two turn on 1 Sam. xvi. 2-13. The boy David who is left in the field to tend the sheep, while his brothers are brought before the Prophet, but who is fetched at the request of the latter, corresponds to the boy Muhammed left behind with the luggage. Baḥira's enquiry as to *the redness in his eyes* is only a misapplication of the words (v. 12) "he was *ruddy*, fair of *eyes*," and even the repast prepared by Baḥira is a reflex of the sacrifice to which Samuel invites Jesse and his family. It may not be superfluous to remark that the term *bâḥar* ("has chosen")[16] occurs three times (vv. 9, 10. 11) in the report of the proceedings. With this we must connect Ps. lxxviii. 10, lxxxiv. 4, 20, where the word *b'ḥirî*, whilst referring to David, gives a clue to the meaning of the name *Baḥirâ*.

[10] *Muh. and Kor.* p. 54 *sq.* [11] *Leben und Lehre*, II. p. 365 *sq.* [12] *Muh. and Kor.* p. 58.

[13] II. p. 367. [14] I. 178-83.

[15] In the version of I. I. p. 115, the form of the seal was like the mark made by capping glasses, but the scholia add that it had the shape of an apple. The use of capping glasses was so common among Arabs that their employment as a simile is quite natural. The traditions on the subject are collected in *Uyûn alâthâr*, Brit. Mus. Or. 3015, fol. 17ᵛᵒ *sqq.*

[16] *Qor.* ii. 248 with regard to Sau : Allâh has chosen him (اصطفاه).

It is conspicuous enough that Baḥîra plays the part of Samuel in 1 Sam. xvi. 1-13. Although the name of this prophet is not mentioned in the Qorân, and it is uncertain whether Muhammed knew of him, we can see in the *Iqra'*-legend that at least one episode of his career is reflected in Moslim tradition. The circumstance that persons and sayings are mixed up without the least discrimination, far from being strange, is characteristic of the method employed by the author of the homilies. And that we have to deal here with one author only, is to be concluded from the fact, that the legends of *iqra'*, the Cleansing of the Heart, and Baḥîra have several important elements in common.

Now as to the *seal* in the shape of an apple and the trees that bowed to Muhammed, they are a homiletic application of the verse Cant. viii. 5-6: "Under the *apple tree* have I awakened thee . . . . Set me as a seal upon thine *heart*, as a *seal* upon *thine arm.*" With this we have to connect Ḥaggai, ii. 23: "I will make thee a *seal* for I have chosen *(bâḥarti)* thee."[17] Lastly the situation of the seal between the shoulders is a reflex of Deut. xxxiii. 12: "He covereth him all day long, and he dwelleth *between his shoulders.*" This verse refers to the tribe of Benjamin, and the Talmud (Zebâḥ. 37vo) builds a homily upon it connected with the circumstance that, although small and wedged in the province of Judah, the territory of Benjamin gave shelter to the Temple. It must be borne in mind that the term *shakhên* ("dwelleth") furnishes the allusion to the *Shekinâ*, and in one version of the legend of the cleansing of the heart Muhammed says: "They washed my heart, and the one asked the other for the *Shekinâ* which was white. They put it in my heart, sewed my body up, *and pressed the seal of prophecy between my shoulders.*"

A literal application of the verses quoted cannot be expected, but their common bearing on the legend is unmistakeable. The name Baḥîrâ is thus nothing but the personification of the (New) Hebrew term bḥîrâ ("Election") which is quite common. Now Muhammed was acquainted with several verses in the O. T. in which the form *b'ḥîr* ("chosen") is used in reference to Israel (Is. xlv. 4), "my servant" (*ib.* xlii. 1).[18] Moses (Ps. cvi. 23) as can be seen from *Qor.* vii. 141; xxvii. 60 (*cf.* xxxv. 29; xliv. 31). The Arabic translation of *b'ḥîr* is *almuṣṭafâ*, one of Muhammed's names. He is himself the *Baḥîrâ*, just as the *seal*, which was supposed to have been a mark on his body, was subsequently used — as described in the verse of Haggai quoted above — to denote his whole personality. He is therefore the Seal of prophecy himself.

The hermit Baḥîrâ thus disappears from history, although Sprenger[19] regards him as historical whilst treating Nestor as a mythical person. According to my opinion Muhammed's interview with the latter, which Sir W. Muir rejects as "puerile,"[20] was a real fact. The hermit Nestor was a Nestorian Christian whom Muhammed had met somewhere in Syria and who had probably tried to convince him of the truth of his religious views. We shall see on a later occasion, that Muhammed, whilst unconditionally rejecting Eutychianism, was less hostile to Nestorian ideas which he adapted to Islâm as well as his conscience allowed him. Muhammed's discussion with the Nestorian recluse was not without consequences, and to him the former owed part of his knowledge of Christian Scripture and doctrines.

But who is the author of the legend or rather of the homilies of which it is composed? Since the Syriac version of the quotations referred to above do not contain *bḥîrâ* or any other form of that root, Christian origin is improbable. A Jewish source only remains, and, indeed, we find a homily on the verses of Canticles and Ḥaggai quoted before *(Shîr hashshîrîm rabbâ)*, the main features of which seem to have been known to Muhammed himself, since they are reflected in the Qorân. He relates in several places (ii. 60, 87; iv. 153, i. vii. 170) that when revealing the Law to Israel, God lifted the mountain over their heads. This the Midrâsh expresses *(l. c.)* they

[17] Refers to Zerubbabel, a descendant of David, Ḥaggai, i. 1.

[18] *Cf.* St. Matth. xii. 8, "my servant whom I have chosen, my beloved." In the Syriac version to all the passages quoted the word *b'ḥîr* is not used, because the root has a different meaning altogether.

[19] *Cf.* ii. 384. The etymology of *Baḥîra* on the basis of Q. V. 102 is obviously futile. The existence of other persons of the same name (one of them a Jew, *ib.* p. 387) is supported by unreliable evidence.

[20] *Life of Mahomet*, 4th ed. p. 20.

stood *under the apple (tree)* and said: we will do and be obedient (Exod. xxiv. 7; *cf.* Deut. v. 24). Both these themes are discussed in *Qor.* ii. 87 (*cf.* 285 and often), and the second was, as we shall see later on, misinterpreted by Muhammed into: "We have heard and are disobedient."[21] Now all these passages were revealed in Medina, from which we conclude that the material from which they were composed had come to Muhammed's knowledge from Jews. The phrase "under the tree" had a special attraction for Muhammed, who always loved to express himself in poetic figures. When discussing the allegiance sworn to him by all his followers at Ḥudaibiya (in the year 7 H.) he only speaks of his standing "under the tree (*Qor.* xlviii. 18),"[22] a position peculiar to prophets. "For out of the tree" Moses is called (*Qor.* xxviii. 30), and "under the tree" Abraham prepared the repast for his celestial visitors (Gen. xviii. 8) just as Baḥîrâ did for the travellers.

As we now see the Baḥîra legend represents a profusion of Biblical ideas blended together in a manner similar to the Jewish Agâda. There is, however, another point which occurs in various versions of the legend, *viz.*, the tree casting its shadow wherever Muhammed sat. This situation is described, Cant. ii. 3, where we find the *apple tree*, the sitting under its shadow, and the word *ḥimmadti* in which it should not be difficult now to recognize the embryo of the name *Muhammed*, the roots *ḤMD* and *BḤR* being in some degree synonymous in Hebrew (see Ezek. xxiii. 6, 12, 23) the former makes an appropriate rendition in Arabic for the latter which has quite a different meaning.[23] From this we may conclude that the time when the Prophet assumed the name *Muhammed* coincides with that when the first elements of the Baḥîrâ legend were produced, which can only have been very shortly before his death. The name Muhammed, it is true, occurs several times in the Qorân, but there are grave doubts as to the genuineness of the verses in question which we will discuss later on.[24]

Now as regards the author of the legend, it can only have been one of those Jews who embraced Islâm during Muhammed's lifetime. Out of the list of these converts there is only one whose knowledge of the Jewish Agâda was extensive enough to enable him to produce this kind of Moslim variation. This was Abd Allâh b. Salâm of the tribe of the B. Qainoqâ who did not embrace Islâm until the year 8 H., or two years before the death of Muhammed.[25] The latter was during this period so fully occupied in extending the secular as well as the spiritual power of the faith, and so little trained to produce homilies of this kind, that we can hardly tax him with having contributed more than scraps from his autobiography, which Abd Allâh idealised in the composite manner of the Agâda. But even the latter will hardly have given more than the simplest form of the legend. It is remarkable that Ibn Isḥâq, who is the first to relate it, hands it down without mentioning any authority, and with the very vague introduction: "they assert." From this we can only gather that the author of the legend launched it anonymously among the Believers, probably because at his time there were some persons alive who were acquainted with the events of Muhammed's earlier life, and it was not until the following generation, that the homily assumed its various fantastic forms.

A more direct proof of the author of the legend having been a renegade Jew may be found in the warning Baḥîrâ gives Muhammed's friends to beware of the Jews, who would endeavour to injure him. If the conversation Muhammed had with the Nestorian divine is really historical, this would also explain why the chief part is played by a Christian, *i. e.*, a follower of a monotheistic faith. Tradition says nothing of open attacks of Christians on Muhammed, on the contrary, it was a Christian, Muhammed's cousin Waraqa, who is supposed to have encouraged his prophetic claims.[26] The attitude of the Jews, however, was different from the outset, and it was therefore impossible to make them speak favourably of their arch enemy.

[21] See Ch. IX.

[22] See Ch. XII

[23] *Cf.* further for בחר 2 Sam. xxi. 6 (Saul), Ps. cvi. 23 (Moses) for מחמד Ex. xxiv. 16; Hos. ix. 16: Lam. ii. 4. Dan. ix. 23, x. 11, 19.

[24] See Ch. XIII.

[25] See Iṣâba and *J. Q. R.* Vol. X. p. 111.

[26] This is the reason why in some traditions Waraqa is confounded with a Baḥîra. The Iṣâba *(s. v. Addâs)*; relates on the authority of Ibn Abbâs that Khadîja heard of Muhammed's call from Baḥîra, and went to ask him about Gabriel; *cf.* Sprenger, II. p. 386.

The name Baḥîrâ must be struck out of the list of the teachers of the Prophet on account of its mythological character. I believe that the charge made against the latter and reproduced in various revelations (xvi. 105; xxv. 5)[27] of having employed teachers in Mecca, far from being embarrassing, was not unwelcome to Muhammed. It gave him an opportunity of leading his accusers off the track, and throwing the suspicion on persons whom no one would otherwise have thought capable of having assisted him in his studies. His remarks in replying to the charge, that his alleged teachers spoke in a foreign tongue, is explained by AlBeidhâwi with good reason as referring to Greek,[28] because the term *ajam* could not be used in speaking either of Jews or Christians within the Peninsula. The learning which those men — whose names can be seen in Al-Beidhâwi's annotations to the passage of the *Qorân* quoted above[29] — could have imparted to Muhammed, can only have been limited to Christian lore. No one will assert that this was much spread among laymen, and how much could the artisans living in slavery know? Add to this the difficulty of meeting Muhammed in secrecy, and there remains very little to justify the probability of a teacher in or near Mecca. It is unreasonable to assume that a conscientious teacher would have been content to remain in the background, whilst allowing his knowledge and talents to be used by a person of inferior faculties, who according to Sprenger not only frequently misunderstood his words, and misinterpreted his statements, but had to be corrected on more than one occasion. Is it probable that the Mentor knew the learning he imparted and the aims he fostered to be safe in Muhammed's keeping, whilst he was satisfied with an ideal success alone? Did such a man ever live? It is more likely that, if the supposed Mentor concealed his identity, he did so in order to escape unpleasant consequences in case of failure; he would then have been but a miserable coward and incapable of the high idealism which marks Muhammed's exertions in the Meccan period.

Now I consider it very improbable that a mentor of any kind *could* have remained unknown in a place like Mecca. Muhammed was also much too independent a character to be a party to such a policy, or to rely on one single instructor. And how awkwardly would so complicated an oracle have worked! The passages in the *Qorân* referring to earthly teachers — "other people"[30] — were not revealed until the descriptive period, *i. e.*, in the eighth or ninth year of Muhammed's ministry, when the greater part of the Meccan portion of the *Qorân* had already been divulged.

From whichever point of view we regard the alleged Meccan tutor, there is no evidence for his existence. Muhammed knew his cue before he appeared on the stage, but the difficulty lay in the circumstance that he could not summon up courage to speak. That he did so at length, being fully aware of the consequences, is a sign of greatness, but what a struggle must it have cost him! In Mecca he could neither learn anything, nor did he wish to do so. The first revelations must have existed in his mind long before the moment he clothed them in words, and there is little doubt that he not only already knew stories of ancient prophets, but also held a series of practical precepts in readiness. Elements of both are to be found in the oldest revelations.[31] He never expected the

[27] Those passages of the *Qorân*, in which the charges of employing a prompter are refuted, form the chief source for critical analysis of the Mentor. In xxv. 5 it is "other people who help him," and in xvi. 105 it is "a man who teaches him." See the *Commentaries*.

[28] One might apply the term *ajam* to the Greek words occurring in the *Qorân*; but it is doubtful whether Muhammed asked for instruction about these.

[29] *Cf.* Sprenger, II. p. 388.

[30] See also I. I. p. 260. The — hardly unfounded — charge made by Al Nadhr b. Al Ḥârith who narrated the Meccans' stories of Persian heroes has been dealt with in Ch. I. Of some inte[illegible]t is the tradition related by I. I. who refers *Q.* xiii. 29 to the insinuation of employing a prompter of the [illegible]ame *Raḥmân* of Yamâma, who according to Bagh. is indentical with Museilima, a rival to Muhammed. The [illegible]ter's reply هوربى had in this case better be translated in Rabbinical fashion: "He (*viz.*, God) is my teacher," [illegible]oreover, the verse must be a late Medinian one, as indeed it is considered to be by Qatâda, Muqâtil, and Ibn [illegible]j who refer it to the treaty of Ḥodeibiya. Al Baghawi, however, refutes this theory and declares the verse [illegible] Meccan, and no allusion is to be found in it to a teacher. *Cf.* Bokh. III. 382.

[31] See above.

inhabitants of Mecca to be willing at a moment's notice to exchange their very sociable gods—gods satisfied with scant reverence, and not even objecting to an occasional chastisement, for a stern incomprehensible Deity. The new God, they heard, would not submit to disrespectful treatment, but demanded unconditional obedience.

If Muhammed was cognizant of the careers of Biblical prophets, he must have been tempted to compare his own position with theirs. This was particularly the case with Abraham and Moses. The former he called *Ḥanîf*, which does not mean, as Sprenger asserts,[32] the follower of a sect, but a man who holds heterodox views regarding certain ecclesiastical matters. This was precisely the attitude which Muhammed wished to adopt. He proclaimed his secession from the paternal gods in the same words, which the Bible attributes to the Patriarch. On the other hand his refusal to "read" in the legend mentioned before, is in every word an almost literal imitation of Moses' hesitation to undertake his mission. Moses too had been "chosen" in the solitude of the desert, but, as Muhammed was well aware, by means of a vision, besides which Moses was also enabled to perform certain miracles. Muhammed greatly missed the aid he would have derived from such factors. As far as the vision[33] was concerned, he vaguely alluded in an early revelation to some apparition in which a *tree* plays a part;[34] but to perform miracles was quite beyond his power. This made his position particularly unpleasant. When later on sceptics demanded miracles, he could only give evasive answers which counted for nothing. The foreboding of this dilemma must have troubled him considerably.

There is yet another point to be taken into consideration. Professor Palmer has raised the question why Muhammed did not act as an apostle[35] of Judaism or Christianity. This question may be simplified by another, why he himself did not embrace either of these faiths, as so many others had done. His own relative, Waraqa, we are told, adopted that course, apparently meeting with no protest on the part of any leading Meccan citizen.[36] I believe his influence on Muhammed should not be overrated, since the latter was his superior both in talent and knowledge. Now had Muhammed followed the example of his cousin, no Meccan would have interfered with him, but it was impossible for him to do so. Muhammed seems to have looked upon Judaism as well as Christianity as degenerated forms of pure Abrahamism. The superficial conversion of other Arabs he could not imitate, and the dogma of the Trinity never appealed to him. We shall presently perceive that his ideas about the development of both Judaism and Christianity were anything but clear, and did not gain in lucidity in the course of time. This becomes apparent from a revelation pronounced many years later in Medina, when he endeavoured to define the difference between Abrahamism on one side and Judaism and Christianity on the other in the following words (iii. 60): Abraham was neither a Jew nor a Christian, but a faithful *Ḥanîf*, and did not belong to those who ascribe to Allâh a companion. — The verse forms the summing up of the many preceding ones, in which Abraham is described as protesting solely against the idolatry of his family and compatriots, but not as the adherent of any dogma or ritual except the worship of one God.

Now Muhammed entertained peculiar ideas on the origin of the Jews, being unaware of the fact that they connected themselves historically with the "Sons of Israel." He saw in them only the representatives of a ritual code which, on account of its severity, was not at

[32] I. p. 45 *sqq.*, but see p. 68, the explanation on behalf of Ibn Abbâs. Beidhâwi on *Q.* ii. 129; xxii. 32; xcviii. 4. Of Meccan revelations *Ḥanîf* only occurs in vi. 79, 162; x. 105; xvi. 121, 124; xxx. 29.

[33] *Q.* xx. 8 *sqq.*; xxviii. 6.

[34] *Q.* liii. 7 to 15.

[35] Muhammed certainly assumed the role of an "Apostle" of a very high standard. The term *rasûlu-(l-lâhi)* is after all nothing but a rendition of Aram. *sh'lîḥâ*. To the Apostles, however, he gives no higher rank than الحواريون (iii. 45), because he looked upon their master as a human being, whilst he claimed to be sent by Allâh himself.

[36] See *Commentaries* on xcvi. 1 and the traditions. Religious tolerance — or rather indifference — was so great in Mecca, that no one interfered with Waraqa, when he embraced Christianity, especially as he did not try and make converts. Moslim theologians are indeed a little embarrassed about his not having acknowledged Muhammed's mission, but they excuse him on account of age and blindness. *Cf.* Bokh. I. 4.

all to his taste. Being likewise ignorant of the character of the name *Yahúd*,[37] he gave it an Arabic etymology signifying that they were *repenting*[38] for some iniquity committed by them at some previous epoch of their history, for which they suffered exile and were "cursed" by Allâh.[39] He, therefore, altered the name from its verbal form into *allad̲îna hâdû*, "those who repented," or *Hûd*[40] of similar signification. All these names are not once mentioned in the whole Meccan portion of the *Qorân*, which only means that the Jews as such did not come under Muhammed's consideration until he lived amongst them in Medina. The *Banû Isrâîl*, on the other hand, represent in his eyes but a historical remembrance; they are the people to whom God has shown His grace and sent down to them "the Book" through Moses. They disappear at the time of Jesus. In Medinian revelations, therefore, they are only mentioned either in historical passages, or in connection with Jesus (iii. 43; v. 15, 82, 110; lxi. 6, 14), whilst the first and second destructions of the Jewish State are alluded to in a Meccan revelation (xvii. 2-9).

If Muhammed's notions with regard to the ancestors of the Jews of his era were rather confused, and he shrank from adopting their strict ritual law, there were two additional reasons for his dislike. He charged them with having falsified the *Tôrâh*[41] and with having relapsed into a kind of heathenish practice by offering divine reverence to the Rabbis. What he meant by the first reproach is hard to say, as he did not express himself distinctly enough on the subject. The truth seems to be that in this case also he was not able to explain the nature of the accusation in question, or rather he could bring no evidence to bear out the reproach hurled already in Meccan revelations against "the Possessors of the Writ." We will, therefore, try and do it for him, as he was not sufficiently versed in the history of Rabbinical doctrine to grasp the development it had undergone. It is to be noted that the reproach of having falsified the *Tôrâh* occurs several times in the *Qorân* in connection with the laws regarding the Sabbath. As we shall see, Muhammed seems to have considered the institution of the day of rest as a punishment for disobedience.[42] The practical observation of this command, however, as well as others did not tally with what he knew about them from the meagre information he had received of the Pentateuch. Moreover, he had probably heard the Jews pronounce many word, in the *Tôrâh*, and the name of God in particular, differently from the way they were spelt. Finally when travelling through Jewish communities and visiting a *Midrâsh* he may have listened to lectures in which plays upon words of the text and Agadic applications of verses of the Bible struck him as distortions of the holy word. Yet he entirely overlooked the fact that when reproducing Biblical tales in the legendary garb in which they had been imparted to him, he not only adapted the same method of the Agâda himself, but indirectly produced a similar literature of which we have illustrative samples in the legends of the "cleansing of the heart"[43] and the monk Baḥira. The second charge we shall discuss later on.

Under these circumstances Muhammed had no other choice but either to remain silent or to create an entirely new religion, and the perseverance he shewed in upholding and proclaiming his conviction is greatly to his credit. Had his training but been more systematic and thorough, Islâm would have been free from much objectionable matter.

Now if Muhammed could not apply to Meccan teachers for instruction, we must consider from what other source he gathered it. Only one assumption is possible, *viz.*, that his years of real study were past long before he proclaimed the *Iqra'*. His own statements that all his knowledge was imparted to him directly by way of heavenly revelations are better left alone. Sprenger

---

37 The Aramaic form of the word.

38 *Cf. Q.* vii. 155. Moses prays: behold *we return* to thee هدنا اليك.

39 *Cf.* ii. 83 and often. The matter will be more fully discussed in Ch. IX.

40 Plur. fract. of هائد. Sprenger, II. 364, connects the term *Yahûd* with the Jewish creed which is not quite correct, as it only refers to the ritual law.

41 Only in Medinian passages, *e. g.*, ii. 70; iv. 48. See *Commentaries*. The alteration of the *Tôrâh* by the Jews is very broadly discussed by Ibn Ḥazm in the anterior chapters of his work.

42 See Ch. IX.

43 See the note at the end of this chapter.

is undoubtedly right in calling attention to the (Meccan) verse xxxvii. 137 *sq.*,[44] as the recollection of a journey during which Muhammed passed the Dead Sea when travelling in Khadîjâ's service to Syria. In pursuing his business he must have come into contact with many Jews and Christians,[45] and very probably discussed religious topics with his new friends. Morever, as a child he had been to Medina, and there had many opportunities of witnessing Jewish ceremonies which, on account of their strangeness, made a deep impression on his mind. This and later experiences were sufficient to allow him to judge of the contrast between Jewish and Christian doctrines and forms of worship on one side, and the one he was accustomed to at home on the other. His first entrance into a Synagogue must have produced on him an effect similar to that which according to Tacitus[46] Pompeius experienced when visiting the temple of Jerusalem. There were no images, no holy stone, no augurial arrows, but a devout congregation which met twice daily in order to worship an invisible Being with hymns and prayers. This was most impressive for the open-minded youth. There was nothing to attract the eye but an "eternal lamp," which shed a dim lustre from a niche in the wall. It almost appears that Muhammed saw in this light, which in reality served different purposes, a symbol of the Deity, which, as he had heard, first appeared to Moses in a light (*Q.* xxvii. 7-8). The recollection of this light seems not to have left him the whole of his life, and is expressed in a parable as follows (xxiv. 35):

"Allâh is the light of heaven and earth; the description[47] of his light is as a niche in which is a lamp, and the lamp is in a glass, the glass is though it were a glittering star, it is lit from a blessed tree, an olive neither of the east nor of the west, the oil of which would well nigh give light, though no fire touched it, light upon light. Allâh guides to His light whom He pleases, and Allâh strikes out parables for men, Allâh knows all things. (36) In houses which Allâh has permitted to be raised, and His name to be recorded therein,[48] His praises are celebrated therein mornings and evenings. (37) Men whom neither merchandize nor selling divert from the remembrance of Allâh and from observing prayers and giving alms, who fear a day in which the hearts and eyes shall be upset."

Thus the light represents the reflex of God's glory, and Muhammed believed himself favoured to behold it, and to grasp its secret. A simple mind has many a time been led in a strange way to find the truth. When reading this parable one is reminded of Hebbel's charming tale, "*Kannitverstan.*" The sight of an insignificant oil lamp in a corner of a synagogue had made a deeper impression on the mind of the artless lad than the most elaborate theological demonstration could have done. What a lesson this is for conversionists! A lover of truth is led by spontaneous observation much farther than by indoctrinated one. The power of persuasion in religious matters chiefly promotes hypocrisy.

A rather striking proof of the fact that during his sojourn in the north country Muhammed had visited Jewish houses of study *(Bêth Midrâsh)* is given in his application of the root *darasa*,[49] because he replaced the widely different Arabic meaning of this word by the rabbinical one. In the school-house he heard many a *Derâshâ* or sermon, the method of which he mistook in so far, as he was not able to hold apart plain explanations of the holy text from homiletic discourses adorned with fictitious interpretation, but he looked upon all as a part and parcel of the Scripture. Some cases in which he did find this out, served him, as mentioned above, to base his reproach of the adulteration of the Law on them.

Muhammed's stay among Jews must once have extended over the autumnal period of the Jewish holidays, because only then he could have heard the blowing of the *Shôfâr* even without entering a Synagogue. That he *did* hear it can be inferred from many Meccan revelations (lxxviii. 18;

[44] *Moh. und K.* p. 7.

[45] Jacob, *Das Leben der vorislam. Beduinen*, p. 99, calls attention to Agh. viii. 79, but if Christian merchants in Ḥîra dispensed religious knowledge together with their wares, it does not follow that they did the same at the Meccan fairs.

[46] *Hist.* V. 9.

[47] *Mathal*; *cf.* Ch. VIII.

[48] *Cf.* Exod. xx. 24.

[49] *Cf.* Beidh. on Q. vi. 105. The old Arabic meaning of the root "is to wipe away, or out," *e. g.*, by rain and wind; *cf.* Kâmel ed. Wright, p. 459, "rags of cloth," Schol. الدريسان ثوبان خلقان; with regard to the meaning of the word in the *Qorân* see Geiger, p. 51.

lxix. 13, etc.), in which he describes the "Great Day of Judgment" on which "the bent horn shall be sounded." The conception of the Jewish New Year's Day as day of Judgment is already to be found in the *Mishnâh* (Rôsh Hash. i. 2).[50] The idea at once took root in Muhammed's mind, and in an old revelation of the confirmatory period is mentioned "the day of distinction" on which "the horn shall be blown." This can only have been the result of personal experience, and offered material for very elaborate pictures of the fates of the just and wicked. To the Day of Atonement, however, Muhammed does not seem to have given much attention at first. Fasting could not be to the taste of people who knew not abundance, and it would have been bad policy to recommend to the Meccans a new religion of which abstinence from food formed an important element. In Meccan parts of the *Qorân*, therefore, fasting is mentioned but once (xix. 27) in a passage belonging to the latest period, and, moreover, a historical connection without any hint as to the desirability of imitation. The traditions existing on the fast of *Ashûrâ*,[51] which corresponds with the Jewish *'Asôrâ* (tenth of Tishri)[52] refer to a temporary Medinian arrangement, but it was only later on, that fasting was officially given prominence as a rite.

Part of the well known formula of the Moslim creed (*dikr*) in common use, and also chanted in the call to prayer (*adân*) is: There is no God beside Allâh.[53] The formula is taken from the *Qorân*, and yet it seems strange, that the name *Allâh* is not used in the *Iqra'* verse; it is even more strange that the formula occurs in the *Qorân* only *twice*, once in a late Meccan passage (xxxvii. 34) and the second time in a Medinian verse (xlvii. 21).[54] The earlier passage runs thus: Verily when it is said unto them "There is no God beside Allâh," they get too big with pride and say: "What! shall we leave our gods for an infatuated poet?"—Now, the formula is here, as in the other passage, not an enunciation, but a mere assertion, which only tends to place the unity of Allâh in contrast to the plurality of other gods. This explains also the great care Muhammed took in the choice of the name for God.[55]

---

[50] The real conception Muhammed entertained about the blowing of the *Shofar* by Jews was, however, very prosaic, as he believed it to be only a means of calling the people to prayer. That is why it was all but adopted later on in Medina, I. I. 347. Bokh. I. 83. The blowing of the horn on the Day of Judgment (1 Cor. xv. 52) mentioned so frequently in the *Qorân*, therefore, only implies the roll call of the dead. The Qoranic expression *ṣuwar* seems to me to be only the Hebrew *shôfâr*, but incorrectly heard. In point of the pronunciation of Hebrew sibilants the Arab Jews seem to have very few distinctions. We shall have instances later on where Hebr. ש and ס are rendered in the *Qorân* by ص, see below.

[51] See Tab. 1281 without Isnâd; Bokh. I. 236. The explanation supposed to have been given by the Jews that the Day of Atonement was celebrated in memory of the exodus of Israelites from Egypt is only another reflex of זכר ליציאת מצרים alluded to in the liturgy of the holidays. The Isnâd given by Bokh. (Mushaddad-Ismâîl b. Ayyûb Nâfi, Ibn 'Omar, Urwa, 'Âisha) is not bad, provided that for the "Qoreish" who used to fast the *Âshûrâ*, another name is substituted.

[52] A peculiar misconstruction of the Jewish Day of Atonement is given by Ibn Ḥazm, fol. 72vo. The Rabbanite Jews, he says, congregate on account of their having angered God and being cursed by Him on a day called "The night of the feast of *Kibûr*," which is, of course, the Hebr. *Kippûr*, misunderstood and explained to mean "Great." It is celebrated on the 10th of the first month Jishrîn, which is October. Then stands up الصدرون, which word the Jews interpret as "the Minor Lord"—exalted be He above such heresy! What this word means is difficult to say, but I believe it is a corruption of *Mstatrôn*. This deity, he goes on, stands with dishevelled hair, weeps a little and says: Woe upon me that I have destroyed my house and have dispersed my sons and daughters, and overthrown my people (Talm. Berâkh. fol. 3vo). I will not raise it up until my prophet comes to whom I will restore my sons and daughters.—In these days of October they worship another Being beside God and commit undoubted idolatry, worse than the Christians. One of them told me that Sandalfôn, "the servant of the crown" is "an angel who bewails the destruction of the house" in similar terms.—What I. Ḥ. means by this second deity is quite clear, *viz.*, that during the ten days of atonement (New Year until day of Atonement) in the prayer called *Amîdâh* the formula האל הקדוש is replaced by המלך הקדוש.

[53] I. I. 347; *cf.* Lane, *Modern Egyptians*, II. 89 *sqq.*

[54] In altered forms a little more frequent. I give here all the passages concerned: iii. 55, *cf.* V. 77; vi. 46: xxviii. 71, 72; xxi. 23; *cf.* above; iii. 43. These passages except the two first belong to the later Meccan periods, and from this we must conclude that the formula long remained unsettled. Needless to say that the tradition given by I. I. 298, that at the death of Abu Tâlib Muhammed summoned those present to recite the formula in question s quite unfounded.

[55] Somewhat nearer to the final text of the formula comes the passage xlvii. 21: "Know then that there is no God beside Allâh." But also here it stands in a subordinate sentence.

*Allâh* was familiar also to the pagan Arabs; it would therefore, have been a mistake to introduce the new God under the same name, and this is another proof of the circumspection with which Muhammed set to work. Even in a comparatively late Meccan revelation (x. 90) he lets Pharaoh say: "I believe that there is no God beside the one in whom the children of Israel believe." In other words: not until the unique character of Allâh was generally and firmly established could Muhammed particularise it, just as we do with *God.*

What name, then, was to be substituted? Muhammed helped himself in a very ingenious way, which again clearly demonstrates how systematically he proceeded. He simply adopted the method of Jews and Christians, who used the terms *Adônay* and *Mâryâ* respectively, both signifying *Lord* (ὁ κύριος). Muhammed translated both by Rabb with a genitive or a possessive pronoun after it. In Arabic *alRabb* (with the article) is rare in pre-Qoranic texts,[56] and is in this manner not used in the *Qorân* at all, whilst when connected with another noun it is quite common and means *Master*, also in secular poetry. Now as in Syriac *mâryâ* represents the form with the article, whilst the Hebrew *Adônay* has a pron. suff. instead, it is clear that the Qoranic form *(rabbika)* is an adaptation of the latter, rather than of the former. The change from the first person of the *pron. suff.* into the second became, however, necessary, as Allâh was the speaker himself and Muhammed the addressed person.

In the employment of a name for God by Muhammed we can distinguish three stages which developed from one another. It seems very appropriate that the first proclamation should have been spoken in the name of the *Rabb who has created*, but it became essential to have an independent term for God also without reference to a person or "the worlds."

In a very old revelation (lxxiii. 9) Muhammed makes an interesting attempt to formulate a creed in the following manner: The *Rabb* of east and west, there is no God beside *Him*. But even this formula remains isolated until a rather late Meccan passage (xx. 7) which runs: Allâh, there is no God beside *Him*, to Him belong the most excellent names. A few verses after this (v. 14) we read: There is no God except *anâ* (*I, cf.* xvi. 2; xxi. 25), and in another place (xxi. 27): There is no God except *anta (Thou)*. Those "most excellent names" form the object of the well known enumeration of the ninety-nine names found in all works on Moslim theology, and of which Prof. Palmer has given an English version in the introduction to his translation of the *Qorân* (p. lxvii.), but Muhammed's object in employing the personal pronoun can only be explained by his inability to decide which name to choose. In the *Qorân*, both in Meccan as well as Medinian revelations, a strong inclination prevails to use *He* and — less frequently— *I*,[57] and *Thou*, rather than *Allâh* for the formula of the creed.

This peculiarity cannot be accidental, and is, I believe, to be explained as follows. Everyone knows that the Jews in post-Biblical times pronounced the Tetragram as *Adônay*, and in some cases abridged it to *Hû* (or *Hô*), after models found in Biblical names such as *Hôshêâ* and others. Subsequently they also shrunk from the too frequent use of *Adônay* and substituted synonyms for it or abridged it to *Anî*. In the *Mishnâh* (*Sukkâh*, iv. 5) we read that at the procession with the palm-branches in the Temple the worshippers sang: *Ani and Hû. Hôshiânâh*. The Palestinian edition of this passage spells *Hû* [והו] exactly like the third person of the masculine personal pronoun, just as *Anî* corresponds to the first person. The Babylonian Talmud (*Shabbâth* 104 ro) contains the passage: "*HU* is the name of the Holy One, blessed be He," and another (*Sukkâh* 83vo) in which Hillêl says: *If Anî (AdôNaI) is here, all are here, if Anî is not here who is here?*[58] — The constraint the Jews put upon themselves in dealing with the names of God was relieved by an alteration which, practically resulting in the use of personal pronouns, not only expressed the divine individuality much more concisely than any name could have done, but for which also the

[56] Meaning *king*, but see Sprenger, I. 299 *sqq.* Kâmil, 593 كلّنا نعبد ربّا واحدا, fem. ربّة الخدر, Hassân b. Th. p. 38; thus also in these instances either indetermined or with genetive following. Wellh R², p. 145, therefore hardly correct.

[57] See Anz, *l. c.* p. 21 (Ishtar): *Mein erster Name ist Ich, die Himelskönigin.*

[58] *Abôth*, I. 14. See also Isaiah xxxiv. 16 אני ש which Jargum and Septuag. refer to God, and seem to have read accordingly, *cf. ibid.* xliii. 10.

Pentateuch itself furnished a model in sentences like *anî anî hû* (Deut. xxxii. 29). This gives a very interesting instance of popular etymology. The real derivation of the substitutes *anî* and *hû* was forgotten, and the people looked upon them as personal pronouns, which took the places of the divine names.

Now there seems to be little doubt that the very frequent use of the personal pronoun in the *D̲ikr* stands in connection with the Jewish custom of shortening the Tetragram, or it may be an attempt to find a substitute for the same in the *Qorân*. Whether the mâsôretic vocalisation of the Tetragram was communicated to Muhammed by some one, is too uncertain to allow us to draw any conclusion, but *Huwa* sounds very much like the abridged form of the former. If in the first stages of Islâm the use of Allâh was avoided for some reason, the choice of an appropriate name for God was a cause of perplexity. To assume that Muhammed found the idea of the personal pronoun independently is not probable. *Rabb* with a suffixed pronoun did very well in the first proclamation. It was, however, not a name, but an attribute, and could not be employed in the creed, whilst the phrase: *There is no God beside Huwa* is a formula of a very expressive character.

The employment of *Huwa* thus marks the second stage in the establishment of a divine denomination, and the relation prevailing between it and *Rabb* is best seen in a phrase like (xiii. 29) *Huwa rabbi* ("HE is my Master"),[59] *there is no God beside Huwa.* Even in phrases such as (xxix. 25):[60] *innahu Huwa-l-'azîzu* ("Behold Him, He is the Almighty"), the inserted Huwa, although generally explained as a grammatical nicety, seems to come under the influence of the sacred application of *huwa*, rather than of a linguistic rule, athough the grammarians have only taken it in the latter sense.[61] It is natural that the pronominal conception was strengthened also in Muhammed's speech to such an extent, that the words, (xx. 12) *innani anâ rabbuka* ("Behold me, I am thy Lord"),[62] are given as rendition of Exod. iii. 6. If the pronouns *huwa* and *anâ* thus in a certain fashion represent Allâh, the Ṣûfic motto *Anâ l-ḥaqq* ("I am the Truth") loses a good deal of its pantheistic character, and stands simply for "Allâh is the Truth," then resembling the saying of Hillêl quoted above. In a similar light, I believe, must be regarded the Ṣûfic ejaculation *Huwa huwa* which must be compared with Exod. xxxiv. 6, being a nominal sentence rather than a repeated ejaculation. The Ṣûfic *Huwa* was then individualized to such an extent, that with the article *(alHuwa)* it was used as a name of Allâh.[63]

It is thus clear that the employment of Allâh in the *Qorân*, considered historically, is not so much a "*Grundlehre*"[64] of Islâm, as the final crystallisation of the formula, after several attempts to condense the first sentence of the Moslim creed into a motto. If it is of Biblical character, it is only indirectly so, since Muhammed left all other Biblical appellations of God, and returned to that with which the Arabs were already familiar. It is easily seen how much more tempting it must have been to pagan Arabs to listen to the call of the *Muad̲d̲in*, who did not invite them to worship a new Being, but Allâh, although only Him exclusively. What a sign this is of Muhammed's knowledge of the human mind, of shrewdness and calculation! A host of traditions exists on the importance and felicitous consequences in this world and the next Muhammed is said to have attached to the ejaculation of the formula.[65] Even in our days it is well known that several orders of Dervishes rouse themselves to the highest pitch of enthusiasm by nothing else than incessantly repeating *lâ ilâh illâh Allâh*,[66] until they are thoroughly exhausted.

---

59 Perhaps the common Jewish abbreviation יי״ה (Exod. xxxiv. 6); *cf.* *Q.* xliii. 64.

60 *Cf.* lii. 28, etc.

61 The so termed *d̲amîr-ul-faṣl* which is also applied to other persons, sing. and plur. As the majority of instances of *d. f.* are taken from the *Qorân*, it appears that its use originated from Muhammed. *Cf.* Sibawaihi, ed. Derenbourg, I. p. 346 *sqq.*, and *cf.* 1 R. xviii. 39.

62 It is to be noted that *huwa* and *anâ* interchange in this *sûra* three times within a few verses.

63 *J. R. A. S.* 1880, pp. 5, 68; 1892, pp. 661.

64 Nöldeke, Q. p. 6.

65 Mishk, I. 544. The tradition Bokh. III 315 on the authority of AlMussayyab; *cf.* Silâh AlMûmin, fol. 14ʳᵒ *sq.*

66 Lane, *Modern Egypt*, II. 63.

To return to the *iqra'*, we see that Muhammed managed to compress the two chief dogmas of every monotheistic creed into *five words*, even including the creating word *(bârâ)* of the beginning of Genesis. It would have been impossible for any one else to equal this in terseness and precision. It is quite unlikely that this should have been the result of spontaneous meditation without the aid of Biblical knowledge. If the traditions that the *iqra'* represents the commencement of the *Qorân* needed any confirmation from within, here it is, because no other sentence in the whole book would approach this in appropriateness of being the first. Fuller explanations Muhammed could reserve for later occasions, but for the present it was all important to give the quintessence of the belief in One God, who is the Creator of the world.

It is now almost superfluous to demonstrate in detail that *iqra' bismi rabbika*[67] is nothing but the literal translation of the Biblical phrase which the Jews read: "*wayyiqrâ b'shêm adônay*" and the (Syrian) Christians "*waqrâ bash'mêh d'mârya.*" It makes no difference whether the former or the latter furnished Muhammed with the original, probably they did both, but a Presbyter or sword-maker in Mecca certainly had no hand in it.

Finally there is the linguistic evidence to be added. The Arabic root *qara'a* does not mean: "to read," but "to gather," and is in this sense frequently used in pre-Islamic literature. The object of the verb furthermore is grammatically not joined by the preposition *bi*, which, however, is common in the Hebrew and Syriac handling of that root. Every word in the *iqra'* verse, taken singly, is pure Arabic, but united they give a new sense, and in this way Muhammed has also implanted a new spirit in the old language.

What remains now of epileptic or hysterical influence on the origin of Islâm? Absolutely nothing. Never has a man pronounced a sentence with more circumspection and consciousnes than Muhammed did in the *iqra'*. Should he have proclaimed it with nothing but prophetic enthursiasm, he must have been the greatest genius that ever lived. This he was not; but he was clever, full of discretion and tact, and also desirous of communicating his knowledge to the world. If we have to take the epileptic fits as historical, then Islâm arose in spite of them, but not by their means. Muhammed's greatness consisted in the recklessness with which he publicly exclaimed what he had recognised to be right. How many would have the courage to do this? He stood, however, firmly on Biblical ground, and there he remained through the whole Meccan period. The bulk of the narratives, descriptions, and laws contained in Meccan sermons are bone from the bone and flesh from the flesh of the Bible, and are responsible for all that is good and recommendable in Islâm.

The late A. Geiger has dealt with the question whether Muhammed "wished, could and dared to borrow from Judaism." Wellhausen, on the other hand, claims to have found "the soul of Islâm in Christianity." They are both equally incorrect. For the most vital portions of the new faith Muhammed was *forced* to depend on the *Old Testament*. It is quite a secondary matter, whether he derived his knowledge of the Bible from Jewish or Christian assistants. The Jews in North Arabia and Syria read the Bible in Synagogues in the Hebrew original, but for domestic study they probably used Aramaic translations as did the Christians. Many Biblical words which occur in the *Qorân*, have evidently gone through an Aramaic channel. It made no difference to Muhammed whence he received his material. He took everything which came into his way, Jewish and Christian, Hebrew, Aramaic and Ethiopic, even Greek and Latin;[68] all that was not known in Mecca was welcome to him. It became all so mixed up in his memory, that later on he was himself unable to distinguish his sources. Any successful attempt to make up for the loss would assist greatly in lifting the veil from over many obscure passages of the *Qorân*, though they often have but a literary interest.

---

[67] A parallel phrase to this is *wa'dkur isma rabbika*, lxxiii. 8; lxxvi. 25, and often. "Mention the name of thy Lord." This phrase is a modification of the other and is also moulded on a Biblical pattern; *cf.* Ex. xx. 24; Josh. xxiii. 7; etc. Whilst (Hebr.) *qârâ* and (Arab.) *qara'a* are constructed with the prepos. *dâkar* rules the accusative pure and simple.

[68] *Cf.* Fraenkel, *De vocabulis in antiquis Arabum carminibus et in Corano peregrinis*, p. 24 sq., though the st is not quite complete.

All this considered, some strict enquirer may yet ask, whether Muhammed was not morally obliged to reveal to his Meccan hearers the sources upon which he had drawn. On this point we must first of all remark, that the ideas about mine and thine were not very highly developed in early Arabia. Even when living in Medina, Muhammed found it perfectly in order to arrange plundering raids against peaceful caravans, going so far as to violate the sacred month, and so we must not wonder that he abstained from divulging the names of his instructors. There is for him, of course, the plea, that no teacher is obliged to reveal to his pupils the names of his own masters, and the school-books from which he learnt. Indeed, he did not even mention the *Tôrâh* and Gospel which were almost within reach of the more intelligent Meccans, till he was in Medina, but in very old revelations he alluded to the more inaccessible *Sheets of Moses and Ahron*, *Zubur of the Ancient* (lxxxvii. 18-19 ; xxvi. 196), and, later on, to the *Kitâb of Moses*. He hinted that the acquaintance with the contents of these writings — which of course are but mysterious names for *Tôrâh* and Gospel — had come to him by way of supernatural revelation (xxvi. 192 *sqq.*).

On the basis of the *iqra'* we may now hope to arrive at an apposite translation of the word *Qorân*. The grammatical form of this word is the infinitive of the same (simple) stem, of which *iqra'* is the imperative. "Proclamation," therefore, seems to be the most faithful translation. Each individual revelation pronounced by Muhammed is a *Qorân*, and as the amount of the existing revelations went under the same name, it was but natural to ascribe it also to the whole book.

## NOTE.

### The Legend of the Cleansing of the Heart (Rem. 43).

This legend has several important points in common with that of Baḥîra, and it is, therefore, probable that both originate from the same source. The various traditions on the legend of the cleansing of the heart have been collected by Sprenger, I. 166 *sqq.*, and it will be sufficient to reproduce the chief elements in it, which will also help us to trace their origin. The nucleus is, in short, this, that Muhammed, when a boy and pasturing the cattle, was seized by two angels who took his heart out of his breast, removed a black clot of blood from it, laved it with snow, and put it back again. Another version (Tabari) adds, that the angels weighed him and found him heavier than the rest of his people. When they had taken his heart out, they threw the part away which belonged to Satan, and a black clot of blood, then they put the *Shekina*, which is as white as snow in his heart, and *stamped the seal of prophecy between his shoulders.*

The last noteworthy variation, mentioned in the Uyûn al Âthâr, connects the affair with a dream. Muhammed tells Âisha that his heart had been taken from him, been washed and put back again. Then the miraculous animal alBorâq appeared, which carried him, accompanied by Gabriel, to heaven. Thus the main part of the legend, *viz.*, the cleansing of the heart, takes place at various epochs of the Prophet's life, from his earliest childhood till the time when he entered his ministry, whilst the stamping of the seal of prophecy between his shoulders is taken from the Baḥîra legend.

According to traditions Muhammed said that there existed no prophet, who did not pasture cattle (I. I. p. 106). This must be collated with the statement in the first form of the legend, that he was pasturing cattle, when the two angels came. Now of the Biblical prophets mentioned in the *Qorân* there are Moses and David, who received the divine call when minding their flocks. The Legend of the Cleansing of the Heart is thus nothing but a homily on Ps. lxxviii. 70 to 72, of which we have chiefly to notice the words: "He *chose* David his servant and took him from the sheepfold, etc.," and "the integrity of his heart." Here there is another point of connection with the Baḥîra legend. See further, Ps. li. 4, 9, 12 to 13, *viz.*, "snow," "clean heart," "cast me not away," etc.

## CHAPTER III.

### THE CONFIRMATORY REVELATIONS.

EXAMPLES — The treaties on the arrangement of Meccan revelations criticised — Pragmatical arrangement — Confirmatory, Declamatory, Narrative, Descriptive and Legislative Revelations — First elements of the "Hijra" — Life, Death, Soul, Eternity, Hell, Paradise and Heaven in the *Qorân*

The first proclamation announcing in a few words a new divinity, a new prophet, and the first elements of two important dogmas could not but be followed by others intended to deepen the impression made and to strengthen the position of Allâh and his Prophet. The connection between both was so close, that the existence of one necessitated also the belief in the other, and it was but natural that the authority of the Prophet was at that stage almost on a level with that of Allâh. No matter whether hearers of the first proclamation received it in public or private, whether they were relatives or strangers, they had first of all to be convinced of the speaker's sanity. Everything depended on the success or failure of the assurance given on that point, as Allâh himself was unapproachable, whilst the would-be Prophet stood as a tangible object of criticism. In two subsequent revelations Muhammed not only repeated the leading ideas of the first proclamation, but added the assurance that he was in full possession of his mental faculties. These revelations[69] again show how systematically he proceeded, and how carefully he weighed every word before uttering it. They run as follows: —

lxxxvii. 1. Praise *the name of thy Lord*, the Most High,
2. *Who has created* and made perfect,
3. Who has determined [everything] and guided.
4. Who produces the pasture.
5. Then he changes it into dry stubble.
6. Surely *we cause thee to proclaim*, so do not forget,
7*a*. Except what Allâh pleases [that thou shouldst forget],[70]
7*b*. He knows what is manifest and what is hidden.
8. We will facilitate[71] unto thee that it be easy for thee [to preach].
9. Admonish, if thy admonishing shall be profitable,
10. Let those be admonished who fear [Allâh].
11. But the most wretched will keep aloof therefrom.
12. He shall roast in the fiercest fire.
13. Then he shall neither live in it nor die.
14. Happy, he who remains pure.
15. He who *mentions the name of his Lord*[72] and prays.
16. But you prefer this present life.
17. Yet the last one[73] is best and of longest duration.
18. Thus it is written in the ancient sheets *(suḥuf)*[74]
19. The *sheets of Abraham and Moses*.

lxviii. 1. N. By the pen, and what they write!
2. Thou art not, through the grace of the Lord, mad.[75]
3. Verily thine is a reward that is not grudged,
4. Verily thou art a grand nature, etc.

It cannot, of course, be said with absolute certainty, that no other address was spoken between the first one and the two just quoted, but there is no doubt, that they were revealed with a view to supplementing the *iqra'*-revelation. It was Allâh who charged the Prophet to "proclaim," and who had the power to withdraw one or another revelation after it had done its work. This was a very diplomatic

[69] It is understood that "revelation" is here and further on a mere technical term. The Arabic equivalents are تنزيل, an ucas "sent down" from heaven, and آية "sign," "miracle" and "verse," see below.

[70] See below. [71] See below. [72] See Ch. II, p. 32. [73] *Viz.*, the next world. [74] See Ch. II.

[75] See also v. 51. I believe, however, that this and the following verses which are evidently of later date were added to this address; see *S.* li. 39, 52; liv. 9; xliv. 13, etc.

clause, arranging at once for the suppression of a revelation in the event of its proving troublesome. On a later occasion this idea was expressed in a much blunter form.[76]

The Moslim theologians assert that after the *iqra'* an interval of several months[77] — or, according to others, years[78] — elapsed, before the Prophet received another revelation, and that this made him very despondent. This theory which has already been rejected by Sprenger and Nöldeke,[79] but is upheld by Prof. Palmer and Sir W. Muir, has indeed no basis, nor is there any reason to account for such a pause. On the contrary nothing could have been more detrimental to Muhammed's prophetic claims than a deadlock, whilst possessing a plan of action and the means of putting it into execution, His silence would have been unintelligible for us, and a moral suicide for himself. The oldest tradition indeed, limits this interval to a few days, which seems much more likely, as it is very probable that after the first proclamation Muhammed waited a day or two in order to watch its effect, and to seize the right moment for a second address.

Example being always more effective than precept, it is probable that Muhammed proceeded to arrange a ritual without delay. To teach the faithful in what manner to worship Allâh, in contradistinction to the idols, was scarcely less important than the belief in him. Such a service, as simple in form as possible, perhaps only consisted in invocations and prayers, of which *Sûra* cxii. furnishes a very appropriate sample. It contains nothing but the declaration of the Unity of Allâh, and is probably modelled on Deut. vi. 4, which verse begins the *Sh'ma'* of the Jewish prayer book. There cannot be the slightest doubt that Muhammed had heard the latter read this prayer many a time, and omitting, of course, the introductory words "Hear O Israel," he rendered it as follows: —

1. Say : *Huwa* [is] Allâh, One,
2. Allâh [is] the Eternal.
3. He has not begotten and was not begotten
4. Nor has there ever been anyone like Him.[80]

It is, indeed, extremely perplexing to assign to this invocation its exact place in the series of early revelations. Its date is so uncertain, that some traditionists go so far as to believe it to be Medinian; but it bears the stamp of great age,[81] and I feel inclined to place it among the first revelations. Now the attempts I have made to fix the dates of the three addresses quoted are rather a bad beginning for a critical examination of the chronological order of such in the *Qorân*. We must even go further and confess from the outset, that there is very little hope of ever obtaining trustworthy results in this respect, however desirable they might be for gauging the gradual development of Islâm. The natural division of the *Qorân* into a Meccan and a Medinian portion marks but roughly the two great epochs of the formation of the Moslim church, but we have already met with one instance at least which even baffled the attempts of the compilers of the book to decide to which of the portions it belonged. There are also similar cases. For a very great number of revelations there is absolutely no evidence as to the time of their birth, and the standard rules are few and but little reliable.

As regards the order of the Meccan revelations some general points of view have been set up by Weil and Sir W. Muir, which were mostly adopted by Nöldeke, to serve as guides in the chaos. They divide the whole mass of addresses rather abruptly into *three* periods[82] according to the apparently

---

76 See S. ii. 100.

77 I. Isḥ. فترة; فتر الوحى; afterwards S. xciii. was revealed as a consequence of v. 3: Allâh has given thee leave. I. Isḥ. gives no Isnâd, but Tabari, p. 1155, reproduces the tradition on the authority of AzZohri, and again according to Abu Salama b. Abderraḥmân from Jâbir b. Abdallâh al Anṣâri from Muhammed.

78 See Sprenger, *Muh. and K.* p. 11. *Leben*, I. p. 304 *sqq.*

79 *Z. D. M. G.* xiii. p. 173 *sqq.* *Cf.* Nöld. *Q.* p. 67 *sq.*

80 See Ch. II.

81 *Itqân*, p. 30; see Muir, p. 46, and Nöld. *Q.* p. 34. Al Beidhâwi مختلف فيها. The tradition on the origin I. Isḥ. p. 400.

82 Muir divides the Meccan portion of the *Qorân* into *five* periods: (1) — *sûras* before *S.* xcvi. *(iqra)*: (2) those until Muhammed's public ministry; (3) ill the year 6 afterwards; (4) till the year ten; (5) till the Hijra. *Cf.* Nöld. *Q.* p. 58.

declining enthusiasm of the Prophet, the decreasing pathos and increasing length of the sentences. Since we have seen, however, that calm consideration governed the oracles from the beginning, the degree of enthusiasm furnishes a criterion of no great reliance. Now if we subject this enthusiasm to strict examination, we must distinguish between the genuine warmth for an idea which thoroughly captivates a man and makes him pursue it regardless of the consequences, and the hollow pathos which does not survive the word that carries it. The former Muhammed had fostered in his breast years before he opened his mouth as a prophet, and it lasted therefore even when his language had grown calmer. Enthusiastic passages are not unfrequent even in Medinian addresses, bearing on the greatness and the glory of Allâh, whilst the merely pathetic Meccan revelations repeat to weariness the same topics on which the speaker had but little to say, and left his hearers cold.

The different degrees of enthusiasm apparent in more or less fiery language must be judged in the same manner, as the changes to which the mood of an individual is subject. Exterior circumstances often have great influence in this respect. Temporary enthusiasm is sometimes kindled by a mere accident or an encouraging word. It does not follow, therefore, that the more pathetic *sûras* are older than others in which cold reflection predominates. There are many *sûras* of later date which show a language as glowing as that of a prophet in the best sense of the word. In consequence of the history of the *iqra'* we must deny to Muhammed the naïve passion from the outset, otherwise that first proclamation can retain neither its place nor its character. Tradition and evidence, however, bear out a contrary theory. Whenever we find Muhammed's language fervent, we must at once enquire, whether it was dictated by the loftiness of an idea, or whether it was mere bombast, which the unwary will often take for genuine enthusiasm. In this way the pathos of many addresses is, after all, a better help for the critical study than the lasting enthusiasm.

A more natural order of the revelations than those hitherto attempted may be derived from the following points of view. The first and most startling proclamation had to be followed by others to *confirm* the speaker's title to prophecy, and to bring the credentials of his mission. Doubts about his sanity had to be allayed and incredulity disarmed by valiant assurances. For obstinate unbelievers there existed, however, as yet no other proof than threats of heavy punishment. As on this topic the Prophet's imagination was unchecked, the language became stilted and high flown, and the addresses were introduced and intermingled with the strongest oaths. This is the striking feature of a large group of addresses which I should like to style the *declamatory*. When the Prophet's stock of pathos was exhausted, he resorted to tales which he accompanied with morals and admonitions. From these resulted the *narrative* period which Muhammed endeavoured to render as attractive as possible both by variety of subjects and miraculousness of plots in order to illustrate the omnipotence of Allâh. His prophetic zeal did not, however, prevent him from occasionally adding that the knowledge of these strange stories had come to him by divine revelation. Having well nigh used up his supply of tales, he started showing the rule of Providence by a group of *descriptive* speeches, which picture the wealth and grandeur of Nature. Is not gratitude due to Allâh who created all for the benefit of man? When this period had terminated, the hearers were sufficiently prepared to listen to a series of *legislative* addresses which taught the Believers how to lead the life of devout Moslims.

These five groups follow each other in natural sequence; nay, there is a direct evidence in a tradition handed down on behalf of 'Âisha, that many descriptive revelations preceded the legislative ones. She said:[83] "Allâh, has revealed first descriptions of hell and heaven in order to win men for Islâm, and he only revealed laws later on. Had he forbidden wine and fornication (chief representatives of ritual and moral laws) from the beginning, people would have said: we will not abstain from either." Nevertheless, one must not think that these groups are clearly divided; on the contrary they regularly encroach upon each other, so that elements of each group may be traced in the oldest addresses, and later ones contain repetitions of former paragraphs. Instances of two descriptive verses we have already encountered in *Sûra* lxviii. 4-5 quoted above. As we must give up the idea of ever reconstructing the chronological order of the sermons, we may hope, by means of a division according to subjects,

[83] See Sprenger, *Leben*, III. p. xix.

to obtain something like a survey over the material of which the *Qorân* is composed. If we succeed in carrying out this task, we can dispense with an accurate knowledge of the date of each revelation. Of a good many of them it is indeed quite irrelevant to know when they were revealed. For Medinian revelations the course of events serves as sort of guide, although not of a thoroughly assured nature.

In his exertions to confirm his mission Muhammed had to proceed in a negative as well as a positive manner. He had to convince his hearers that he was neither a madman, a poet, a soothsayer, nor a liar. To disprove charges by mere protestations is a hopeless task, but Muhammed had no other means at his disposal. Miracles refused to be forthcoming. The first protest against the allegation of being insane quoted above[84] is repeated in a declamatory address belonging to the following period,[85] but had to be reiterated over and over again during the next years.

Still harder to refute was the reproach of being a poet, because it was provoked by the *saj'*-like manner of the oracles. The general form for any sort of public announcement being poetic, Muhammed had to avoid all imitation of it, and this gave him immense trouble. The pathetic addresses in particular with their short, rhymed phrases of nearly equal length, which so much resembled the popular form of an *urjûza* or a ditty, betray the pains Muhammed took *not* to speak in verse. There is no reason to assume that he was unacquainted with the old poetic literature, even without taking into account traditions which report the contrary. Many of the standard features of these poems had become so familiar to him, that he had some difficulty in freeing his style of them. A remnant of this — which to some extent might help to fix the date of the passages in question — seems to me left in the apostrophe *let me* which in poems frequently forms the bridge from the *nasîb* or the amatory introduction to the proper subject of the song. This "let me" we find no less than three times in the oldest revelations, applied in a manner very similar to that of the pagan poems, *e. g.*, lxviii. 44 : So let me alone, etc.[86]

The protestation that "it was the word of a noble messenger" does not seem to have made the expected impression; the Prophet therefore repeated it a little later (lxix. 40) with a supplement: —

V. 41. Nor it is the word of a poet — little ye believe

" 42. Nor the word of a soothsayer, etc.[87]

To this period probably belongs the severe criticism passed on the poets who "say that which they do not do." (*Sûra* xxvi. 221-228.)

The refutation of one reproach only provoked another, as is always the case with a narrow-minded crowd. If Muhammed was neither a liar, nor a poet, nor mad, he must be a soothsayer. This he endeavoured to disprove in

lii. 29. So remind them, for thou art, not, by the favour of thy Lord, either a soothsayer or mad.

30. Or will they say 'A poet'? etc.[88]

It was perhaps not by accident that Muhammed made no refutation of the charge of deception in these sentences. The speaker must have felt that this was dangerous ground. Yet the more the

---

[84] *S.* lxviii. 2, see v. 51 which seems to be of much later date, but was placed in this *sûra* on account of v. 2 The word *al dikr* (v. 51) is already a technical term here, and Beidh. explains it rightly as equivalent to *Qorân*. Therefore v. 52 and *S.* lxxxi. 27, "It (the *iqra'*) is but a *dikr* for the worlds. Other recapitulations of the refutation of the same charge see xxvi. 26; xliv. 13; li. 39, 52; liv. 6; xv. 9; xxxvii. 35; lii. 29.

[85] *S.* lxxxi. 22, see Ch. IV.

[86] See Ch. I. Such passages are also metrically marked, at least in the beginning, *viz.*, lxviii. 44 ⏑ – – ⏑ – – – ; lxxiv. 11 – – ⏑ – ; lxxiii. 11 ⏑ – – – ⏑ –. These passages give the impression that the speaker was endeavouring to free himself by force from the meshes of the metre. For other parts of verses which by accident have assumed metrical shape see Wright's *Arabic Grammar*, 3rd ed. II. p. 359.

[87] V. 52. فَسَبِّحْ evidently leads on to prayer which is to follow; see next remark.

[88] *Ibid.* v. 48 to 49 containing the same invitation to offer up prayers. *Cf.* liii. 62.

ranks of the Believers swelled, the bolder became his answers also to this reproach, and these replies form in some cases a ready criterion for fixing the dates of certain revelations.

Now we see that soon after the *iqra'* Muhammed found himself in the midst of a fierce struggle, and his position was anything but secure. The traditionists describe this as despair at the non-arrival of new revelations, but the truth is that Muhammed could not bring forward such revelations as would effectively silence the adversaries, and be followed by universal acknowledgment. Whether the mental anxiety caused by the doubtless unexpected antagonism so greatly increased his excitement that his nerves failed and he had an epileptic fit, or whether he simulated one, must be left undecided. It appears to me he was subject to nervous headache, accompanied by shivering fits which compelled him to wrap himself in warm garments. When he recovered, he felt himself so refreshed that he broke into the following repetition of his prophetic call:

lxxiv. 1. O thou *wrapped!*[89]
2. Rise in order to give warning!
3. And *thy Lord* magnify!
4. And thy garments cleanse!
5. And detach thyself[90] from abomination

. . . . . . . . . .

11. *Leave me alone* with him I have created single-handed.[91]

To this belongs its twin oracle published under similar circumstances with all but identical beginning, *viz.*, lxxiii. 1-14.

Whether Muhammed only projected or really introduced vigils cannot be decided from the respective second verses of the two last mentioned addresses. I should feel inclined to explain the two "Rise" as illustrating the excitement which deprived him of his sleep, in the consciousness of "the heavy task he had in store" (lxxiii. 9). Upon this point the Commentators throw no light. To *Sûras* lxxiv. and xxiii. I oppose *Sûra* xciv. in which Muhammed encourages himself to hold out, since he had gained some followers to stand by him.

1. Have we not expanded thy breast?
2. And taken off thee thy load,
3. Which weighed down thy back?

[89] The traditions about the origin of this address are of contradictory character. I. Hish. p. 184, relates on very uncertain authority ("a scholar told me") that one day when going out, no one met Muhammed without calling him a liar. He returned home, wrapped himself up, and was addressed by Allâh: O thou wrapped up, etc. — Al Beidh.: It is handed down that Muhammed said: I was at Hira and heard myself called. I turned right and left, but saw nothing. Then above me I saw Him (فاذا هو) sitting on the Throne between heaven and earth, *viz.*, the angel who had called me. I returned to Khadîja and said دثروني. — Al Beidh. adds: he wrapped himself in his garment when reflecting, *or he was asleep.* — According to Tabari, p. 1155 (al Zuhri) this vision was followed by the revelation of *S.* lxxiii. Then follows the remark وزملناه اى دثرناه. Bokh. *ibid.* repeats the same tradition with the Isnâd give in Tab. 1153, but winds up: I said دثروني; they wrapped me up and sprinkled water over me. — Beidhâwi's additional note is evidently the safest to follow in the confusion of wondrous traditions, and receives further evidence from *S.* lxxiv. 4, which I should take literally rather than metaphorically which a view to performing a symbolical action. See Sprenger, I. 309, rem. 1. — A tradition Bokh. III. 365, that *S.* lxxiv. forms the first revelation is of doubtful authenticity.

[90] فاهجر repeated *S.* lxxiii. 10 واهجرهم هجرا جميلا "detach thyself from them completely as befits thee." In the older Meccan revelations the term is applied in a more general sense, *e. g.*, xxiii. 69; xix. 47. In xxv. 32, the *Qorân* is described as *shunned* (مهجور) by the Meccans. *S.* xxix. 25, is Lot a مهاجر "to his Lord;" xvi. 43, refers to those who had on Muhammed's advice gone to Abyssinia in order to avoid the persecutions of the Meccans.

[91] See Beidhâwi; Palmer inaccurate.

4. And exalted for thee thy renown ?
5. Verily with difficulty is ease
6. Verily with difficulty is ease
7. But when thou art at leisure then toil
9. And hope patiently unto *thy Lord !* etc.

lxxiii. 8 forms a distinct repetition of the *iqra'* verse with the slight variation into *wa'dkur*. The choice of this word points not less to the Pentateuch than the *iqra*, *e. g.*, Exod. xx. 24; xxiii. 13, etc.,[92] and it is particularly noteworthy that in both cases the construction of the Hebrew terms are faithfully retained in the Qoranic imitations.

Of very great interest, however, is the early indication of the first shadow of the great rupture which ten years later ended in the departure of the Prophet and his friends from their native town. "*Detach thyself (fa'hjur)* from abomination (lxxiv. 5);" "Endure patiently what they say and *detach thyself* completely as befits thee (lxxiii. 10)," the former passage referring to the gods, the latter to kinsmen and alliances. It is the same root which supplied the term *Hijra* not only for the temporary retirement of a large portion of early Moslims to the hospitable shelter of the Ethiopian king, but also to the final exodus to Medina. What is known in universal history as *Hijra* proves to be not an episodic event, but the completion of the local Hijras[93] which accompany the whole of the Meccan period of Islâm. Muhammed fostered no false hopes with regard to the consequences of his onslaught against the worship of his forefathers. The public proclamation of the single word *fa'hjur* had cost him dear, and he knew it well, but its repetition shows that he was firmly determined to stand by it. Here, if ever, he showed greatness of mind and deserves to rank with the great men of History. Upon those Meccans who were at all capable of conceiving ideas that word must have made a deeper impression than continual pathetic assurances of the divine origin of the revelations.

To return to the charge of fraud, in *S.* lxxiv. 24, Muhammed complained that some influential Meccan citizens had made allegations of this nature. In this instance his remonstrances are not of a general character, but are, as tradition tells us, launched against Walîd b. alMughîra of the family of al Makhzûm.[94] The attack was very strong, taunting Muhammed with the human origin of his rhapsodies. He could only parry it with a wild threat of hell fire. In a supplementary speech (lxxiii. 11 *sqq*., he compared himself to Moses (without, however, mentioning his name), only stating that his mission was also discredited by Pharaoh.[95] His challengers were destroyed, and from this Meccan scoffers were invited to take an example.

It is certainly not without purpose that at this comparatively early stage in his career Muhammed should have likened his own position to that of Moses. He could hardly have chosen a better means of strengthening his hands. Moses did not go on his own account, but was unwillingly sent by Allâh,

[92] See Ch. II. (and above rem. 84). اذكر is thus originally parallel to اقرا, and consequently ذكر قرآن. Later on the former was restricted to the ejaculation of the formula of the Unity; *cf.* Sprenger, I. 319, and Q. lxxxvii. 9, 10; lxxxix. 24, etc. — In *S.* xciv. ذكر has a profane meaning.

[93] The translation, "Flight" made popular by modern authors, is not correct. The *Hijra* was much more than that, as it was a complete cutting off of every bond of kinship, that connected Moslims with former friends and relatives remaining faithful to paganism. Bagh., therefore, explains very appropriately (according to Mujâhid, Ikrima, Qatâda, Al Zuhri, Ibn Zeid, and Abu Salma): give up the worship of the idols, and do not come near them.

[94] According to Bagh. on v. 11 al Walîd was called الوحيد. Beidh. explains وحيدا to be Ḥâl of 1st person, *viz.*, ذرني وحدي معه. In I. Isḥ. 171 alWalîd calls Muhammed a charmer in the better sense, "because his speech is bewitching and fit to separate man from his father, brother, wife and family." The tradition is evidently coloured.

[95] *Cf. S.* lxxiii. 15 *sqq*.

and in a like manner Muhammed tried to convince those around him that he did not preach of his own free will, but obeyed the command of Heaven. The reproach of fraud was, therefore, as unjust as it was insulting to Allâh, and liable to heavy punishment. This is another clever move and again shows with what deliberation Muhammed selected his words. In lxxiii. 5 we read that Allâh had thrown upon him "a heavy speech," and in lxxvii. 6 he says: Certainly *we* cause thee to proclaim, so that thou shouldst not forget. Finally, lxxvi. 23 *sqq.* again re-echoes the first call to prophecy accompanied by the admonition to be patient, and xciv. 1-8 are revealed to inspire him with new courage to brave the difficulties.

The unwillingness of Biblical prophets to undertake their missions was no secret to Muhammed, although he did not cite the most striking instances, *viz.*, those of Moses and Jonah until somewhat later (xxvi. 11-13; xxxvii. 140) in the narrative period. He may have hoped that there would be no necessity for this, yet the pains he took to satisfy the Meccan public that his own attitude was passive and that he was but a tool in the hand of Allâh forms the main idea connecting many of the revelations of this period.

With the first address Muhammed had introduced a series of abstract notions such as heaven and hell, eternity, death, soul, immortality, reward, and punishment after death. Although not all of these notions were covered by corresponding terms, he discussed them and endeavoured to impart to his hearers a more or less clear conception of them. He could not achieve this by giving definitions, which in the first instance he was incapable of doing, and which, moreover, would not have served his purpose. The practical theologian is no philosopher, and hearers of a sermon decline to be regaled with metaphysical demonstrations. Muhammed in particular was preacher to an unlettered crowd; the *Qorân* was, therefore, not the place to discourse on abstract ideas. He was more successful in expressing the same in as concrete a manner as possible.

The common pre-islamic view recognized a kind of shadowy after-existence. Otherwise the materialistic opinion is prevalent, that death is the end of everything. Muhammed himself dwelt on this point in a late Meccan revelation as follows:

> xlv. 23. And they say: there is only this present life, we die and live,[96] and only time kills us,[97] . . . . etc.

Some commentators not unfitly refer the words: "we die and live," to the pagan belief in the transmigration of soul[98] and the words which follow they apply to the common notion, that there is no other life after death. Muhammed tried to combat these views not with arguments, but simply by putting others in their places. This he did when he threatened transgressors with sufferings in purgatory, which in itself presupposes a kind of after-existence. The fire of hell being a very familiar conception to Christian (S. Matth. v. 22) and later Jewish doctrine, there can be no doubt that Muhammed had during his years of study heard much on this subject. Now he himself appears to have believed that those sufferings were physical rather then spiritual, as may be seen from many passages in the *Qorân* (xcviii. 5; lxxxix. 24; lxxii. 15, 24; lxxxv. 10; lxxviii. 21, etc.). If, however, he held more abstract views on the matter, it was as well for him not to dilate on them, since the people cared very little about agonies inflicted on their souls after the destruction of the body. The *whole* sinner shall "be dragged by the forelock (xcvi. 15-16)" to hell, he taught, and in this manner Muhammed condemned his uncle Abd alUzza, body and soul, branding him as "Father of the flame" in that fiendish execration which forms the contents of *Sûra* cxi.

---

[96] Beidh. finds particular difficulties in the words: *we die and live*, which he endeavours to explain in different ways: (1) the being born of what was not alive before; (2) we die and live in our children; (3) some of us die, whilst others live, etc.

[97] Beidhâwi. مرور الزمان وهو في الأصل مدة بقاء العالم من دهره اذا غلبه; *cf.* also Beidh. on *S.* lxxvi. 1 الدهر طائفة ممدودة, and see Lane, *s. v.*

[98] Beidh. *Ibid.*

1. Perish the hands[99] of Abû Lahab, and perish he
2. His wealth shall not avail him nor what he has earned,
3. He shall broil in a fire that flames *(lahab)*
4. And his wife carrying faggots,
5. With a rope of palm fibres on her neck.

A malediction couched in such terms could not fail to strike superstitious people with terror of the unknown hereafter. Tradition[100] tells us that the hapless uncle had provoked the Prophet by cursing him in no more measured terms, and this may not have been the only imprecation which came to Muhammed's ears, but he was careful only to retaliate on a near relative, and to burn him in effigy with such broadly drawn features, that he might be taken for any other infidel.

The language of the *Qorân* has no more terms to describe the immortality of the human soul than the Bible. Nevertheless, as early as in the confirmatory period Muhammed began to expound theories which teach that spiritual life outlasts physical death. This gives us an opportunity of briefly outlining the manner in which Muhammed rendered those transcendental portions, indispensable to every theological system.

In a revelation already quoted (lxxxvii. 12 to 13), Muhammed says that the wicked shall "broil in the fiercest fire, then he shall neither live nor die."[1] If the modern reader finds it difficult to understand such a situation, how puzzled must the Meccan hearers have been. It is characteristic of the eschatology of the *Qorân* that the tortures of hell are depicted in endless variations, with glowing colours and in all details, whilst the pious are simply "happy" (v. 14)[2] without any further description, and it is only intimated that for them there is in store a "last life" which is "the best and of longest duration" (v. 19).

Thus the conditions of the wicked and pious are contrasted with each other. The former are, according to the Commentators, to lead a kind of semi-life, which is neither rest in the grave nor a life that avails aught, but not until they have gone through purgatory, whilst the latter shall enjoy the eternal pleasures[3] of the "last life." This is repeated over and over again (xcii. 13; xciii. 4)[4] especially in the later Meccan *Sûras*. Although it is doubtful whether Muhammed himself had any clear conception of his own theory of the hereafter, it was indifferent to him whether the Meccans grasped the meaning of it or not. It is much more probable that he hoped to work more successfully on their minds by vague fears and hopes.

Muhammed himself betrays the fact that he had derived his knowledge of the nature of the last life" from the most ancient sources, *viz.*, "the *Suḥuf* of Abraham and Moses." That these terms do not mean certain books of a religious character which in the pre-islamic period were held sacred by various communities, as Sprenger believed, I have intimated above.[5] *Suḥuf* are nothing

---

[99] The Commentators, of course, felt themselves obliged to correct this concrete conception, and put "soul" and "fortune" in the place of "hands." Thus Bagh. يديه والمراد به نفسه علي عادة العرب فى تعبير ببعض الشى كله و قيل اليد صلة كما يقال يدا الدهر ويدا الزرايا والبلايا و قيل المراد به ماله وملكه يقال فلان قليل ذات اليد يعنون به المال. The tradition in I. Isḥ. p. 231, is badly accredited, as instead of giving the Isnâd, he only says وحُدِّثتُ. In this tradition Abu Lahab calls the Prophet "Muhammed" and charges him with not believing himself that the things he foretells will be realized after death.

[100] Beidh. with reference to S. xxvi. 214; but cxi. seems to be older.

[1] This only means that *after* the wicked have left purgatory they shall neither live nor die. The Commentators who evidently did not understand what Muhammed meant by the phrase, are silent on this point. Bagh. فيستريح ولايحى حيوة تنفعه; Beidh. similarly.

[2] *Cf.* S. xci. 9.

[3] Beidh. (v. 17) فان نعيمها تلذذ بالذات خالص عن الغوائل لا انقطاع له. *Cf.* xliv 56.

[4] As a contrast to this, the last punishment (lxiii. 33) is the strongest.

[5] See Ch. II.

more or less than the Bible. Now it is well known, that the idea of an eternal life is nowhere explicitly taught in the Bible, and is only inferred indirectly. The belief in it was, however, firmly established both among Jews and Christians, and when Muhammed heard them speak of it, he considered it tantamount to its being written down in their holy Scriptures.

The term "last life" implies that there is no other to follow, it is therefore eternal. Muhammed expressed eternity approximately through the synonyms for "space of time," or "remaining in a place or state."[6] This is about the same in all languages. In a very early revelation (civ. 3), Muhammed censures him "who thinks that his wealth has made him lasting [for ever]." The Commentators explain this to mean, that he shall not die at all. When, to choose another case, Satan induces Adam to disobey the divine command, he promises to show him "the tree of duration, and a dominion which shall not cease" (xx. 118). "To no man before have we given perpetuity *(alkhuld)*, shall they remain for ever, when thou diest" (xxi. 35 ; *cf.* v. 8) ? These and similar expressions answered Muhammed's purpose well enough, because when applied to mundane subjects they express the immutability of a condition, and were perfectly intelligible to everybody. To describe, however, Allâh as eternal Muhammed did not attempt except in one case (cxii. 1), but even this is open to grave doubts, and has caused much discussion among the Commentators, many of whom bring the expression used in this passage *(aṣṣamad)* in no connection with eternity at all.[7] Muhammed himself was uncertain as to the distinctness of this word, and, therefore, hastened to explain in the next verse that "Allâh was not born." Later Moslim theology developed an appropriate terminology to express eternity with regard to past and future.

Heaven[8] as the abode of God is a conception to be found frequently in the Bible, and transplanted by Muhammed into the *Qorân* at an early epoch. He, therefore, had to alter the old Arab meaning of the word which only comprehends the sky, the reservoir of the heavenly bodies and clouds and rain. In this sense it is used by poets[9] and also in the oldest portions of the *Qorân*. In *S.* lxxxviii. 18 heaven as a piece of creation is paralleled to the camel, the mountains and the earth. Allâh has created the seven heavens[10] in storeys, and has set the moon therein for a light, and the sun for a lamp (lxvii. 3). Allâh has built the heavens (lxxix. 27), and their government belongs to Him (lxxxv. 9). It must have caused Muhammed some difficulty to change the theories in which he had been brought up, into the abstract ones that Allâh sits in heaven on His throne,[11] which is borne by eight angels (lxix. 17). He is possessor of the lofty throne (lxxxv. 15).[12] The anthropomorphistic side of this

---

[6] Synonyms for "eternal" الدهر xlv. 23; lxxvi. 1, *cf.* rem. 97; سرمد xxviii. 71, 72; الصمد cxii. 2; خالد frequently, الخُلد xxi. 35; further قديم , ديمومة , ازلية.

[7] According to Ibn Abbâs, Mujâhid, Al Ḥasan, Sa'îd and Ibn Zubeir (Bagh. on cxii. 1) الصمد means a person who has no "inside" (لاجوف له) ; according to Al Sh'obi it means one who neither eats nor drinks ; according to others it means ما بعده. Abu l Âliya handed down on behalf of Ibn Abi Ka'b that الصمد means a person who was neither born nor has begotten, because he who is born must die, who inherits has heirs. Al Suddi explains الصمد as one who is sought after for presents and assistance. According to Qatâda it means : the remaining after the death of the physical part of the body. Ikrima الذي ليس فوقه احد. — Mewâqif, p. 168, has several other explanations : (1) Lord, king (relative attribute) ; (2) Sage, whom the deeds of the disobedient neither excite nor trouble (negative attribute) ; (3) Standing on the highest step ; (4) He who is invoked and implored ; (5) He who has no internal parts (not compact, synon. المُصْمَت with change of د with ت).

[8] Gen. xix. 24 ; xxii. 11, 15 ; xxviii. 17, etc.

[9] Ḥassân b. Thâbit ed. Tunis, p. 8, l. 7, تعفّيها الروامسُ والسّماءُ. "its traces have effaced the winds and the *rain.*" Ibn Koteiba (Sprenger, I. 544) explains it as what is above us. *Cf. Itq.* 692 *sq.*

[10] *Cf. S.* lxxi. 14 ; lxxviii. 12 ; and St. Lucas x. 20.

[11] In Meccan *Sûras* Muhammed exclusively uses the term العرش, whilst the Aramaic الكرسى is employed only once in Medina (*S.* ii. 253). In xxxviii. 33 it means an *earthly* throne.

[12] *Cf. S.* lxxxi. 20 ; xl. 15 (xvi. 1). The Mutazilite school had some misgivings about Allâh being represented as sitting on a throne. Beidh. takes العرش asa synonym for "dominion;" see his notes on S. vii. 52 : Upon the throne abides His Rule (*amr* see above). Our fellow-thinkers believe that the abiding upon the throne is an

phrase will occupy our attention later on.[13] If Allâh "sends down" revelations (lxvii. 9; xcvii. 1),[14] this means that they come from heaven. This way of expressing it is, however, rare in older *sûras*, and does not become more frequent until the narrative and descriptive periods, *e. g.*, vii. 38, "the gates of heaven shall not be opened for the infidels."[15]

Popular belief places the souls of the righteous in heaven. One can easily perceive how such a belief grew, a belief which made the aëtherial component of the human body leave this *irdische Jammerthal* and fly away[16] above the clouds. The idea is based on the manner of describing certain extraordinary forms of death in the O. T. Elôhim takes Henoch away, and Elijah ascends in a chariot of fire. In the *Qorân* Allâh "takes away" the soul of man (xxxix. 43), and in harmony with the Rabbinical way of expressing the idea, "every soul tastes death."[17] Muhammed concreted the soul in the same manner as did ancient and modern poets without much discernment, and placed hell so close to paradise, that its inhabitants were within hail of those of the former, from which they were separated only by a curtain (vii. 42-44),[18] which permitted conversation between them.

The resemblance of death to sleep is so striking, that it could not fail to enter pre-Islamic Arab speech also, but with the difference that the hope of awakening from the sleep in the grave was discarded. "If we are dead," the Meccans said, "and have become dust and bones, can we be awakened (xxxvii. 16)?[19] If thou speakest to them: you shall be aroused after death, the infidels will surely say: "this is nought but clear deceit (xi. 10)." Of course, Muhammed could not tolerate such views in Islâm, and could not sufficiently call to the minds of his hearers "the day on which they would be awakened,"[20] and to enjoin the belief in resurrection after death (lxxv. 1-4; lxviii. 39; lvi. 60).

The way in which Muhammed pictured the resurrection of the dead was very similar to the notions popular among Jews and Christians, *viz.*, that the body should share in it as well as the soul. The "collecting of the bones" (*Qor.* lxxv. 3) recalls vividly the vision of Ezekiel (ch. lxxxvi.) with which every Jew was familiar enough owing to its forming part of the liturgy on the Sabbath of the Passover week. There is nothing surprising in the fact that Muhammed should have heard of this.[21] Above the assurance that on the day of resurrection "man's bones shall be gathered" he gives for the present no further description,[22] and confines himself to vague hints at the time when this should take place, after being announced by the most miraculous signs. This was also to be the great "Day of Judgment on which the horn should be blown," etc. (see above). From all this we see that Muhammed wished to show his hearers the aim of human life in a rather serious perspective. The tortures of hell are described in the *Qorân* long before any of the more cheerful pictures of the "last life" are painted.

Although the "Garden" is spoken of in verses which are inserted in older *sûras*, these are evidently later and more prolix (lxxxv. 11; lxviii. 17, 34; lxxiv. 42). The older passages mention "the garden" without any further additions (lxxxviii. 10; lxxxix. 30; lxxxi. 13; lxix. 22). Fear Muhammed calculated to be more impressive than hope, and as a rule when depicting the two contrasting conditions of man after death, he not only placed punishment in the foreground, but made it much

attribute to Allâh without How. It means that His abiding on the throne is to be understood in a manner which exalts Him above resting and dwelling. The throne is the body which surrounds all other bodies, and is called thus, because it is elevated or compared to the royal couch from which government and commands descend. *Cf.* xxxii. 3-4; xvi. 2.

13 See Ch. VIII.

14 See lxvii. 16 to 17, "He who is in heaven."

15 *Cf.* Gen. xxviii. 17.

16 *Cf.* Ps. xc. 10.

17 *S.* xxi. 36; xxix. 57.

18 As to the people of the intervals, see next chapter.

19 See v. 51; *S.* xix. 67: Man says: when I am dead, can I be brought out in the end alive?

20 *S.* xliv. 34: This is but our first death, and we can not be aroused. Beidhâwi explains: the first death ends the life on earth, and there are no means by which to awake for another. The answer is given in v. 56: they (the righteous) only taste the first death; He guards them from the punishment of hell fire.

21 *S.* xxxvii. 144; xxxviii. 80; lxxxiii. 4; xxvi. 87; xvi. 85. The Commentators, of course, bring Gabriel on the scene, and Palmer wrongly follows them.

22 See next chapter.

more elaborate and energetic in tone than that of reward.[23] Experience proved here also to be the best teacher. For after the disaster of Uḥud Muhammed could give no greater comfort to the demoralised Believers than the assurance that those who had been slain were not dead but alive (iii. 163).

From the foregoing observations, we can gather that during the time of the struggle to confirm his missionary title, Muhammed had to handle a number of abstract subjects which to a real thinker would have been so many problems to solve. The circumstance that they all had been thoroughly familiar for some time to large multitudes entitled him to operate with them as with known quantities, and he left it to his hearers to digest them as best they might. He would have been infinitely more successful, had he been able to achieve something like a miracle, but, of course, he could not divine that the existence of Islâm was all the better assured, the harder it had to fight its way through difficulties of every description.

A miracle was the great, but unfulfilled, longing of Muhammed, and the disappointment he felt through his impotence to perform a miracle penetrates not only the whole of the *Qorân*, but many occasional sayings. Tradition, nevertheless, managed to record a great number of such, and the Moslim church officially recognizes a series of miracles which must be believed in.[24] Not quite so difficult was the problem to be favoured with a vision and those who already believed could easily be served with one. Many years afterwards, when the figure of the Archangel Gabriel was introduced into the revelations, they became very numerous indeed, but they were not nearly so important as in the earlier periods. Now Muhammed's great model, Moses, not only furnished him with the material for the first proclamation and the reluctance to enter upon his mission, but also with the pattern of a regular vision which it was not very hard to copy. In the evidently very early revelation, which forms part of *Sûra* lxxix.,[25] he expresses himself thus?

15. Has the story of Moses come to you
16. When *his Lord* called him in the holy valley of *Ṭuwâ:*
17. "Go to Pharaoh, verily he transgresses.
18. Say: Hast thou a wish to purify thyself?
19. And that I may guide thee unto *thy Lord*, that thou mayst fear?"
20. So He (Allâh) showed him the *greatest sign*, etc.

We conclude from it that the scene described in Exod. ch. iii. was known to Muhammed already, and that he reproduced it more elaborately in a short address which he significantly styled "an inspiration" taught to him by the Almighty. The hazy description of the scene, the principal figure of which is the speaker himself, was calculated to impress hearers as a vision granted to him. It forms the first portion of *Sûra* liii.[26]

1. By the star when it falls,
2. Your comrade errs not, nor is he deluded,
3. Nor speaks he out of lust.
4. It is but an *inspiration* inspired
5. Which taught him One mighty in power
6. Endowed with sound understanding; he appeared,
7. And was [seen] in the loftiest tract;

[23] He could find models for it in Lev. xxvi. 3 to 43; Deut. xxviii. 1 to 68. The maledictory portions of these two chapters are likewise much more elaborate than the benedictory ones and bear the popular name *tôkhêḥâ*.

[24] Ibn Ḥazm, fol. 122ro. *Cf. Umdat Aqîda*, p. 16 sq.

[25] It seems to be an independent revelation, whilst v. 1 to 14 belong to the declamatory, and v. 27 to 45 to the descriptive periods, but placed here on account of v. 34 الكبرى = v. 20.

[26] V. 62 an introduction to prayer.

8. Then he hung down and so drew near,

9. Until he was two bows length off or nigher still,

10. Then he inspired his servant what he inspired.

11. The heart belies not what he saw.

12. What will ye dispute with him on what he saw ?

13. And he saw it another time

14. By the Sidra-tree which none may approach,

15. Near which is the Garden of the Abode,

16. When something covered the Sidra-tree —

17. The sight swerved not nor wandered —

18. He saw then of the *signs of his Lord the greatest.*[27]

The positive information contained in this address is very meagre, and the vagueness of the description is concealed as much as possible by prolixity. Muhammed only states that he had seen something *covering a certain tree.* This was indeed quite sufficient for those who already believed in his mission, but not so convincing for others. Yet to judge from S. lxxxi. 22,[28] one might at any rate give him credit for having at least *imagined* that he had had a vision. The wish was father to the thought, and made him look upon a vague apparition as a real prophetic vision.

Muhammed need not have troubled to enquire whether his hearers believed in his statement concerning the vision, if he had been able to perform a miracle, which would have convinced even the most stubborn. His boast was, however, a two-edged tool, as in his zeal he had made known that previous prophets had confirmed their missions by miracles. He therefore felt that he had exposed himself to the demand to perform one, and for this reason styled his vision a miracle (lxxix. 20, see above). He had not long to wait and the doubtless satirical tone in which he was called upon to exhibit his powers is still reflected in one of the latest Meccan revelations (xxix. 49).[29] His answers were so timid that he had to refer the importunate querists to the *Suhuf.* This was just as unsatisfactory to his great grief, and nothing remained but to style the revelations he boasted to have received, miracles. He, therefore, chose a term for them which at the same time served to designate each revealed sentence as a "Sign" or miracle. In his philippic against Walíd b. al Moghíra Muhammed describes him as "hostile to our signs" (lxxiv. 16). The infidels rejoined that the "Signs" were "old folk's tales" (lxviii. 15 ; lxxxiii. 13) or even "lies" (lxxviii. 28), which can, of course, only refer to the revelations. The marvel to be discovered in the "Signs" could, then, only consist in the circumstance that a man in so humble a position and grown up in ignorance and already past the prime of life should suddenly develop the qualities of a prophet and spiritual leader of his people. This is admirably expressed in *Súra* xciii.[30]

6. Did He not find thee an orphan and give thee shelter ?

7. And find thee erring and guide thee ?

8. And find thee poor with a family and nourish thee ?

The proof of the veracity of the miracles performed by Moses before Pharaoh was given in the fact, that the magicians were not able to imitate them (lxxix. 25 ; xxvi. 43). Muhammed therefore boldly challenged scoffers to bring forward a "Sign" of the same kind as his. "Let them bring a

---

[27] *Cf. Beiträge*, p. 8. A manifest external resemblance also exists between this piece and S. lxxix. 15, 27, not only as regards the rhyme, but esp. v. 20 with S. liii. 18. The latter oracle is evidently the youngest of the two.

[28] "Your companion is not mad, (23) He surely saw him on the distinct horizon," another echo of lxxix. 20; *cf.* also xx. 24.

[29] *Cf.* xxvi. 187 ; vii. 202.

[30] V. 9 to 11 added later, and are legislative.

*hadîth*[31] of the same kind (lii. 34)." We have, in the first chapter, discussed the subject, and need only to add here that the Prophet felt himself on so safe a ground, that he repeated the challenge several times. This, however, increases the evidence that he had prior to his first proclamation possessed himself of a considerable stock of learning unknown to any Meccan, and that he also held in reserve sayings, tales and regulations which he intended to divulge piece-meal. However limited his learning was from our point of view, never was the proverb that knowledge is power more splendidly confirmed than in Muhammed's case. It remained his chief support, and won him more followers than assurances, threats, and declamations could have done.

The passages of the *Qorân* alluded to in this chapter — as indeed in all others — are given in but approximately chronological order, as it is sufficient to sketch out the course which Islâm took in its initiatory stages. The line of conduct was given to Muhammed by circumstances. He had to weather the storm of public opinion and to uphold his claim under the most disadvantageous conditions. His position was for a time one of defence rather than attack, and the desire to be left alone with his convictions is expressed in a short address which seems to belong to this period, and which is another disclaimer of the old worship:

cix. 1. O ye infidels!
2. I do not serve what you serve,
3. Nor will ye serve what I serve,
4. Nor will I serve what ye serve,
5. Nor will ye serve what I serve,
6. Ye have your religion, and I have my religion.

The term *dîn* (religion) which appears here for the first time, is applied indiscriminately both to Islâm and Meccan paganism. The wide signification allowed to the word is undoubtedly due to the circumstance that Muhammed had heard it employed both by Jews and Christians in various fashions. The former meant by the same term a rite as well as a judgment both religious and profane. To Jews and (Syrian) Christians "Doomsday" was familiar as the "Day of Judgment" *(yawm aldîn)*.[32] Also later on Muhammed treated *dîn* as a synonym for Islâm,[33] but on this occasion he paid the infidels the compliment of styling their belief a *dîn*.[34] What he had to say about the "Day of Judgment" will form the chief object of the next chapter.

[31] *Hadîth* is otherwise tale, and in this manner the term is applied to Moslim tradition in general; here, however, I should take it = Hebrew חדוש, "something newly produced."

[32] See Ch. I.

[33] See next chapter.

[34] Equivalent to ملة which is also applied to paganism, see Ch. I., note 2.

## CHAPTER IV.

### The Declamatory Revelations.

Character of Muhammed's prophecies — Messianic oracles — The "Day of Judgment" — Great variety of expressions for the same constitutes an essential feature of the book — The problem of the Freedom of Will — Redemption — Predestination — The Heavenly Book — Declining pathos. (Criticism of the theory of strophic forms in the *Qorân.*)

---

The Prophet's exertions were not entirely without success. Led by his wife Khadîja, a small but devoted band rallied round him. The majority, it is true, consisted of people in the humblest circumstances, but there was also a fair sprinkling of members of the foremost families of Mecca. Among these was Aliy, son of Abû Tâlib, Muhammed's uncle and foster-father. This latter, however, did not join the new faith himself. Of greater importance still was the conversion of Abû Bakr,[35] a wealthy and much esteemed merchant of the clan of the Qoreish. This was indeed most encouraging, yet the adversaries still commanded an overwhelming majority, and held the welfare, even the lives, of the Faithful in their hands. Muhammed dared not remain inactive, but had to go on with his work and produce fresh credentials.

As regards the performance of miracles he had hitherto been somewhat unfortunate. A still greater difficulty remained to be overcome, concerning another indispensable apanage of a prophet, *viz.*, the faculty of foretelling future events. Of this he must have been aware through his knowledge of Scripture, especially as many passages from Biblical prophecies held — and still hold — prominent places in the Jewish liturgy.[36]

It appears to me that the series of oracles in the *Qorân* which describe the condition of things at the end of time, were modelled on Messianic prophecies in the Bible, although not attaining to their loftiness and grandeur. Muhammed could only use such portions as touch on the sinfulness of mankind and the punishment awaiting them, the reward of the pious and the general transformation of Nature as intimated in Isaiah xxiv. 18-23; Zach. xiv. 4, *etc.*

Vaticination was common in Arabia,[37] and we have seen how Muhammed had to defend himself against charges of soothsaying. To a certain extent he was unable to avoid giving some colour to these, as his manner of speaking greatly resembled that of the Kâhins who, with mystic ceremonies, foretold the future to individuals. Muhammed himself disclaimed any share in such proceedings, but Moslim tradition will not allow him to be behind other prophets in this line, and records two cases in which his prophecies were verified.[38]

The reader of the *Qorân* cannot fail to note that, when speaking of other prophets, Muhammed in only a very few instances refers to their prophetic gifts,[39] and as a rule only represents them as warning against idolatry and wickedness. As a matter of fact he was unable to predict anything, and least of all a general conversion, after the manner of Isaiah ch. ii., or xi. 6-9. All his prophecies are of an eschatological nature and beyond the control of any human being, so that no one could hope to find an opportunity of charging him with fallacious predictions. He gave weight to these prophecies by making them axioms of faith like those incorporated in the religious codes of the Jews and Christians.

In the oldest epoch of the *Qorân* the "Day" is not mentioned at all, but only hinted at in the description of the events which are to take place when this dawns. An instance is given by *Sûra* lxxxi. which, in spite of the forced pathos and the mannerism of the diction, represents the best

---

[35] See I. I. p. 160 *sq.*, where also the names of the other early believers are given.
[36] With regard to the Messianic hopes entertained by the Jews of Medina *cf.* I. I. 286 and R. E. J. VII. p. 91.
[37] *Cf.* Wellh. R. p. 130. [38] *Cf.* Mishk. II. p. 682. [39] *E. g.*, *S.* xxvi. 155 on the she-camel of Ṣâliḥ.

type of the declamatory period. The Messianic apostrophes, the vague warning that reckoning awaits every soul, and his protestations of being "a noble Messenger" might have made some impression. This *sûra* is divided into two strophes of unequal length, the cadence is all but metrical, and the whole declamation so thoroughly original of its kind, that it deserves to be reproduced in full.[40]

1. When the sun is folded up
2. And when the stars fall down
3. And when the mountains are moved
4. And when the *'ishâr*[41] shall be neglected
5. And when the beasts shall be crowded together[42]
6. And when the seas shall surge up
7. And when the souls shall be paired [with bodies]
8. And when the [female child that was] buried alive shall be asked,
9. For what sin she was slain,
10. And when the sheets shall be opened
11. And when heaven shall be flayed
12. And when hell shall be set ablaze
13. And when Paradise shall be brought nigh:
14. The soul shall know what it has produced.
15. Therefore I swear not by the heavenly wanderers,
16. That move on and backwards,
17. Nor by the night when it draws on,
18. Nor by the morn when it first breathes up;
19. Verily this is the speech of a noble Messenger,
20. Of great power with the Lord of the Throne,

[40] The *sûra* itself is composed of two strophes of about equal length, *viz.*, v. 1 to 14 and 15 to 29, but in such a manner that the second strophe is logically subordinated to the first. This circumstance has been overlooked by D. H. Müller, *Die Propheten in ihrer ursprünglichen Gestalt*, p. 57. Müller's theory, altogether, adapts itself to the *Qorân* on a very limited scale. To suppose that Muhammed knowingly arranged *sûras* in strophes with *Responsionen* would mean that he deliberately exposed himself to the opprobrium of being called a poet. The *Qorân*, of all Semitic literatures, is least appropriate for a theory of the kind in question, as the composition of most *sûras*, and certainly of many quoted by Müller as patterns, is anything but perspicuous. Müller is doubtlessly right in denying that Muhammed borrowed the formation of strophes from a Jew, but then the question arises, where does pre-Islamic poetry offer a single instance of strophes with *Responsionen?* Surely, any ancient tradition among Arabs on such a form of poetry would have left some traces, but to assume that so primordial a custom should, after falling into oblivion, have been revived again at so late an epoch, and without any visible link connecting it with the past, is against common sense. I should rather think that wherever we find strophes in the *Qorân*, they are of a very crude character, and unconsciously constructed rather than artistically. *Sûra* lxxxi. gives an example of this. The stock of rhymes on the same consonant being exhausted, the speaker made a *Kunstpause*, and dropped his voice. In the second strophe there is a marked falling off both as regards vigour and poetic expression, but the speaker felt instinctively that the second part of the oracle must continue on the same strain as the first, and be of equal length. In every *sûra* quoted by Prof. Müller we shall have an opportunity of judging how far he succeeded in proving his case, however, *Strophentrümmer oder doch nicht ganz durch-und ausgebildete Strophenformen* is too elastic an expression to serve as conclusive evidence. Other patterns of strophic structure in the *Qorân* not noticed by Müller are S. lxxxvi. 1 to 10, 11 to 17, both strophes beginning with "by the heaven"; lxxxviii. 1 to 16, 17 to 23, strophes of unequal length; xc. 1 to 10, 11 to 20, the second strophe likewise being subordinated to the first. No further division is justified.

[41] Camel in the tenth month of pregnancy.

[42] *Cf.* Isaiah xi. 6 to 7. It is not at all unlikely that Muhammed should have heard of this famous chapter, which the Jews read in the Synagogue on the last day of Passover.

21. Obeyed and trusty too.

22. Your comrade is not mad!

23. He saw Him on the plain horizon,

24. Nor does he grudge [to divulge] the unseen.

25. This is not the speech of a pelted Satan,

26. Now whither do you go?

27. It is but a reminder to the worlds

28. To whomsoever of you pleases to be steadfast.

29. But you will not, unless Allâh, the Lord of the worlds should please.

The almost artistic structure of the *sûra* alone shows that it cannot have been the product of spontaneous enthusiasm. Muhammed himself was evidently so pleased with this fine performance, that he shortly afterwards tried to imitate it by another which was, however, far inferior, *viz.*, lxxxii. 1-19.[43]

In this *sûra* the "Day of Judgment"[44] is mentioned twice by name (v. 15 and 18), and once more in a paraphrastic manner (v. 19). Subsequently Muhammed got into the habit of circumscribing the "Day" alone, choosing the strangest epithets and paraphrases. This does not refer to the declamatory period alone, but extends over the whole *Qorân*. On account of their large number I have arranged all the instances into groups. It is noteworthy that of the first two groups only one example (lxiv. 9), and of the following but a small number belong to Medinian revelations, the latter being marked by an asterisk.

A. 1. 15, 33. The day of the well known term (*cf.* 38, 82)

2. 19, 40. The day of sighing[45]

3. 20, 61. The day of adornment[46]

4. 26, 189. The day of the scorching heat

5. 30, 56. The day of arousing

6. 32, 29. The day of victory

7. 38, 15, 25, 53. The day of reckoning (*cf.* 40, 28)

8. 40, 15. The day of meeting

9. 40, 18. The day of the approaching hour

10. 40, 34. The day of crying out

11. 42, 5. The day of gathering[47]

12. 44, 40. The day of decision (*cf.* 77, 13)

13. 50, 19. The day of appointment

14. 50, 33. The day of eternal duration

15. 50, 41. The day of coming forth

16. 54, 19. The day of continuous ill-luck

---

[43] Müller, *l. c.* p. 57, three strophes, *viz.*, 1 to 5, 6 to 12, 13 to 19.

[44] Al Ghâzâli, *Iḥyâ*, iv. p. 443 *sq.*, gives a lengthy description of the duration, the names, and calamities of the Day of Judgment.

[45] Epilogue to the story of the mission of Jesus, *cf.* St. Matth. viii. 12; xiii. 42, *etc.*

[46] Palmer takes it as day of festival, but the words are evidently Messianic. The root حشر is frequently used in the *Qorân* in this sense.

[47] With the addition: on which there is no doubt.

17. *64, 9. The day of gathering, this is the day of deceiving
18. 75, 1. The day of Resurrection
19. 82, 15. The day of Judgment (and often)

B. 1. 6, 15. A great day (*cf.* 10, 16; 19, 38; 83, 5)
2. 11, 3. A grand day
3. 11, 28. A painful day (*cf.* 43, 65)
4. 11, 85. An encompassing day
5. 22, 54. A barren day
6. 26, 37, 155. A well known day (*cf.* 56, 50)
7. 29, 35. The last day
8. 54, 8. A hard day (*cf.* 74, 9)
9. 76, 10. A severe day
10. 76, 27. A heavy day
11. 85, 2. The promised day
12. 90, 14. A foodless day

C. 1. *2, 45, 117. The day wherein no soul shall pay recompense for another soul
2. *2, 255. The day on which there is no bartering (*cf.* 14, 36)
3. *3, 7, 24. The day whereof there is no doubt
4. *3, 28. The day that every soul shall find what it has done
5. *3, 102. The day when faces shall be whitened, and faces shall be blackened
6. *5, 108. The day when Allâh shall assemble the apostles
7. *5, 119. The day when their confession shall profit the confessors
8. 6, 22, 128. The day when we shall gather them altogether (*cf.* 10, 29, 46; 41, 18; 27, 85)
9. 6, 73. The day when the horn shall be blown
10. 6, 159. The day when some signs of thy Lord shall come
11. 7, 13. The day when they shall be raised
12. 7, 51. The day when its interpretation shall come
13. *9, 35. The day when it shall be heated in the fire of hell
14. *9, 78. The day when they shall meet him
15. 11, 11. The day it comes to them there is no turning it away from them
16. 11, 107. The day when it shall come no soul shall speak, *etc.*
17. 14, 42. The day when reckoning arises
18. 14, 43. The day on which all eyes shall stare
19. 14, 44. The day when the torment shall come
20. 14, 49. The day when the earth shall be changed into no earth
21. 15, 36. The day when they shall be aroused (*cf.* 37, 144; 38, 80)
22. 16, 86, 91. The day when we shall send from every nation a witness
23. 16, 112. The day when every soul shall come to wrangle for itself

24. 17, 54. The day when he shall call on you

25. 17, 73. The day when we shall call all men by their leader

26. 18, 45. The day when we will move the mountains

27. 18, 50. The day when he shall say, *etc.*

28. 19, 39. The day when they shall come to us

29. 21, 104. The day when we will roll up the heaven

30. 22, 2. The day you shall see it

31. *24, 24. The day when their tongues and hands and feet shall bear witness against them

32. *24, 37. A day when hearts and eyes shall be upset

33. *24, 64. The day they shall be brought back to him

34. 25, 18. The day He shall gather them (*cf.* 10, 29, 46)

35. 25, 24. The day they shall see the angels

36. 25, 27. The day the heavens shall be rent asunder

37. 26, 88. The day when wealth shall profit not, nor sons

38. 28, 62, 74. The day when he shall call them

39. 29, 55. The day when the torment shall cover them

40. 30, 11, 13, 54. The day when the Hour shall rise

41. 30, 42. A day which there is no averting (*cf.* 42, 46)

42. 31, 32. The day when a father shall not atone for his child

43. 32, 4. A day the measure of which is as a thousand years

44. *33, 43. The day they shall meet Him

45. *33, 66. The day when their faces shall writhe

46. 34, 29. A day of which you shall not keep back an hour

47. 40, 35. The day when you shall turn your backs

48. 40, 54. The day when the witnesses shall stand up

49. 40, 55. The day when their excuse shall not avail the wicked

50. 41, 18. The day when the enemies of Allâh shall be gathered together into the fire

51. 41. 47. The day when He shall call to them

52. 44, 9. The day when the heaven shall bring obvious smoke

53. 44, 15. The day when we will assault with the great assault

54. 44, 41. The day when friend shall not avail friend at all

55. 45, 26. The day when the hour shall arise

56. 46, 19, 33. The day when the infidels shall be exposed to the fire

57. 46, 34. The day when they shall see what they are threatened with

58. 50, 29. The day we will say to hell 'Art thou full?'

59. 50, 40. The day when the crier shall cry

60. 50, 41. The day when they shall hear the shout

61. 50, 43. The day when the earth shall be cleft asunder

62. 51, 13. The day when they shall be tried by the fire
63. 52, 9. The day when the heavens shall reel about
64. 52, 13. The day when they shall be thrust away into the fire of hell
65. 52, 46. The day when their plotting shall avail them naught
66. 54, 6. The day when the caller shall call
67. 54, 48. The day when they shall be dragged to the fire
68. *57, 12. The day when thou shalt see believers, *etc.*.
69. *57, 13. The day when the hypocrites shall say
70. *58, 7, 19. The day when Allâh shall raise them
71. *64, 9. The day when He shall gather you (*cf.* A, 11)
72. *66, 8. The day Allâh will not afflict the Prophet and the Faithful
73. 68, 42. The day when the leg shall be bared
74. 70, 4. A day whose length is fifty thousand years (*cf.* 32, 4)
75. 70, 42, 44. Their day which they have been promised
76. 70, 43. The day when they shall come forth in haste
77. 73, 14. The day when the earth and the mountains shall tremble
78. 76, 7. The day the evil of which shall fly abroad
79. 77, 35. The day when they may not speak
80. 78, 18. The day when the trumpet shall be blown
81. 78, 38. The day when the Spirit and the angels shall stand in ranks
82. 78, 41. The day when man shall see what his two hands have sent forward
83. 79, 6. The day when the quaking quakes
84. 79, 35. The day when man shall remember what he strove after
85. 79, 46. The day they see it (*viz.*, the hour)
86. 80, 34. The day when man shall flee from his brother
87. 82, 19. The day when no soul shall control aught for another
88. 83, 6. The day when man shall stand before the Lord of the world
89. 86, 9. The day when the secrets shall be tried
90. 101, 3. The day when men shall be like scattered moths.

D. On that day (*alyawma* and *yawma'idin*) very frequent

E. 1. 79, 42. The Hour (and about forty times more)
2. 80, 33. The Calamity (*aṣṣâkhatu*)
3. 88, 1. The overwhelming due (*alghâshiyatu*)
4. 90, 11. The steep (*ala'qabatu*)

From this extraordinary variety of names and elaborate definitions of the "Day of Judgment" something must be learnt. Muhammed would certainly not have taken the trouble of continually finding new epithets without some distinct purpose. It is therefore clear that they represent nothing less than Messianic prophecies, the only kind of predictions in which he could safely indulge. Although they are distributed over the whole *Qorân*, their actual development belongs to the declamatory period, whilst their inception may be traced to the period of confirmatory revelations.

Another imitation of *Sûra* lxxxi. is *Sûra* lxxxiv.,[48] both as regards contents and form, also describing the "Day" without distinctly mentioning it. It begins thus :

1. When the heaven is split,
2. And gives ear to its Lord and is dutiful
3. And when the earth is stretched
4. And casts forth what is in it and is empty,
5. And gives ear to its Lord and is dutiful :
6. O man ! verily thou are toiling hard after thy Lord, *etc.*

*Sûra* xcix.[49] is devoted to the same subject, but is obviously weaker. The description loses it poetic vigour, but refers twice tò "that day."

In the first chapter I have already alluded to the incident which caused the revelation of *Sûra* lxxx.[50] It belongs to the declamatory period. The very brief but graphic introduction is followed by a soliloquy which leads up to the subject of the address proper. This is a recapitulation of the second sentence of the first revelation (xcvi. 2),[51] but in a more detailed and descriptive manner. By inserting an appeal to man's gratitude towards the Creator for the comforts of life, Muhammed introduced a new element of discussion, which at a later period became a very important subject in his sermons. A short description of the "Calamity" of the "Day of Judgment" and the varying demeanour of the pious and wicked "on that day" concludes an address, which is distinguished not only by variety of topics, but also by high flown diction and even originality, whilst forming a united and well rounded sermon.

If Muhammed introduced into his delineations of the "Day of Judgment" the changes to which sun, moon and stars are to be subjected, he may have followed Biblical models (*e.g.*, Isaiah xxiv. 23 ; xiii. 10 ; lx. 19 ; Amos viii. 9), but it seems that, at the same time, he wished to protest against the worship of heavenly bodies. He teaches that, being but component parts of the created world, they are subject to the divine will which can utterly annihilate them. The sun shall be "folded up," the stars shall "become black," the mountains be "removed," the moon be "split" (liv. 1 ; lxxv. 8-9 ; lxxxiv. 18), or "gathered in."[52] All this, however, was not to take place until some very remote period, but it was important to point out that the cosmical powers, and particularly the meteorological phenomena connected with certain constellations, were but the work of Allâh. He alone makes man die, causes him to be buried, then, if he wishes, raises him up again (liii. 45-50 ; lxxx. 21-3 ; lxxv. 8-9, 40). He has created from a clot, and He is the Lord of the Sirius.[53]

[48] Likewise overlooked by Müller. The *sûra* is divided into two strophes (v. 1 to 15, 16 to 25) of unequal length and little internal coherence. Verse 16 corresponds in every respect to lxxxi. 15. Verse 25 does not seem to have originally belonged to the *sûra*, but was added in order not to allow the *sûra* to end with a verse containing something evil.

[49] According to some traditionists the *sûra* is of Medinian date, *cf. Itqân*, p. 22 *sq.* According to Ibn Abi Ḥâṭim from Abu Sa'îd Al Khaḍri it was not revealed until after the battle of Uḥud (*Itq.* 30). Fihrist, p. 251, call it Medinian. It is, however, very improbable that a *sûra* of this style should have been first revealed so late. To v. 7 *cf.* x. 62 ; xxxi. 15.

[50] See Müller, *l. c.* p. 86, *Wie die beiden disparaten Theile zu einer Einheit geworden, weiss ich nicht. Weder Sinn noch Strophik geben eine Lösung dieses Räthsels.* The *sûra* has evidently been a whole one from the beginning. Verse 16 is not only through the rhyme, but logically connected with the preceding verses ; *cf.* v. 34 to 42. — Verse 21 (connected by فل) begins the second strophe which draws the moral from the contemplations of the first.

[51] Verse 13 = lxxxvii. 18 to 19 and lxxiv. 52.

[52] In *S.* vi. 75 to 78 this is in a more popular manner demonstrated by the tale how Abraham worshipped a star, the moon and the sun, each in their turn, but seeing them set could not believe in their divine nature.

[53] See Ch. I. p. 9.

There now follows a series of addresses which Muhammed always begins by conjuring heaven and earth and all they include. One of the best specimens of these is *Sûra* lxxxvi.[54] which contains the remarkable sentence (v. 4) that "every soul has a guardian over it, but let man consider for what he has been created," *etc.* — The inferences drawn from this and similar passages shew that the views which Muhammed held at the earlier period with regard to the freedom of human will, differ from the later theories which considerably limited man's own responsibilities in matters of belief, and the shaping of his fate. The former idea was not only inborn in Muhammed, but also strengthened by his studies, the latter was an axiom artificially cultivated and foisted upon the believers for practical motives. At the time when the Prophet was anxious to gain the goodwill even of the humblest member of his audience, he would have been ill advised to teach that their guidance depended solely on Allâh.[55] It was more prudent to preach that he was charged to show them the right way, and that those who refused to listen, did so on their own responsibility and to their own hurt.

lxxv. 1. I swear not by the Day of Resurrection,
2. Nor do I swear by the self-accusing soul,
3. Does man think that we shall not collect his bones?
4. Yes, we are able to arrange his finger-tips
5. Nay, but man wishes to be wicked;
6. He asks: When is the Day of Resurrection? *etc.*

Now in the sentence quoted above it is stated that every soul has a guardian over it, who gauges its actions, but which are otherwise quite unfettered.[56] Far from teaching salvation through a vicarious agent, Muhammed at this period entertains the theory, also rife in Jewish belief, that man is answerable for his actions, and must give an account of them on the Day of Judgment. The idea is more clearly expressed in *Sûra* liii. 39-46 given in the form of a quotation from the *suḥuf* of Moses and Abraham,[57] *viz.*, that "no burdened [soul] shall bear the burden of another, and that man shall have only what he strives for." This is clearly nothing but the Rabbinical sentence: "With what measure man measures, shall be measured unto him."[58] This axiom so thoroughly penetrates all phases of Rabbinical literature, that it had undoubtedly become proverbial, also among those Jews with whom Muhammed had come in contact in Syria and elsewhere. As already intimated, post-Biblical tradition made the first day of the seventh month (Lev. xxiii. 24; Numb. xxix. 1) into a "Day of Judgment," on which "the children of man pass by before Him like lambs"[59] in order to be judged according to their merits.

Similar ideas are expressed in the the *Qorân* not only in the oldest epoch, but through nearly the whole Meccan period. "Every man is hostage for what he deserves" (lii. 21);[60] "on that day shall every soul earn what it deserves" (xl. 17). Sentences of this kind stand in opposition to what is called the "fatalism" of the Moslim creed. Even as late as almost at the end of the Meccan period Muhammed pronounced: "Leave those who treat their faith as play and mockery, this life deceives them, but remind them that a soul is offered what it has earned, and has, beside Allâh, no friend nor intercessor; and though it should compensate with the fullest compensation, it would not be accepted. Those who are given up for what they have gained, for them is a drink of boiling water, and painful punishment for their disbelief" (vi. 69). Finally: "Whoso does evil, he shall only be recompensed with the like thereof" (xl. 43).

---

[54] *Cf.* above.
[55] *Sûra* lxxiv. 34 a very late, in fact Medinian, revelation.
[56] The Commentators (Bagh.) naturally refer to celestial guardians.
[57] *Cf.* S. lxxxvii. 13 *sq.* and frequently repeated.
[58] See *Mishna*, Sôtâ I. 7.
[59] See *Mishna*, Rôsh Hash. I. 2.
[60] *Cf.* S. lxxxiii. 14; lxxiv. 41; xlv. 21; xlii. 29; cxi. 2. The expressoin كسب stands in its material sense; *cf.* xli. 46: Whoever does good, it is for himself, and who does evil, upon him it comes; see also li. 59.

Opposed to these verses stands a long series of others which describe man as dependent in his actions entirely on the will of Allâh. It cannot be said that the latter doctrine replaced the former, as in a revelation belonging to the oldest periods it is already stated that Allâh "makes enter into His mercy whomsoever He wishes" (lxxvi. 31), and later on, "thus leads Allâh astray whom he wishes and guides whom he wishes" (lxxiv. 34). "If Allâh wished He would guide all mankind [to belief]" (xiii. 30). There are many more passages alluding to the following subjects, the creature of man (xxviii. 68), providing him with food (xiii. 26; xiv. 13, 32; xvii. 32; xxviii. 82; xxix. 62); granting mercy (xxix. 20; x. 107), or inflicting punishment on him (xiii. 14) solely on the ground of Allâh's will.[61] Any attempt to reconcile this paradox will fail, and it only remains for us to try and find out how Muhammed came to reveal theories so antagonistic to common sense.

Muhammed had evidently meditated on the problems of human free will and predestination as taught in Jewish as well as Christian writings. On the relation of man to his deeds in the former we have treated above, and even a sentence, like Exod. xi. 10, is regarded by Rabbinical doctrine as punishment for sins committed before voluntarily.[62] But with regard to man's fate Jewish doctrines are likewise absolute in giving them unconditionally in the hands of Providence, whilst it stands in no connection with his piety or wickedness.[63] No accident, great or small, befalls man which is not ordained by the will of God.[64]

The fundamental doctrines of the Christian Church remained either unknown to Muhammed or else did not appeal to him, and therefore we find few traces in the *Qorân.* Even in the Medinian revelations he repeatedly denied that one soul could atone for another, and that intercession would be accepted (ii. 45, 117, 255-6), although a mediator is not unknown both in the Old and New Testaments.[65] It is, however, possible that Muhammed had found support for his fatalistic inclinations in sentences (like Romans ix. 14-18) that "he hath mercy on whom he will, and whom he will he hardeneth" (*cf.* v. 21). In fact, this phrase greatly resembles those of the *Qorân* quoted above. Yet the effect of true penitence is clearly laid down in the *Qorân*, although I believe in one passage only.[66]

It is difficult for untrained minds to speculate on the problems of human free will and predestination taken singly, and to acquire any clear idea on the connection which exists between the two, is beyond the capacity of the large majority of believers in the latter. Being important factors in every religion it was advisable to render these promblems more conceivable to the common mind by introducing them in the shape of a book. This idea which is first expressed in a Biblical metaphor (Exod. xxxii. 32), subsequently assumed two different forms. In one book man's fate is inscribed (Isaiah iv. 3; Ps. lxix. 28, cxxxix. 16); whilst the other records his actions for which he must give account hereafter (Abôth iii. 16). It is easy to see that the notion of such a book was most tempting to Muhammed, and he took the first opportunity of making use of it. Although according to the *Qorân* the Book contains everything, the oldest *sûras* only state that its purpose is to chronicle the deeds of man. Its functions are, however, increased later on to such an extent, that "there escapes Him not [a thing of] the size of a seed in the heavens or in the earth, or smaller or larger than it, that is not recorded in a manifest book."[67] Muhammed's own notions were rather dim, and when asked what the Book

---

[61] *Cf. S.* x. 99: If thy Lord had wished, everyone on earth would be a believer; but wilt thou force men to become believers? (100) It is not in the power of a soul to believe unless Allâh grants it, and He places disbelief on those who do not understand (see Sprenger, II. 313 rem.). *Cf. S.* lxxxi. 29: You will nothing except the Lord of the worlds will it; *cf.* xlii. 6.

[62] *Cf.* Gen. iv. 7; Deut. xxx. 19.

[63] "It is not in our power to explain the welfare of the wicked nor the trials of the righteous" (*Abôth* iv. 15).

[64] "Even the distributer of water is appointed by heaven" (*Talmud, Berakhoth* 58vo).

[65] Exod. xxxii. 11 to 14; Deut. v. 25; Job xxxiii. 23; Gal. iii. 19 to 20.—Moslim tradition has, however, reserved to Muhammed the right of interceding on behalf of those for whom permission is granted to him by Allâh; *cf.* Kremer, *Gesch. der herrschenden Ideen*, p. 285. Al Ghazâli, Iḥyâ, IV. 453.

[66] *Cf. S.* xlii. 24.

[67] *Cf. S.* x. 62, nearly literal repetition; lxxviii. 29: Everything have we recorded in a book.

meant, gave only vague answers with which, in the declamatory period, he endeavoured to cloak his inability to give a clear definition.[68]

The problem of predestination gave ample food for discussion and hairsplitting theories to the Muhammedan theologians. A good deal of what was then written on this subject has been made accessible in modern works,[69] and I can therefore omit it here, especially as my aim is only to give in outline that which concerns the *Qorân*. Suffice it to say that the orthodox Moslim forms, from the inferences which he draws from these sentences of the *Qorân*, tenets which show that man's actions as well as his fate are entirely dependant on what is inscribed in the celestial Book.

Descriptions of the Day of Judgment, scarcely differing from each other except in the endless variety of torments for the wicked which they depict, form a prominent feature of the declamatory addresses. Yet Muhammed did not allow his imagination to run away with him, but very shrewdly endowed Paradise with ever-flowing springs of fresh water, shady bowers, and tempting fruits. Knowing the sort of people with whom he had to deal, he wished first of all to attract them, and it was strategy rather than sanctity which induced him also to add more sensual pleasures than one would expect in celestial regions. Revelations of this nature are to be found in *Sûras* lxxxviii.,[70] lxxix., and lxxvii., the last named being built on *Sûra* lxxxiii.

lxxvii. 1. By those sent in a series,
2. And by those who speed swiftly,
3. And by the dispensers abroad,
4. And by the separators apart,
5. And by those who instil the reminders
6. As an excuse or warning.
7. Verily, what ye are threatened with shall surely happen !
8. When the stars shall be erased,
9. And when the heavens shall be cleft,
10. And when the mountains shall be winnowed,
11. And when the Messengers shall have a time appointed for them !
12. For what day is the appointment made ?
13. For the day of decision !
14. And what shall make thee know what the decision is ?
15. Woe on that day for those who say it is a lie ! *etc.*

This is but one-third of the *sûra*, yet all originality is already exhausted. Although devoted to the "Day of Decision" the *sûra* gives no other explanation of it, but that therein the infidels shall be woe begone, and that they shall neither speak nor receive permission to excuse themselves (v. 35-36). The words: "woe on that day," *etc.*, form a refrain which is repeated after groups of two or three verses.

Looking at this refrain from an artistic point of view, it does not seem justifiable to regard it as marking the division of strophes, as it does not form an integral part of the paragraphs, but is, if anything, out of place in many instances. It is probably but a *Kunstpause*, serving to prolong the address and to allow the speaker time to think of new phrases and expressions for a subject which was commencing to lose its freshness.

[68] See *S.* lxxxiii. The *sûra* consists of *four* strophes, *viz.*, v. 1 to 9, 10 to 20, 21 to 28, 29 to 36.

[69] See Kremer, *l. c.* p. 280 *sqq.*

[70] Two strophes, *viz.*, v. 1 to 16, 17 to 26. The second strophe being quite out of connection with the first, does not seem to have belonged to it from the beginning, but to the descriptive period. The poetic value is certainly much smaller than that of the first strophe.

In introducing "the Book" Muhammed made quite a new departure in the *Qorân*, both with respect to matter and name. For the inhabitants of Mecca a book of any sort possessed all the charms of novelty, as not many of them had ever seen one, whilst that mentioned in the revelations, although invisible to mortal eyes, was yet made palpable by the vivid description given of it.[71] This book which contains the fate of every living being, is to be opened and read on the Day of Judgment. As is the case with the latter, Muhammed liked to change the name of the "Book," although less frequently. In one of the last mentioned *sûras* (lxxxiii.) we had the names *sijjîn*[72] (v. 8) and *illyyûn*[73] (v. 19); other names are *suḥuf*[74] and *lawḥ*.[75]

On the Day of Judgment the Book[76] shall appear as a book for each individual. The pious shall hold it in his right hand, and the wicked in his left.[77]

lxix. 19. As for him who is given his book in his right hand, he shall say: Here! take ye and read my book, etc.

25. As for him who is given his book in his left hand, he shall say, etc.

Subsequently, however, this was changed. Instead of giving the book into the right or left *hand*, the pious and wicked are placed respectively on the right or left *side* to be chosen for Paradise or for hell. This is the description given in *Sûra* lvi. 8-9, 26, 40, where, however, *three* groups are mentioned, although only the fates of two are enumerated. This omission of the third party, I believe, is due to the circumstance that v. 10-25 form an independent address belonging to the same period, and were inserted here for some reason unknown to us, perhaps on account of vv. 13-14[78] resembling vv. 38-39.

In v. 77 of the same *sûra* (lvi.) a "Book" is mentioned which is not the book of fates, but the heavenly archtype of the *Qorân*. Later on it is frequently used in this sense, this being the third signification of the word. It also becomes an object to swear by in

*Sûra* lii. 1. By the mount![79]

2. By a Book inscribed.

3. Upon an outstretched vellum! etc.

The *sûra* concludes:

48. And wait thou patiently for the judgment of thy Lord, for thou art in our eyes; and celebrate the praises of thy Lord what time thou risest

49. And in the night praise Him, and at the fading of the stars.

I believe the recitation of the last verses was an invitation to join in common prayer, as was probably the case with other addresses which conclude in a similar manner.[80]

---

[71] See S. lxviii. 37: Have you a book in which you study.—Later on الكتاب refers to the Holy Writ in general. "Possessors of the Book" means Jews and Christians.

[72] Probably etymologically identical with سجّيل (cv. 4; xv. 74; xi. 84).

[73] Seems to be adaptation of Hebr. *'elyôn*. *Cf.* Fränkel, *Aram. Fremdwörter*, etc.

[74] See S. lxxxi. 10; lxxx. 13; lxxiv. 52.

[75] Hebr. לוח. *Cf.* lxxxv. 22.

[76] *Cf.* lxxviii. 29. The *sûra* consists of *three* strophes, *viz.*, v. 1 to 16, 17 to 30, 31 to 41. The second and third strophes begin with إنّ; v. 38 is to be divided (after صفّا) in two.

[77] *Cf.* lxxxiv. 7 and 10.

[78] The integrity of the *sûra* is very doubtful in spite of Müller's (following Nöldeke, *Q.* p. 83) taking it as a whole. If this be the case, we would have the same description repeated. That والسابقون (v. 10) may very well form the commencement of an address we gather from S. lxxix. 1; c. 1. It would also be strange that the three groups mentioned should be the first treated of. The *sûra*, I believe, is composed as follows: v. 1 to 9, 26 to 43 to which belong 54 and 55, 56 to 73, 74 to 96 (*cf.* lii. 48 to 49).

[79] The *sûra* contains several reminiscences of previous addresses: v. 11 = lxxvii. 15; v. 39 = liii. 21; v. 45, فذرهم, *cf.* lxxxii. 11; lxxiv. 11.

[80] Also lvi. 96.

Here we may place *Súra* lxx.[81] which in its entirety is devoted to pictures of the Day of Judgment. Again the pious appear on the right side, the wicked on the left (v. 37).[82] The beginning of this *súra* was due to the tiresome questions[83] of a hardened sceptic, who wearied the prophet with such unpleasant insinuations that the latter had a hard struggle not to lose patience (v. 5).[84] The address is of certain practical importance, as it inculcates the desirability of prayer, almsgiving, chastity, honesty and truthfulness (v. 22-34).[85] Otherwise the *súra* shows visible marks of declining fervour which, however, revives once more in a series of shorter addresses belonging to this period as *Súras* c., ci., cvi.,[86] cvii.,[87] cviii. *Súra* xc. is a fine composition consisting of two strophes.[88] Similar as to form and contents is *Súra* xcii.[89] In *Súra* xci. the speaker begins by calling on the sun and moon, day and night, heaven, earth, and soul[90] to witness his innocence of the charges of spreading falsehood. This is illustrated by the example of the prophet of the tribe of Thamúd whose warnings were derided, whilst those who scoffed at him were heavily punished.

We now see distinctly how this leads up to the narrative period, as the time had come when Muhammed had exhausted his stock of objects to swear by. Yet this *súra* must still be counted among the declamatory ones on account of its beginning. Its antiquity is guaranteed by the fact that the fate of the Thamudenes was a matter well known in Mecca. For a similar reason I here mention *Súra* cv. Perhaps *Súra* cii. is also of declamatory character, but its shortness gives no clue as to the place to which it belongs.

Narrative elements are further visible in *Súra* lxxxix., although its beginning is decidedly of declamatory character, and v. 27-28 form a reflex of Ps. cxvi. 7.

Still are to be mentioned the beginning and end of *Súra* lxxxv. The verses 4-8 are referred by Geiger to Dan. iii. 8 *sq.*,[91] but there is no historical allusion at all in these verses, and they seem only to contain a malediction against infidels. The verses 12-22 harmonize with the first portion (v. 1-8) as to rhythm and rhyme, and belong together, whilst v. 9-11 are evidently of later date. Finally *Súra* ciii. is rather weak, and verse 3 very theological.

81 Verse 42 = lii. 45; see Ch. III.

82 *Cf.* xc. 18 to 19.

83 See Nöldeke, *Q.* p. 83.

84 Bagh., on the authority of قيل, refers v. 5 to 7 to Abu Bakr.

85 *Cf. Súra* xcii.

86 Nöld. *Q.* p. 72.

87 *Ibid.* p. 74.

88 Verses 1 to 10, 11 to 20; see above.

89 Two strophes, *viz.*, v. 1 to 11; 12 to 21; Müller, *l. c.* p. 58, has six strophes.

90 See *S.* lxxv. 2.

91 Verses 9 to 11 do not belong here; to v. 22 *cf.* rem. 75. Nöld. p. 77 is in so far right, as Christians are styled Believers" as late as in the Medinian passage ii. 59, but this passage is purely rhetoric.— قتل is optative. *cf.* lxxx. 16.

# CHAPTER V.

## The Narrative Revelations.

Narrative fragments in the oldest revelations — Historical recollections — Morals of the stories — Alterations of Biblical tales — Intentional obscurities — Various methods of narration — Analysis of various narrative addresses — Transition of the descriptive period — *Al Fátiḥa.*

---

In the development of the *Qorán*, the part of which we are going to treat in this chapter stands above others of the Meccan period as far as variety of topics is concerned, and was undoubtedly more effective than any of the preceding ones.

Although the East is the home of the public narrator (and Muhammed's aim was to instruct and overawe rather than amuse), yet in Arabia he was able to inaugurate a new era in the art of the story-telling. In pre-Islamic times public recitations were poetic, but prose narrations cannot have been quite unknown, at any rate in certain circumscribed areas, since the Meccans used the (Greek) term *asâtîr* for stories, which they disparagingly applied to those told by the Prophet.

The reason why Muhammed introduced tales into his sermons is obvious. A large part of his knowledge of the Bible was of historical in character. He could not fail to realize quickly that by inserting small historical fragments he aroused the curiosity of his hearers. Although these served at first solely as examples to illustrate his warnings, they became gradually longer, and ultimately — being provided with a rich stock of tales of prophets and others who could easily be stamped as such — he simply reversed his tactics. Thus the tale became the chief object of the address, and the morals to be drawn were interspersed.

The short quotations from other books to be found in earlier revelations gave Muhammed opportunities of showing an acquaintance with past events and miracles which must have come as a great surprise to the Meccans. In the primary stages of Islâm, however, tales would have been out of place. Muhammed's first object was to introduce himself as the Messenger of Allâh, to preach His unity, and to confirm his own position. When all he had to say on these points was exhausted, repetition would but have wearied and repelled his most faithful adherents. Interesting tales were, therefore, not only a powerful attraction for his old friends, but an effective means of gaining new ones. They were suited to every capacity, and in an agreeable way induced reflection, whilst working considerably on the superstition of untutored savages.

In the preceding chapter we noticed that these early historical fragments[92] refer to the ancient tribes of 'Âd and Thamûd. Legendary reminiscences of the latter were extant among the Arabs, who had lost the faculty of reading the records engraved in the stones of Al Ḥijr. The frustrated expedition of King Abraha gave rise to *Sûra* cv., but although the incident had occurred within the memory of living persons, Muhammed dared to transform the plague which had decimated the forces of the enemy, into birds sent down from heaven. In *Sûra* lxxxv. 18. Pharaoh is mentioned for the first time,[93] and in other places either alone or together with other persons.[94] Abraham and Moses we encountered in connection with the *Suḥuf* ascribed to them.[95] It must, however, be noted that the two passages in question belong to the confirmatory period, and are not again repeated. I believe this is not accidental. Muhammed may have found it necessary to show that he knew of the existence of previous prophets and their books, but he may not have cared to speak too much about them at that time. He was more interested in

---

[92] S. lxxxv. 18; xci. 11.

[93] *Cf.* S. lxxxix. 9.

[94] S. lxxiii. 16; lxxix. 17; lxix. 9; liv. 41.

[95] S. lxxxvii. 19; liii. 37; *cf.* Ch. IV.

trying to focus all attention on himself and his new doctrine. People had to become accustomed to see in him first and foremost the bearer of the monotheistic idea, whilst other prophets moved like satellites around him. Finally "the people of Noah" appear in *Sûra* liii. 55.[96]

The Qoranic tales in so far resemble their Biblical models, as they show a marked tendency to demonstrate that the believer is rewarded whilst the infidel meets with severe punishment. Both are portrayed in such vivid colours, that the moral of the story stands out sharply defined against the background. It frequently appeals to the lowest instincts in human nature. When the tales become longer, the thread does not run smoothly, but is at certain intervals interrupted by contemplations.[97]

To demonstrate more clearly the meaning of the first verses in *Sûra* lxviii., Muhammed relates an anecdote of two agriculturists whose harvest was destroyed as a punishment for their having announced their intention of reaping without having exclaimed first: if Allâh please! and with the determination not to give any to the poor.[98] Somewhat later but still of a very early period are v. 34-52 with an allusion to Jonah, "the man of the fish."

The first revelation of distinctly narrative character is *Sûra* li. The beginning reminds us of a good example of the declamatory period.[99] Then follows a brief description of the torments of hell and the pleasures of paradise. To an observant person signs of a divine Providence are to be found on earth as well as in man's own soul. This is illustrated by a *résumé* of Gen. xviii. The comparison of the account as given in the *Qorân* with its legendary form in Rabbinical literature has been made by Geiger.[100] Evidently in order to make the sermon a little longer, brief accounts of the wickedness of Pharaoh, the people of 'Âd, Thamûd, and the generation of Noah are added. The keynote of the address is probably to be found in v. 52:[1] "There never came a Messenger unless they said: he is a sorcerer or mad." This shews that not only had the old reproach been revived but another had been added, *viz.*, that Muhammed was prompted by a desire for material gain.[2] The latter he refuted in the concluding verses winding up with a threat for the wicked.

If the narration of the strangers' visit to Abraham be examined a little more chosely, we observe that Muhammed altered his original to suit his purpose. The message they brought to him with regard to the birth of a son is treated as a matter of secondary importance, whilst their chief object is represented as being to inform Abraham of their intention to destroy a wicked people among whom there is only "one house of Moslims" (v. 36). The whole is meant to represent a "sign" for those who fear the punishment.

There is scarcely a single revelation of narrative character in which the "sign" is not mentioned. This proves how keenly Muhammed felt the disappointment of being still unable to perform a miracle. Hence the employment of *âya*, the term for "sign" also for "verse." The "sign" is the main object of all the Meccan *sûras* following and many Medinian ones. Not less than ten Meccan *sûras*, all of which are narrative, begin with the words: "These are the signs of the manifest Book," or something similar.[3] A veritable lecture on the sign is

---

96 *Cf.* S. lxxi. 1 more in detail.

97 To this rule even S. xii. makes no exception, *e. g.*, v. 34, 38, 40, *etc.*

98 See Ch. VIII.

99 V. 10 قُتِلَ ; *cf.* lxxxv. 4; lxxx. 16; lxxiv. 19, 20. Nöld. *l. c.* p. 83 regards v. 24 *sqq.* as a later addition.

100 *Was hat Muhammed, etc.*, p. 129 *sqq.* Beidh. draws attention to the grammatical character of ضيف which is used for sing. and plur. alike. It is possible that Muhammed chose a singular form on purpose with respect to Gen. xviii. 3, which gave the Jewish commentators also opportunities of attaching remarks to it. — Another direct reference to the original is to be found in v. 26 أهله = הנה באהל; *ibid.* v. 9.

1 Application of v. 39.

2 *Cf. I. Ish.* p. 1000 and the interview of Otba with Muhammed: *cf. ibid.* p. 185 *sq.*, and *Qor.* xli. 1 to 3; xxxviii. 86.

3 Meccan *Sûras*: x. to xv., lxxvi., xxvii., xxviii., xxxi.; Medinian: xxiv., lxii.

*Sûra* xxvi., which is as elaborate as it is methodically constructed. In the beginning the speaker describes his mental condition as follows:[4] —

1. Those are the Signs of the manifest Book.
2. Haply thou art vexing thyself to death that they will not be believers.
3. If we please we will send down upon them from heaven a Sign, so that their neck shall be humbled thereto.

This most impressive introduction[5] is followed by a very detailed relation of the message of Moses to Pharaoh. As credentials he and Aaron receive Signs in word and deed similar to Exod. iv. 1-17. They perform their task to the astonishment of all present, and lead the Israelites through the sea. The tale ends then with the same words as v. 7, which return regularly as refrain after the stories of Abraham, Noah, 'Âd, Thamûd, Lot, and Shueib. The appearance of each prophet being connected with a "sign" wrought upon the people to whom they were sent, was to prove to the Meccans that Muhammed's knowledge of those facts was miraculous, and therefore likewise a "Sign." This can be inferred from the following words: —

v. 192. And verily it is a revelation from the Lord of the worlds.
193. The faithful spirit[6] came down with it.
194. Upon thy heart, that thou shouldst be of those who warn.
195. In plain Arabic language.
196. It is [to be found] in the *zubur* of the ancient![7]
197. Shall it not be a Sign unto them, that the learned men of the children of Israel recognise it.

There is an obscurity in these verses which is intentional rather than accidental. Such strange things as the *zubur* and "the faithful Ruh" were better left unexplained as food for general contemplation and wonder. The assurance that the revelation had been brought down "in plain Arabic language" did not help to make matters clearer, nor did it follow that everyone understood it. It is, on the contrary, an endeavour to hide the un-Arabic look of the whole paragraph. The same assurance is repeated about half a dozen times in the next few years,[8] and three times at the beginning of addresses. As a Sign must also be regarded that already "the learned of the children of Israel" knew it.[9] This is as vague an expression as can be, since, as we saw above, the Children of Israel were for Muhammed only a historical reminiscence and nothing more. The Meccans were the last to know anything at all about them.

The verbosity of *Sûra* xxvi. is in itself a sign of the severe struggle which raged in the bosom of the Prophet. He saw himself compelled to amend the deficiency in quality by quantity. He represents himself as being sent to warn his nearest kinsmen and to spread his

[4] As to the initials see Ch. XIII.

[5] V. 6 descriptive. — The verses 7 to 8, 67 to 68, 103 to 104, 121 to 122, 139 to 140; 158 to 159, 174 to 175; 190 to 191 form eight refrains which include the seven narrations. The intervals (59, 35, 17, 17, 18, 14, 15 verses) are so unequal that this *sûra* does not give much to support O. H. Müller's assertions (*l. c.* p. 40 *sqq.*). It is to me more than doubtful that Muhammed, in the composition of this *sûra*, followed any tradition of olden times. The *sûra* has a second refrain, *viz.*, v. 109, 127, 145, 164, 1680: "I expect no reward."

[6] الروح v. 193. In the older passages الروح is only mentioned in the connections with the angels (الملائكة); *cf. S.* xcii. 4; lxx. 4; lxxviii. 38; *cf.* also xvi. 2 (and standing alone, xxxviii. 72). الملائكة without الروح liii. 28; xvii. 97. All these passages do not go beyond the declamatory period. *Al Rûḥ* is, of course, the same as in Exod. xxxi. 3, *etc.* — The روح القدس of rabbinical origin, is not mentioned until xvi. 104 (descriptive). The original Arabic form is الرّوح.

[7] الزبر used here for the first time; *cf.* liv. 43, 52. The verses 79 to 84 appear to be a reflex of various paragraphs from the Jewish prayer called *'Âmidâ*, or "Eighteen Benedictions."

[8] xx. 112; xliii. 1; xii. 2; xxxix, 29; xlvi. 11; xvi. 105; xli. 2. See Ch. I. p. 6.

[9] Suffixum in يعلمه refers to تنزيل (v. 192).

wings over all those who follow him in belief (v. 214 to 215), but is not responsible for the perdition of the disobedient (216).[10] These words betray more self-confidence than real potency. Muhammed was hardly able to protect himself, much less others, and, indeed, he could not have succeeded in giving shelter to one of them, had they not enjoyed the protection of influential families. It is therefore better to take v. 215 purely in a spiritual sense, with which the admonition of v. 217, to put his trust in Allâh, agrees very well.

If one peruses the narrative revelations, it is soon perceived that these are of two classes. Some there are which name quite a number of prophets, to each of whom only a few verses are dedicated, whilst others mention but one or two altho' with far more detail. Yet even those of the latter class seldom give complete biographies, but are contented with one or two episodes out of the life of the prophet under discussion, whilst they save other noteworthy incidents concerning the same prophet for other occasions. Thus it happens that larger episodes of the lives of men like Abraham, Moses and Jesus[11] are scattered piecemeal through the whole book. Muhammed exercised a wise economy in not exhausting his material too quickly in order to sustain the interest of his hearers with an ever fresh display of learning.

The narrative element is so essential, that it must be carefully investigated especially with regard to its bearing on Islâm in general. Since the bulk of it belongs to the Meccan portion of the *Qorân*, we may conclude that those who had the greatest influence on Muhammed's theological views, were the persons who are oftenest discussed. Now the foremost of these is Moses who is mentioned about *twenty* times; then follows Abraham with *fifteen*, Noah, Lot, Shoeib with *ten to seven*. The birth and mission of Jesus are mentioned in the Meccan *sûras* only twice, but both times without acknowledgment of his divinity (xix. 36; xliii. 58-9). This proves that Muhammed was little influenced by the New Testament. In the face of this fact Wellhausen's assertion, that Christianity had sown the seed of Islâm, is untenable. Nor was it Rabbinic Judaism, but Mosaism of which Islâm is a weak imitation. Therefore Moses and Abraham are frequently placed before Believers as the representatives of an uncompromizing monotheism.

Here again method and systematic dealing manifest themselves, and out of the apparent chaos of incoherent stories emerge distinct forms which Muhammed has set up as his models. It is not accidental that those who appear next in frequency to Moses and Abraham are Hûd and Ṣâliḥ, the two legendary prophets of 'Âd and Thamûd, because they are taken from the history of Muhammed's own country; nor is it even by chance that the latter is mentioned not only alone, but earlier and more in detail than the former, probably because the ruins of their dwellings in Al Ḥijr were known to all travellers.

Typical of older narrative *sûras* is liv. Beginning with a solemn reminiscence of the declamatory period it announces that "the Hour is near and the moon rent; although[12] they might now see a Sign, they would turn away and say: 'deception without end' "! — Subsequently the speaker mentions the people of Noah, 'Âd and Thamûd, without, however, stating the names of the apostles belonging to the two last, a proof that Hûd and Ṣâliḥ have allegorical meanings, *viz.*, Penitent[13] and Pious. Sin and punishment of Thamûd are more minutely described than of the others, including Lot and Pharaoh. The narrator also bestowed a certain amount of care on the forms. The stories are divided into paragraphs each ending with a refrain which runs:

16. Then how was my punishment and my warning.

17. We have made the *Qorân* easy as reminder — but is there anyone who will mind?[14]

---

[10] I believe the sermon ended v. 220, whilst v. 221 to 228 form an independent address.

[11] The number of prophets mentioned in the *Qorân*, is five and twenty (*Itqân*, 790), whilst there occur about forty names of persons.

[12] Rückert's *Doch wenn sie schon* is wrong.

[13] هود plur. of هائد; *cf.* Ch. II.

[14] V. 21 to 22, 32, 40. Also here I can see no strophes, as the paragraphs are of very unequal length. Besides the refrain in vv. 30 to 32 is interrupted by v. 31, which describes the punishment of the Thamûd. The whole is a rhetorical play. Palmer omits the refrain several times.

*Sûra* xxxvii. begins with a completely declamatory introduction to support the proclamation of the Unity of Allâh. Signs would be disregarded by the infidels who hold that death is the end of everything.[15] "When they are told, there is no God beside Allâh, they behave haughtily and say: shall we forsake our gods on account of a mad poet" (v. 34[16] to 35)? This charge which had evidently not died out yet, provided Muhammed with another opportunity of a very realistic description of the pleasures of Paradise and the tortures of hell.

After this homiletic overture follows the essential part of the lecture which is of narrative character. Having briefly mentioned Noah, the sermon proceeds to relate the rabbinical legend of Abraham's adventure with his father's idols.[17] On this occasion the speaker treats on an episode in Abraham's life differing from that given in *Sûra* xxvi. Whilst the tone in the latter is solemn and pathetic, the former is anecdotal and in part even satirical. Abraham taunts the idols as well as their worshippers, and the latter construct a furnace into which he is thrown. Being rescued by divine interference, Abraham recites a prayer and receives tidings that "a son" is to be born unto him.[18] In a dream he is commanded to sacrifice his son (v. 101 to 104), but finally he is absolved from performing this painful task and is rewarded for his obedience.

In the course of the sermon Moses and Aaron are alluded to, and Muhammed hurries on to introduce a new personality in the figure of the prophet Elijah.[19] The citation of this man in the *Qorân* has another interest for us, as the worship of Ba'al is mentioned in connection with his name.[20] There can be no doubt, that Muhammed's acquaintance with the history of Elijah could only have come from Jewish sources, as *ba'l* in Arabic is only known in its original meaning of *husband*.

It is rather confusing to find in this part a few verses devoted to Lot and his wife,[21] but Muhammed had another new person to introduce, *viz.*, Jonah. We read about his adventures on the ship, his being swallowed by a fish, his illness,[22] his gourd, and his mission to hundred thousand[23] people who are saved from destruction by embracing the true faith. — A general feature to be noted in the latter part of the *sûra* is the refrain which terminates the account of each messenger in the words: Peace be upon N. N.,[24] *etc.*, which at the end of the *sûra* is repeated in a more comprehensive manner thus: Peace be upon the messengers, and praise to Allâh, the Lord of the worlds.

---

[15] *Cf.* v. 51 and xliv. 34 opposed to v. 56; see Ch. III.

[16] The passage is one of the two expressing the *Dikr*, see Ch. II.

[17] The anecdote is reported in full by Geiger, *l. c.* p. 122 *sqq.* — Moslim theologians of the Zahirite school (see Goldziher, *die Zahiriten*, p. 116 *sqq.*), which interprets the *Qorân* strictly according to its literal sense, are greatly concerned about several apparently sinful sayings and doings of Biblical persons. Ibn Ḥazm, therefore, takes the trouble to remove these difficulties. Abraham, he points out, made several misstatements, *viz.*, *S.* xxxvii 87; vi. 76; xxi. 64, to which Ibn Ḥazm adds Abraham's statement that Sarah was his sister. The last statement does not occur in the *Qorân*, but Ibn Ḥazm must have learnt it from a private source, which did not reveal him Gen. xx. 12. As a consequence of his rigid method of exegesis Ibn Ḥazm's explanations are rather hair-splitting. In a similar manner he treats Adam's disobedience, Noah's error (*S.* xi. 47), and Lot's impious remark (*S.* xi. 80). The untruth Joseph's brothers told their father (*S.* xii. 8 to 18) is dismissed with the declaration that they were not prophets. In the same way Ibn Ḥazm speaks of the transgressions ascribed to Moses, Jonas, David and Solomon (fol. 323$^{vo}$ to 333$^{ro}$).

[18] This son is not Isaac but Ismael, as the former is mentioned, v. 112 sq.

[19] Mentioned only once more (vi. 85).

[20] Baghawi و هو اسم صنم لهم كانوا يعبدونه لذلك سُمّيت مدينتهم بعلبك قال مجاهد عكرمة و قتادة البعلُ الرّبّ بلغة اهل اليمن. In the *Qorân* itself بعل occurs several times in its original meaning *husband* (pl. بعولة), ii. 228; xxiv. 31. *Sûra* xi. 75 وهذا بعلي شيخاً, however, seems to be translation of (Gen. xviii. 12) ואדני זקן The assertion of Al Baghawi that البعل means in the dialect of Yaman *master* is of no consequence, as the original meaning of this word had then already undergone great transformation.

[21] V. 135 is exactly like xxvi. 171. The wife is not mentioned any more.

[22] Jonah iv. 8, יתעלף.

[23] *Ibid.* v. 11, "twelve myriads."

[24] Vv. 109, 120, 130, 131.

Of very similar construction is *Sûra* xliv. The "Book" was sent down in "a blessed night."[25] Then follows a rhapsody ending with the words: There is no Allâh beside Him;[26] He quickens and kills, (He is) your Lord and the Lord of your fathers.[27] — The reproach that Muhammed is only "a trained madman" (v. 13), is refuted by the reproduction of a story of Pharaoh to whom "a noble messenger" came who was in fear of being stoned (v. 19). This is evidently a reflex of Exod. viii. 26. Then follows the rescue of the Banû Israel "whom we have chosen[28] on account of our knowledge of the worlds (v. 31), and gave them the signs." — The objection raised by Meccans that man dies only once, is met by reminding them of the fate of the people of Tobba',[29] whose history was sufficiently known in Arabia. — The address is then concluded by a description of hell, particularly of the tree Zaqqûm, which is in so far significant, as it is mentioned in two preceding addresses.[30]

I here add *Sûra* xxxviii., the revelation of which, according to some commentators, stands in close connection with the conversion of Omar.[31] V. 5 evidently refers to the final seclusion of the Qoreish[32] who claimed that so complete a repudiation of every polytheistic relic[33] was unheard of in "the last religion."[34] This leads up to the argument that also the people of Noah, 'Ad, and Pharaoh ("the man of the stakes") had refused to become believers, as well as the Thamûd, the people of Lôt, and of Al Aika.[35] Quite a new personality s introduced in "our servant David, the man of power." The mountains and birds which praise (Allâh) with him are reflexes of verses like Ps. xcvi. 11 to 12, cxviii. 8, *etc.* The fable related in 2 Sam. xii. 1 to 6 is reproduced by Muhammed in the light of a real incident, but is evidently confounded with 1 K. iii. 27. Another novelty is the introduction of Solomon, whose ove for horses (1 K. x. 28) is hinted at, as well as his predilections for enjoyments as shown in Eccles. Ch. ii. The building of the Temple remains unnoticed, although Muhammed, a little later, alludes to his nightly journey to the same, but the rabbinical legends of Solomon's rejection, repentance, and his dominion over spirits are touched upon, being more entertaining.

New, likewise, is "my servant Job" (*cf.* Job xlii. 7 to 8) who is told by God to stamp with his foot, and a spring gushing forth from the ground should cure him of his disease. There exists no Biblical or Rabbinical equivalent for this, but I believe Muhammed had the story of Na'amân, whose leprosy was cured by bathing in the Jordan, in his mind (2 K. v. 10 to 14). An allusion to this was in so far very appropriate, as the Syrian general had been under the impression that the prophet Elisha (mentioned below) would apply a charm to free him from his disease, and the confusion of the two cases is therefore probable. Subsequently we meet "our servants" Abraham, Isaac, Jacob, Ismael and Elisha. Who Dul-Kifl[39] may be, cannot be made out. The name owes its origin apparently to some misreading on the part of Muhammed of which we have had several instances.

The lecture ends in a sermon on the paradise, "the day of reckoning"[40] and hell. The verses which follow are of special interest; I therefore give the translation.

v. 65. Say: I am only a warner, and *there is no God beside Allâh*,[41] the One, the Victorious.

---

25 *Cf.* xcvii. 1, في ليلة القدر.

26 See Ch. II.

27 Adaptation of Hebrew *Elohênu wêlôhê abhôthênû.*

28 See Ch. II. and *S.* xxxv. 29.

29 Only once more, *viz.*, l. 13.

30 lvi. 52; xxxvii. 60.

31 Sprenger, II. 23, where the traditions are reproduced. I. Isḥ. p. 279 refers to the death of Abû Tâlib.

32 "The aristocracy severed themselves from them and said: Go, confide in your gods, etc."

33 This is meant by v. 6. Sprenger, II. 94 (rem.), refers the multiplicity in آلهاتكم to angels. The word ملة is used here for the first time; see above p. 16.

34 Palmer: "in any other sect" has completely missed the sense of the phrase.

35 أحزاب Sprenger, I. p. 471, rightly compares the word with Hebr. גוים

36 *Cf.* Geiger, *l. c.* p. 183.

37 *S.* xvii. 1.

38 Geiger, *l. c.* p. 188.

39 See above and *S.* xxi. 85. Sprenger, II. p. 270, gives him a Yemanian origin. It is, however, to be observed that also Pharaoh is styled ذو الأوتاد, and Noah ذو النون (xxi. 87).

40 Occurs three times in the *sûra*, *viz.*, v. 15, 25, 53.

41 وما من اله الا الله.

66. The Lord of the heavens and the earth, and what is between them, the Mighty, the Forgiving.
67. Say: It is a grand story, (68) but ye turn from it.
69. I had no knowledge of the exalted chiefs when they contended.[42]

Now the last verse contains a bold statement. Muhammed pretends to have been till then unacquainted with a discussion which took place between the heavenly hosts concerning the creation of man. What he really did know was a Rabbinical legend on this subject, connected with Gen. i. 26 ("let *us* make"), but he did not reveal it fully until a Medinian sermon (ii. 28).[43] In this place he confines himself to reproduce, in Biblical terms,[44] the divine intention of creating man to which he adds the rabbinical tradition that Adam being superior to the angels, the latter had been ordered to pay homage to him. Satan, however, refused to do so, and was cursed and banished. In conclusion Muhammed found it necessary to repeat that, like previous prophets he asked no reward for his ministry, nor was he prompted by mercenary motives. This assertion, which no one will deny, was meant to place him in contrast to professional soothsayers, and could not but be useful to him.

We now come to a batch of *sûras*, which are distinguished by certain features which they have in common. They have no declamatory prologue, and the refrain, which marks the paragraphs, is also missing. Finally they all begin with reference to the " Signs of the Book and a manifest *Qorân*.[45] Of these revelations I mention first *Sûra* xxvii. 4 to 59, in which the refrain has not been omitted entirely, but is visibly disappearing.[46] After a short introduction of irrelevant character we hear quite a new story, *viz.*, Moses' vision of the burning bush. He is instructed how to perform the *two* signs, which shall be among the "nine Signs[47] (to be shown) to Pharaoh and his people" (v. 12). Subseqnently David is mentioned, then Solomon who informed mankind that he had received the power of understanding the speech of the birds (v. 16). In the same sermon the speaker inserted the history of Solomon's meeting with the Queen of Sheba in legendary form, which in the following generations has developed into a beautiful fairy tale. It is interesting to observe that Muhammed puts the formula of Unification into the mouth of the hoopoe.[48] A few verses later we come across the formula which Muhammed subsequently placed at the head of all documents, and which also stands at the beginning of each *sûra*, and since heads every book or document written by Moslims. — To this story are attached short accounts repeating the missions of Ṣâliḥ, the prophet of Thamûd, and and of Lot.[49]

*Sûra* xxviii. having no other beginning than the verse mentioned above, at once proceeds to relate the history of Moses. Pharaoh (v. 2) is charged with oppressing the inhabitants of the *earth* by slaying their sons and outraging their daughters; he and his adviser Hamân must therefore be punished. Moses' mother is advised by Allâh to nurse her child, and if she fears for his safety, to throw him into the sea without any misgivings. Pharaoh's men find him in the water, but his *wife* takes great liking to the boy, and persuades the king to adopt him

42 Sprenger, II. 240, regards v. 68 to 70 as belonging to the time when the mentor had disappeared; *cf.* p. 350.

43 Bagh. يعنى فى شأن ادم عم حين قال الله نع إنى جاعل فى الارض خليفةً قالوا اتجعل فيها من يفسد فيها. See *B'rêshith Rabbâ* to Gen. i. 26.

44 V. 82, ونفخت فيه من روحى; *cf.* (*S.* xv. 29 and) Gen. ii. 7.

45 *Cf.* above.

46 Only v. 14 (not after v. 45), 52; v. 53 is an echo of xxvi. 7. V. 60-95 form an independent address, beginning and ending with الحمد الله.

47 Confused with the ten plagues which are called מופתים. Exod. vii. 3; x. 1.

48 V. 26, لا اله الا هو. The words ربّ العرش العظيم evidently form an intentional contrast to v. 23, ولها عرش عظيم.

49 V. 60 *sqq.* I believe this piece forms a separate *sûra* belonging to the descriptive period, *cf.* 10.

Moses' mother is well pleased, and appoints her daughter to look after the boy, Muhammed evidently forgetting that the latter was already with the royal couple. The child refusing to be fed by a native woman,[50] his sister offers to find a place where he could be reared, and subsequently he is sent to his mother's house. He grows up, and kills the Egyptian, but repents his transgression (6 to 16). The next verses (17 to 18) read almost like a translation of Exod. ii. 13 to 14. An unknown man from "the remotest end of the city" warns Moses against the danger which threatens his life. Afterwards there is a great confusion in the narrative. Moses flees, and meets *two* women whom he assists in watering their flocks. These are not only confounded with Lôt's two daughters,[51] but also with those of Laban, since the father of the two girls, whom he had assisted, offers him one in marriage on the condition, that he serves him *eight* or *ten* years. Then follows the vision of the burning bush, and Moses receives his call (v. 29 to 35). Pharaoh's command to Hâmân to build him a tower[52] on which he could ascend to Moses' God is evidently a reflex of Gen. xi. 4, Isaiah xiv. 13, and perhaps also Esther v. 14.

In none of the preceding accounts of Moses' mission was allusion made to the revelation on Sinai. This does not seem to be accidental, since Muhammed was well acquainted with its history, but reserved it for use on another occasion. An opportunity soon arose for alluding to the scene.[53] but he did not reproduce the Biblical tale, because, to judge from v. 48,[54] several Meccans knew it already, and wished him to arrange a similar ceremony. Being unable to comply with the demand, he at least gave a clever answer, asking whether Moses himself had not met with disbelief.

Now in contradiction to earlier theories concerning man's own responsibility, we read here among observations attached to the story in question that "Allâh does not guide the wicked."[55] This maxim subsequently gained preponderance over the other, and was adopted by the orthodox school. The long sermon of contemplative character, which then follows — and in which the Creed is repeated twice[56] — is broken only by a remark on Qôraḥ's rebellion, and the fabulous wealth attributed to him by the Talmudical tradition.[57]

It would be both irksome and unnecessary to analyse every *sûra* which belongs to this group, and we must therefore be content to draw the main features of each. *Sûra* xv. repeats after a homiletic introduction the story of the disobedience of Iblîs (Satan, 28 to 50), and then proceeds to relate the visit of the angels to Abraham (51 to 77). After this the people of Al Aika are briefly mentioned (78 to 79), and the "people of Al Ḥijr," *viz.*, the Thamûd, whose sepulchral caves[58] (v. 82) Muhammed mistook for houses (80 to 86). A short sermon closes the *sûra*.[59]

A visible effect must have been produced on the hearers by these tales, which not only increased Muhammed's eagerness to recite them, but also induced him to arrange them more carefully for this purpose. Nor did he fail to prepare his hearers for an extraordinary treat, when the story they were going to be told, promised to be of unusual interest. Now an incident had occurred which spurred Muhammed to show his histrionic talent in its best light. Tradition relates that Al Nadhr b. Ḥârith, one of the Prophet's bitterest enemies, endeavoured to outrival Muhammed's stories by telling the Meccans the adventures of Persian heroes. Al-Nadhr himself, accompanied by Oqba b. Abu Mo'eit, were sent to Medina in order to make enquiries about Muhammed's prophetic powers of the Jewish Rabbis of this town. The latter

[50] *Cf.* Geiger, *l. c.* p. 153.

[51] V. 23, وابونا شيخاً كبيراً, is evidently translation of Gen. xix. 31. Geiger overlooked the double confusion.

[52] *Cf.* xl. 38 to 39 more elaborate than v. xxviii. 38 and therefore probably later.

[53] V. 44 to 46.

[54] V. 48.

[55] V. 50 to 56; *cf.* Ch. III.

[56] V. 70 and 88.

[57] V. 76 to 79; *cf.* Geiger, *l. c.* p. 168.

[58] *Cf.* Doughty, *Notes et Extraits*, xxix. p. 4 *sqq.*

[59] V. 87, "seven of the mathâni;" *cf.* Geiger, *l. c.* p. 58. V. 98, فسبّح, invites to joining the preacher in prayer.

are said to have given the messengers certain queries to be put before Muhammed who replied by narrating the stories of the Seven Sleepers of Ephesus, contained in *Sûra* xviii.[60]

However sceptical our attitude may be towards this tradition, thus much is true, tha Muhammed was somewhat downhearted, when he began this sermon. "Haply, he says (v. 5) thou grievest thyself to death[61] after them, if they believe not in this [following] communication." It is very probable that the rivalry of Al Nadhr in entertaining his followers with the attractive tales of daring deeds made his spirits sink. The story of the Seven Sleepers (v. 8 to 25) which he related, was by its miraculous character not only calculated to outdo tales of the most perilous adventures, but was introduced by the words of Allâh (v. 12) "We relate unto thee their story in truth." A homily attached to the tale takes the form of two parables.[62] The next piece (v. 48 to 58), recapitulating the disobedience of Iblîs, is perhaps directed against Al Nadhr, especially the second part of v. 48.[63] The fabulous journey of Moses and his servant (v. 59 to 81) which then follows, is, I believe, based on that of Tobias, intervowen with anecdotes heard elsewhere. The series of tales ends with an account of the journey of the "Two Horned," generally supposed to be Alexander the Great,[65] who is requested by a people of strange speech to protect them against the encroachments of Jâjûj and Mâjûj.[66]

The finest and best rounded tale in the whole book is the recitation styled "Yûsuf," which fills out *Sûra* xii[67]. Muhammed begins with the reference, quoted above, to "the Sign of the distinct Book," and proceeds again: We will relate to thee the finest of stories[68] with which we reveal to thee this *Qorân*. The harmony of the composition is, however, impaired by the daring assertion (v. 103).

"This is one of the stories of the unseen which we inspire thee with, though thou wert not with them when they agreed in their affair, when they were so crafty — and yet most men, though thou shouldst be urgent, will not believe."—Another new tale, the birth of Jesus, is related in *Sûra* xix. Muhammed tells of nothing but the nativity, because he regards the Founder of Christianity in the light of a monotheistic prophet alone, and quotes only such teachings as relate to his mission as a servant of God. He is in possession of "the Book." He is a blessed prophet, charged to teach the propriety of praying, giving alms, honoring parents, and the hatred of oppression. One cannot fail to be struck with the careful manner in which Muhammed weighed each word when lecturing on this delicate subject, and we have here the best opportunity of noticing, how conclusions may be drawn from things which he left unsaid as well as from those which he said. Vv. 34 to 36 show[69] clearly the attitude he adopted towards the New Testament. In v. 38 he speaks of the various sects and their differences.[70]

The story of Jesus being rather short, Muhammed reverts to the history of the Patriarchs Moses, Aaron, Ismael (v. 55), Idrîs[71] (v. 57), Noah, and "his descendants Abraham and Israel."[72]

---

[60] See J. Q. R. Vol. X. p. 100 *sqq.* [61] *Cf. S.* xxvi. 2. [62] See Ch. VIII. [63] "They are foes of yours," *etc.*

[64] Geiger, *l. c.* p. 171, confesses that he is unable to discover the source of the story. It is to be remembered that Moses bears in Talmudical tradition the name of Tobias (Sôtâ, fol. 12vo). According to Itqân, p. 793, the Mûsa of this story is not identical with the Biblical Moses, but is a son of Manasse, which is evidently confused with Exod. vi. 19. — There is another explanation possible. According to a Rabbinic legend, R. *Joshua* b. Levi, a famous Talmudical authority, meets the Prophet Elijah, who journeys with him through paradise and hell. In a parallel Moslim tradition by Al Bokhârî (ed. Krehl, III. p. 276) Moses and *Joshua* b. Nûn meet Al Khiḍr (the prophet Elijah), who advises them on their journey. Now while the Rabbinic legend is focussed round the person of a Rabbi (who from collector of legendary traditions became their hero), the Moslim counterpart of the same tale clung to the better known Biblical *Joshua*, whose master Moses became the chief person concerned in the legend.

[65] Nöldeke. *l. c.* p. 106, seems to have given the right explanation of the name.

[66] Gen. x. 2; Ez. xxxviii. 2; xxxix. 6. [67] V. 2, "Arabic Qorân."

[68] *Cf. S.* vii. 99, iv. 3 *sqq.* Josef gives his fellow prisoners a lecture on Islâm.

[69] V. 34 refers to the resurrection of all flesh in Messianic times, or Muhammed would have stated otherwise. *Cf.* I. Ish. 200 *sq.*, and *S.* xliii. 57 to 59.

[70] *Cf.* xliii. 65; fuller definition of أحزاب is given in xxxviii. 12, xl. 5.

[71] For the etymology of the name see Geiger, *l. c.* p. 106, Itqân, 792.

[72] V. 59; Gen. xxxii. 28 was evidently not known to Muhammed.

A conspicuous feature of this *sûra* is the employment of the term AlRaḥmân for Allâh no less than *eighteen* times. Sprenger is of opinion that the term stands for Christ. This is however, impossible, since Maryam herself places her hope in Al Raḥmân before Jesus is born (v. 18). Besides most of the passages in which that name occurs treat of other prophets.

If the Syrian Christians employed *raḥmânâ* for Jesus, they did the same as the Jews did in speaking of God. *Al Raḥmân* in the *Qorân* is therefore nothing but a synonym for *Allâh* or *Al Rabb*.[73] As long as Muhammed lived in Mecca he treated the name 'Îsâ (Jesus) as one belonging to an ordinary mortal, and it was only when he came to Medina, and had nothing more to fear, that he substituted Al Masîḥ[74] for it. On the other hand Al Raḥmân is scarcely used at all after the *narrative period*, since it is rare in the descriptive group. In Medinian revelations it is only mentioned twice (ii. 158, lix. 22); both times in the earlier revelations of this epoch, and used as an attribute in the Creed, but not as name at all.[75] Muhammed explains this clearly in *Sûra* xvii. 110, where he characterizes *Al Raḥmân* as another word for Allâh, because the Meccans had charged him with adoring two gods.[76] In another place *Al Raḥmân* is identified with *Huwa* (xiii. 29), and cannot therefore be due to Christian influence.

Muhammed could not conclude this sermon without referring to the doctrine of the fatherhood of Al Raḥmân (v. 91 to 93).

The brief account of Jesus given in *Sûra* xix. is supplemented in *Sûra* xliii. 14 to 15,[77] but in a rather antagonistic spirit. Subsequently Abraham and Moses are quoted as examples of true servants of Allâh, after which the discussion on Jesus[78] is resumed.

Very similar to the preceding two *sûras* is *Sûra* xxi. both as regards matter and composition. The chief subject of discussion is the Unity of Allâh which Muhammed, as intimated above, endeavours to demonstrate by way of syllogism. V. 23, "He shall not be questioned concerning what He does, but they shall be questioned," is a reflex of Job ix. 12 (Eccl. viii. 4) a verse made popular through insertion into a Jewish prayer[80] for the Day of Atonement. V. 25 we have mentioned as one of the early attempts to formulate the Creed; v. 26 re-echoes the verse xliii. 59,[81] v. 27 ("they do not speak until He speaks, but at His bidding do they act) is a distinct reflex of Ps. ciii. 20 to 21. The whole passage together with the words "they shrink through fear" (v. 29) may be borrowed from the Jewish morning prayers preceding the reading of the *Shma'*, since there can hardly be any doubt, that the Jews in the Ḥijâz recited the same every day. In spite of these purely theological observations, to which may be added the denial of man's immortality (35 to 36),[82] the narrative character of the *sûra* is maintained in the second half. Moses and Aaron are briefly stated to have received the *Furqân* (v. 49). This word which occurs here for the first time, stands for *Tôrâh*, as it does in all Medinian revelations, excepting *S.* viii. 42 where it maintains its Aramaic meaning "victory."[83] Muhammed evidently confounded the latter signification with that of *Perâqim* into which the Pentateuch was divided for liturgical purposes, and which also guided the interpretations given to the word by the Moslim Commentators.[84] The rest of the *sûra* is taken up with tales of Abraham and other Biblical characters. In v. 105 Muhammed shows his acquaintance with the Psalms by quoting Ps. xxxvii. 29.[85]

---

[73] *Cf.* lv. 1 = xcvi. 1 to 2; see Ch. VI. and XVII. 110.

[74] *Cf.* iii. 40: المسيح عيسى.

[75] The tradition on Muhammed's prayer: O Allâh, O Raḥmân; see Sprenger, II. p. 200.

[76] See the Commentaries.

[77] See Ch. VIII.

[78] On عَلَم (v. 61) see the Commentaries and *S.* iii. 52, where Jesus is compared to Adam.

[79] *Cf.* xxiii. 93; see Ch. II. p. 23.

[80] *Ne'ilâ*.

[81] See above and *S.* xix. 36, 91, 93.

[82] See v. 8 and *S.* xxix. 57.

[83] Geiger, p. 56, only records the Aramaic interpretation of the word.

[84] *Cf. S.* xvii. 107, وقرآنا فرقناه, the resemblance is more noticeable in the spelling than in the pronunciation.

[85] See Sprenger, II. p. 196 (misprint for Ps. xxxvi i. 29) and S. xxi. 105. The Hebrew text has not "*caddîk*" but *ṣaddîqîm*.

The foregoing *sûra* is a fine example of Muhammed's endeavours to relieve the monotony of narrative sermons by introducing meditations on all sorts of subjects. The same policy is observed in *Sûra* xiv. which begins with the remark that no messenger is dispatched except he speak the language of his own people (v. 4).[86] This is a variation of the phrase "*Arabic Qorân*" usually employed. Another and still more noteworthy feature of the *sûra* is that it is rich in parables,[87] which are of Jewish, and indirectly of Biblical, origin. The merely narrative element in the address offers nothing new, except that Abraham prayed to Allâh to make "his house (Mecca)" safe (v. 40).

*Sûra* xx. is more drawn out. It begins with a very detailed account of the message of Moses, which is in so far of interest, as the Israelites are reminded of the covenant received "on the right side of the mountain" as well as of the Mannah and quails.[88] The description of Allâh as "Living and Eternal *(alḥayyu alqayyûmu)*"[89] is new. An account of Adam's sin and forgiveness with the admonition belonging to it close the *sûra*.

*Sûra* xi. commences with a sermon in which the speaker alludes to the creation of heaven and earth in six days,[90] and "His throne upon the water" (v. 9). Now it appears that one circumstance mentioned above, *viz.*, that the stories relating to one and the same person were rich in variations, had given rise to the suspicion that Muhammed took liberties with the facts. This reproach he endeavours to refute in v. 15: "Haply thou art leaving part of what is revealed to thee, and thy breast is straitened thereby lest they should say: why is not a treasure sent down to him? or why did not an angel come with him? thou art only a warner, and Allâh is guardian over all.—16. Or they will say: he has devised it. Speak: *Bring ten Sûrahs* like it devised, and call upon whom ye can beside Allâh, if you do tell the truth, etc.[91]"

This challenge we have already discussed, as also the theological dogma derived from it.[92] A rather stale parable (v. 26)[93] closes the homiletic part of the *sûra*, which then becomes broadly narrative, and takes its name from the first prophet mentioned in it, *viz.*, Hûd. His story (52 to 63) is followed by that of Ṣâliḥ (64 to 71), Abraham and Lot (72 to 84), Shoeib (85 to 98), and Moses (99 to 112). A feeble attempt at a refrain is made by repeating the admonition placed at the beginning (v. 3): "Ask pardon of your Lord, then return to Him" three times.[94] This is a proof of the unity of the *sûra*. At the conclusion Muhammed receives the assurance that all these stories had been revealed to him in order to strengthen his heart (v. 121).

In the following *sûras* the narrative element is visibly on the decline. To these belongs *S.* xxxiv. in which only the first portion (v. 1 to 20) contains references to Biblical persons and is otherwise partly descriptive, partly homiletic.

Several portions, of which *Sûra* vii. is composed, belong to the latest revelations of this period, and are only welded together by a common rhyme. The usual introduction calculated to attract the attention of the hearers contains the phrase (v. 6): "Now let us narrate to them (the Meccans) knowledge, for we (Allâh) were not absent." In a mixture of narrative and descriptive style the creation of the earth and man is touched upon, followed by a repetition

---

[86] See the Commentaries and traditions. [87] See Ch. VIII.

[88] Muhammed uses the Biblical terms, see I. Isḥ. 368. The explanations of المن, given by the Commentators, are wrong.

[89] This is, perhaps, a proof that the Arab Jews pronounced *qayyûm*.

[90] The phrase فى ستة ايام occurs in the following passages: vii. 52, x. 3, xi. 9, xxv. 60, xxxii. 3, l. 37, lvii. 4.

[91] *Cf.* Bagh. ائت بقرآن غير هذا ليس فيه سب الهتناهم النبى ان يدع آلهتهم ظاهرا.

[92] Known in Moslim theology as اعجاز; *cf.* Ch. I. p. 17. [93] Verse 26; see Ch. VIII.

[94] Verses 54, 64, 92; v. 114 is not exactly the same.

of the fall and expulsion of Adam and his wife from paradise (1 to 24). This gives an opportunity of apostrophising the "sons of Adam"[95] into paragraphs of exhortative character with reference to their past life. The middle portion of the *sûra* contains a succession of tales, dealing with Hûd, Ṣâliḥ, Lot and Shoeib (v. 57 to 100), and closes with the repeated assurance that the knowledge of all this is of divine origin. After this, and evidently belonging to the same piece,[96] follows a long account of the mission of Moses. It is interesting to note that Muhammed mentions five plagues or "Signs" (v. 130), *viz.*, the *flood* (either confounded with that of Noah, or the drowning the Egyptian army), locusts, lice, frogs, and blood. Muhammed's information on this subject was, however, so deficient, that later on[97] he confused them with the "nine and manifest Signs," which Moses performed before Pharaoh. Otherwise the narrative closely follows the lines of the Biblical original.[98] The piece comprehending v. 186 to 205 being an independent homily on the "Hour," and stated to have formed one of Muhammed's answers to Al Nadhr b. Al Ḥârith,[99] was probably placed here on account of v. 194 being similar to v. 178. The sermon to which the latter belongs is, however, Medinian.[100] It contains a historical outline of the evolution of man from one pair, and the child born to them. The words of v. 189 "they called on Allâh, their Lord" recall Gen. xxv. 21 to 22.[1] Verse 198: "Endeavour to pardon command that which is merciful, and shun the ignorant" represent the first attempt to formulate a sentence, and this became subsequently of great importance both in theology and jurisprudence.[2] Verse 204 has some slight resemblance to Deut. v. 5 to 7, whilst the last three words of the *sûra* also recall a phrase of the Jewish prayer book.[3]

Apart from the first vision of Muhammed (spoken of in Ch. III.) he now tells of a second, namely, his nightly journey to the Temple in Jerusalem, which under the name *almi'râj*[4] has become famous in Moslim tradition. This forms the beginning of *Sûra* xvii. which was, I believe, very short originally, and only assumed its present bulk through the insertion of large pieces belonging to the following Meccan periods. The mention of the Temple in Jerusalem (v. 1) gives Muhammed an opportunity of surveying briefly the two chief phases of the Israelitish history (vv. 2 to 8). The concluding part of the *sûra* (v. 103 to 111) is narrative, although entirely disconnected from the first piece, whilst several words in v. 106 running parallel to v. 7 and v. 108 to v. 5 show the reason why these two pieces were put in one *sûra*. Here is to be placed *Sûra* lxxiii. 15 to 19.[5] According to the Commentators v. 110 (of *S.* xvii.) was misconstructed by the infidels into a charge of dualism.[6] This suggested the revelation of the docrine that "the most beautiful names" were those of Allâh *(ibid.)*, of which the legend counts no less than ninety-nine beside "Allâh."

*Sûra* xl. is of equally compound character, the portions 1 to 6, 24 to 35, 38 to 59 being narrative.[7] Pharaoh is here not represented as a historical figure at all, but stands as the prototype of a wicked and daring person, combining the characteristics of Nimrod and Nebuchadnezzar. The verses 36 to 37 stand for themselves to represent Joseph as a prophet, thus supplementing *Sûra* xii. in a very important omission. The prophetship of Joseph is evidently an afterthought, as through the romantic character of his history Muhammed had neglected to stamp him as a prophet.[8] For the rest of the *sûra* see below.[9]

---

[95] V. 25, 26; v. 29 and 33 are younger and only placed here on account of the same beginning.

[96] V. 101 ثمّ.

[97] xvii. 103; *cf.* xxvii. 12.

[98] V. 154 = Exod. xviii. 25 (together with Numb. xi. 24) واختار.

[99] See above.

[100] See below.

[1] See Palmer, I. p. 161, rem.

[2] *Cf. Mevâqif*, p. 331.

[3] Bend the knee and prostrate and give thanks.

[4] *Cf. Mishkât* and Sprenger, II. 527 *sq.*

[5] The verses treat also of Pharaoh; *cf.* v. 18 كان وعده مفعولا

[6] *Cf.* Nöldeke, *Q.* p. 114.

[7] The phrase "O my people," v. 30, 31, 34 and again vv. 41, 42, 44.

[8] Joseph's prophetship, which distinguishes him from his brothers, is made the object of discussion by Ibn Ḥazm, fol. 3.

[9] V. 68 *sqq.*, an independent sermon beginning with قل, but placed here on account of ربّ العالمين, v. 66 and 67.

To the same period also belongs *Sûra* xxix. 13 to 42.[10] From the reappearance of Pharaoh with Hâmân we may conclude that the speech in question was revealed almost simultaneously with the corresponding portion of *Sûra* xl. A fine parable breaks the sameness of the topics.[11] V. 47 contains the famous assertion that prior to his ministry Muhammed had been unable to read and write.[12]

The second and smallest portion of *Sûra* x., recapitulating the missions of Noah, Moses and Jonah, shows an attempt at chronological order, which is repeated in *S.* xxiii. 23 to 52 with Noah, Abraham, and Moses. The piece was inserted here on account of *alfulk* ("ships," v. 27; *cf.* v. 22).

I have to mention here several pieces of narrative character which the compilers have inserted into Medinian *sûras*, but which undoubtedly are of Meccan origin. It is improbable *a priori* that Muhammed should have revealed new discourses in Medina on the old topics recited during the service in the Meccan *sûras*, besides which the ministry of Muhammed was of more practical nature, and it is unlikely that he would have returned to these tales. The style is the same as in the other narrative *suras*. These pieces are xlvi. 20 to 35 on 'Âd and Moses, and ii. 200 to 210 without reference to any particular person.

An isolated narrative speech we find inserted in *Sûra* v., which is of Meccan origin in spite of the place allotted to it by the compilers (v. 23 to 38). It consists of two parts, the former (v. 23 to 29) giving a condensed account of Numb. Ch. xiii. to xiv. 34. The second (v. 30 to 38) reproduces Gen. iv. 2 to 9 with the agadic already exposed by Geiger, who also discloses the source of v. 35. The next three represent probably the moral drawn from the foregoing tales, and are meant to impress Meccan foes. The punishments threatened were not executed in Medina, but they had only to choose beween conversion and execution.

It was the narrative period of the *Qorân* which, as I believe, gave birth to the short *sûra* which heads the book and is known under the name *alfâtiḥa*. It consists almost entirely of verses which occur frequently in revelations belonging to this period, and which Muhammed selected in order to form them into a short prayer. V. 1 is one of the two sentences which are used to invite the audience attending sermons to start praying,[13] and is found both at the beginning and at the end of many discourses. It is at the commencement of *Sûras* xviii., xxxiv., xxxv, and xxvii. 60 which evidently marks the beginning of a new speech. In the last named *sûra* the phrase also ends the sermon, as it does in *S.* xxxvii., xvii., and xl. 67 (end of a sermon) and xxxix. *Sûra* lii. 48 is a combination of both sentences used for the purpose, whilst *S.* x. 10 to 11 informs us that

10. Their prayer therein (in paradise) shall be: celebrated be thy praises *(subḥânaka)* oh Allâh, and their salutation shall be: Peace!

11. And the end of their prayer shall be: Praise to Allâh, the Lord of the worlds!

This is quite in accordance with the instances given in other places.

The verses 5 to 6 (of *Sûra* i.)[14] appear in S. xliii. 42, xi. 59, vii. 15; xlii. 52 to 53, *etc.* Now although it is very difficult to fix the date of the *sura* with accuracy, that given to it by Nöldeke is evidently too early.[15]

---

[10] V. 1 to 12 legislative; *cf.* Ch. VII. [11] *Cf.* Ch. VIII. [12] *Cf.* Ch. I. p. 12.

[13] The other being فسبّح بحمد ربك. [14] *Cf.* Ps. xxvii. 11. [15] Nöldeke. *Q.* p. 86 f.; Itqân, p. 54.

## CHAPTER VI.

### The Descriptive Revelations.

Descriptive elements in older addresses — Object and scope of description — Models imitated — Lectures on the "Signs" — Analysis of *Sûra* xvi.

In the first proclamation, as we have seen, only one item out of the Biblical narrative for the Creation of the World was made use of — the one item essential for Muhammed's immediate requirements, *viz.*, the Creation of Man. It was not Muhammed's intention, however, to omit the rest of the narrative; he only reserved it for reproduction on later occasions, as the opportunity or need should arise. He would have neglected an ethical factor of great importance, had he omitted to remind his hearers how much gratitude they owed their Maker for having given them the means of living a comfortable life. So far from making such a mistake, he took the earliest opportunity of touching on this subject, immediately after the first proclamation had been made, although at first only in slight reference.

The descriptive element in the *Qorân*, therefore, is nearly as old as the book itself, although it is not particularly noticeable till the latter part of the declamatory period. It becomes more prominent in the narrative period, when Muhammed's style had lost the charm of novelty. It is impossible to draw a line clearly separating the descriptive from the preceding classes of revelations, since many verses of a descriptive character are interspersed among the narrative lectures. Yet those sermons, in which descriptions of Nature and its bounties form the foremost topic, are distinctly of later date.

Although divergent in character the descriptive revelations agree with the narrative revelations in one important point, that is, in the endeavour to demonstrate the "Signs of Allah," and to form another substitute for miracles which the Prophet was unable to perform. It seems that Muhammed wished to convey to his hearers, that as so many "Signs" of the divine omnipotence already existed, new ones could be dispensed with. The scope of descriptions being rather limited, the number of revelations of this class is smaller than of any previous one, but they also follow Biblical models and abound in repetitions.

Apart from the brief allusion to the Creation contained in the first proclamation, the oldest pieces of descriptive character are found in a few verses in the declamatory *Sûra* lxxx.[16]

24. But let man look unto his foods,
25. Verily we have poured the water out in torrents,
26. Then we have cleft the earth asunder,
27. And made to grow therefrom the grain
28. And the grape and the hay,
29. And the olive and the palm,
30. And gardens closely planted,
31. And fruits and grass —
32. A provision for you and your cattle.

lxxvii. 25. Have we not made the earth to hold
26. The living and the dead
27. And set thereon firm mountains reared aloft, and given you to drink water in streams?

[16] See also S. lxxvii. 25 to 27.

I regard the last portion of *S.* lxxix.[17] which looks like a hasty recapitulation of Gen. Ch. I. as the first independent piece of this class. It speaks of heaven, night and dawn, the earth, water and pastures, man and beast.

*Sûra* lxxi. contains a rather original description of Nature ascribed by Muhammed to Noah. In spite of the narrative beginning, this chapter cannot be placed among the narrative revelations, because with the exception of the first few verses the rest of the *sûra* (the bulk of which is of descriptive character) reproduces a prayer[18] in which Noah tells of his unsuccessful endeavours to make his people believe in God.

The inner connection which exists between the first proclamation and the descriptive revelations of a much later period is unmistakeably illustrated by *S.* lv., which cannot be as old as Nöldeke believes it to be.[19] Now, for this new species of lectures Muhammed required new models. Having chosen for the preceding the form of prayer, he composed this *sûra* after the fashion of Ps. cxxxvi. with a refrain introduced gradually and repeated afterwards at the end of each verse. For a descriptive sermon Muhammed could only use few verses of the body of the Psalm, which I place in parallel columns with the corresponding verses of the *sûra:*

| *The Sûra.* | *The Psalm.* |
|---|---|
| 4. The sun and the moon have their appointed time. 5. And the stars and the trees adore. | 8. The sun to rule by day : for, *etc.*<br>9. The moon and stars to rule by night. |
| 6. And the heavens, He raised them and set the balance. | 5. To Him that by wisdom made the heavens. |
| 9. And the earth He has set it for living creatures. | 6. To Him that stretches out the earth, *etc.* |

The *sûra* gives a more comprehensive synopsis of the Biblical account of the Creation, and that is the reason, why the first proclamation is repeated, and, as a matter of course, placed at the beginning in the words: AlRaḥmân taught the *Qorân* (2) He created man, (3) taught him plain speech. — Another proof of the imitative character of the *sûra* is that the refrain does not speak of "Signs" but of "Bounties."[20] Part of the contents of the *sûra* are taken from another Psalm which will occupy our attention anon. When the material was quite exhausted,[21] Muhammed resorted again to pictures of hell and paradise.

The style adopted in *S.* l. is one of great contemplativeness on the Creation, interspersed with a narrative reminiscences,[22] which also afford an opportunity for the introduction of a fine metaphor.[23] Descriptions of Nature are adorned with pictures of the Last day which, in this short *sûra*, is mentioned by not less than *five* different appellations.[24]

Another lecture on the "Signs" is *S.* xlv., discoursing on the earth and the animated beings that move on it, on the change of night and day, the food sent down from heaven (through rain), and the wind. Dry land as well as sea, the hosts of heaven and earth which serve men, are all subjects which lend themselves to treatment in the usual style.

Nearly contemporaneous with this one is *S.* xlii.,[25] in the rather long introduction of which the "Arabic *Qorân*" (v. 5) is alluded to, and Divine Providence appears several times

[17] Also Nöldeke, *Q.* p. 87, regards this piece as the later portion of the *sûra*.

[18] Nöldeke, p. 95, sees in this *sûra* a fragment of a larger sermon.

[19] *Ibid.* p. 83; *cf.* Sprenger, II. p. 219, with the tradition connected with it. Verse 1 = xcvi. 2, but *Rabbika* replaced by *AlRaḥmân*.

[20] The refrain is evidently nothing but the attempt of a rendition of כי לעולם חסדו. The dual تكذبان has no particular significance, and was only chosen on account of its yielding a rhyme to *Raḥmân*. Verse 7 recalls Isaiah xi. 6.

[21] Verse 58 contains a fine metaphor ; see Ch. VIII.

[22] Verses 1 to 11, 14 to 15, 37.

[23] V. 15, see Ch. VIII.

[24] See Ch. IV.

[25] Verse 9, ليس كمثله, *cf.* Exod. viii. 6, ix. 14, *etc.* — Verses 11 to 12, legislative. Verses 28 (*cf.* xlv. 3) and 31 begin with ومن آياته. — Verses 52 to 53, see Ch. V.

(vv. 13, 20, 23) as *Kalima.*[26] Both the *Kalima* (v. 45) and "Arabic *Qorán*" (v. 2) also appear in *S.* xli., of which several portions (vv. 8 to 11, 37 to 40) are descriptive, and contain, besides, a sketch of hell and paradise. The introduction treating of the "Arabic *Qorán*" is, in the course of the lecture, supplemented by a verse (44),[27] which is intended to explain more clearly an idea expressed some time before,[28] but it only makes it more obscure. It runs thus :—

"And had we made it a 'foreign *Qorán*,' they would have said: 'unless its signs be detailed [we will not believe]; is it foreign *and* Arabic?' Say: 'It is, for those who believe, a guidance and a healing; but those who do not believe, in their ears is dullness, and it is blindness to them. Those are called to from a far off place.' "

The revelation seems to be an excuse for employing a certain number of foreign words in the "Arabic *Qorán*." Perplexity shuffles.

*Súra* xxxv., being of a distinctly descriptive character, begins with the statement afterwards repeated, that Allâh makes the angels His messengers. This is nearly a literal translation of Ps. civ. 4. The same psalm is also re-echoed in other verses.[29] Similar topics, but in shorter form, are dicussed in *Ss.* xxxii.,[30] lxvii., and xxv.[31] I mention the last two together, because their common superscription marks them both as hymns to the Creator.[32] In *S.* xxv., Muhammed replies to a charge that he was but an ordinary mortal eating food and visiting the fairs.[33] This charge was not imaginary, but seems to have been made repeatedly, since it is refuted twice (vv. 8 and 22) in this sermon. A final answer is not given until *S.* xxiii. 53,[34] in which messengers in general are bidden to "eat good cheer." Of this *súra* the first and last parts (vv. 1 to 22, 53 to 118) form one address, but vv. 27 and 34 show why the piece was inserted after v. 22.[35] From the more elaborate arguments employed we gather that this *súra* is later than xxv. The homily embodied in the last part (v. 93) consists only of repetitions, the most important of which is the attempt to demonstrate the Unity of Allâh by argument.[36]

Two verses of this part (99 and 100) contain expressions for exorcising ("I take refuge") Satanic influences, and give perhaps a clue to the placing of the *Ss.* cxiii. and cxiv.,[37] which are formulas of the same character and with the same commencement.

*Súra* xvi. marks the apogee of the descriptive revelations. It not only unites all descriptive recitations scattered through other sermons, but places them before the reader in a really

[26] See Ch. I., note II.

[27] From Beidhâwi's remarks we infer that the reading أأعجمي is uncertain, as other authorities have أعجمي and اعجمى.

[28] See *S.* xxvi. 198 and Ch. I. — The sense of the passage seems to be the following: Had we revealed the *Qorán* in a foreign tongue, their disbelief could not be greater than it is ; *cf.* xvi. 105.

[29] *E. g.*, v. 10, 13, 14. The two, three and four pairs of wings ascribed to angels are evidently modelled after Is. vi. 2 together with Ezech. i, 6. As to the paraphrastic imitation of Ps. civ. see below.

[30] The creation of the world in six days is also mentioned in xi. 9, l. 37, xxv. 60. As to v. 4 see lxx. 4 and Ch. IV.

[31] The expressions تبارك and فرقان (v. 1, *cf.* Geiger, *l. c.* p. 50) seem to be taken from the Jewish prayer called *Qaddish.*

[32] Verse 1: "Blessed be," *etc.*, see lxvii. 1; *ibid.* v. 5: With "lamps" *cf.* Gen. i. 16.

[33] The verses 8, 9 and 22 (*cf.* xxiii. 34) seem to be a justification directed against Exod. xxxiii. 28. Whether Muhammed was really expected to live for some time without food, is hard to say, but this seems to have been the case, and it is supported by a tradition of Bagh. (on v. 22) on the authority of AlDhaḥḥâk and Ibn Abbâs, that the Qoreish reviled the prophetship of a man who consumed food. The matter is probably to be understood as follows : Some Meccan critic had a superficial knowledge of the statement that Moses had passed a certain time without food, and inferred from it that a prophet who could perform miracles, must also be able to dispense with eating and drinking.

[34] There are also other points of connection between the two *súras* ; *cf.* xxiii. 1 to 11, and xxv. 64 to 77.

[35] Verse 21, تأكلون, *cf.* vv. 34, 35; v. 22, الفلك, *cf.* vv. 26 to 29.

[36] *Cf.* verse 117, and Ch. II.

[37] *Cf. S.* xxiii. 99 to 100, xvi. 100, vii. 199.

artistic form. Muhammed must have bestowed much care on its composition, as it is beautiful although not quite original; it is in fact an imitation of Ps. civ. with the verses differently arranged. We must naturally expect to see Muhammed adapt his rendering of the Psalm to the conditions of life in Arabia, as also to his particular theological purposes.[38] The latter are represented by a strong Moslim tendency, and teachings are inserted which are not to be found in the original. Those verses of the Psalm are therefore omitted which describe animals and plants unknown to Meccans. I place the verses side by side :

| *The Sûra.* | *The Psalm.* |
|---|---|
| 2. He sends down the angels with the spirit[39] [which is part] of his *Amr* upon whom He will of His servants (to say): Give warning that there is no God but Me; Me therefore do ye fear! | 4. He maketh His angels winds *(spirits)*; His ministers a flaming fire. |
| 3. He has created the heavens and the earth in truth! Exalted be He above that which they join with Him. | 2. Who covereth [Thyself] with light as with a garment, Who stretcheth out the heavens like a curtain. 5. Who laid the foundations of the earth, *etc.* |
| 10. He it is Who sends down water from the sky, whence ye have drink, and whence the trees grow whereby you feed your flocks. | 3. Who layeth the beams of His chambers in the waters; Who maketh the clouds His chariot; Who walketh upon the wings of the wind. |
| 11. He maketh the corn to grow for you, and the olives, and the palms, and the grapes, and some of every fruit — *verily in that is a Sign unto a people who reflect.* 13. And what He has produced for you in the earth varying in hue, *verily in that is a Sign for a people who are mindful.* (See also vv. 69 to 71.) | 14. He causes the grass to grow for the cattle, and herb for the service of man, that he may bring forth food out of the earth. 15. And wine that maketh glad the heart of man, and oil to make [his] face to shine, and bread which strengthens man's heart. |
| 12. And He subjected to you the night and the day, and the sun, and the moon, and the stars are subjected to His bidding. *Verily in that are Signs to a people who have sense.* 16. . . . . and by the stars too are they guided. | 19. He appointed the moon for seasons, the sun knoweth his going down. 20. Thou maketh darkness and it is night, wherein all the beasts of the Lord do creep forth. |
| 14. He it is Who has subjected the sea, that ye may eat fresh flesh therefrom, and ye bring forth from it ornaments which ye wear; and thou mayest see the ships cleaving through it; and that ye may search after His grace, and haply ye may give thanks. | 25. This great and wide sea wherein are things creeping innumerable, both small and great beasts. 26. There go the ships, [there is] that Leviathan whom Thou hast made to play therein. |

[38] *Cf. S.* xxxv. 1. — Verse 43 may serve to fix the date of the *sûra*, and probably refers to the isolation Muhammed's followers had to suffer for some time in Mecca, or to the emigration of a number of them to Abyssinia. As to the details see Sprenger, II. 128 *sqq.* — Verse 110 *sqq.* I regard (against Sprenger) as Medinian. الذين هاجروا refers to those who had shared the Hijra to Medina, but the piece was placed here on account of these two words. The verses 116 and 119 are nothing if not Medinian, since they were of no interest for a Meccan audience.

[39] Muhammed renders *rûḥôth* by الروح, being unaware of the circumstance that רוח also means *wind.* Verse 1 being introduction, is Muhammed's own; the same is the case with vv. 6 to 8, bearing on the habits of travelling merchants.

| | |
|---|---|
| 15. And He has cast firm mountains on the earth lest it should move with you, and rivers and roads, haply ye may be guided. (See also v. 83.) | 8. They go up by the mountains, they go up by the valleys unto the place which Thou hast founded for them. 18. The high hills a refuge for the wild goats, and the rock for the conies. |
| 40. They swear by their most strenuous oath: Allâh will not raise up him who dies, *etc.* . . . . 50. Do they not regard whatever thing Allâh has created, its shadow falls on the right or the left adoring God and shrinking up? 67. And Allâh sends down water from the sky and quickens therewith the earth after its death; *verily in that is a Sign to a people who can hear.* 72. God has created you, then He lets you die, *etc.* | 29. Thou hidest Thy face they are troubled. Thou takest away their breath, they die and return to their dust. 30. Thou sendest forth Thy spirit, they are created, and Thou renewest the face of the earth. |
| 44. Those who are patient and upon their Lord rely.[40] | 27. These wait all upon Thee, that Thou mayest give them their meat in due time. |
| 51. Whatever is in the heavens and in the earth, beast or angel, adores Allâh, nor are they big with pride. | 33. I will sing unto the Lord as long as I live: I will sing praise to my God while I have my being. |
| 52. They fear their Lord above them, and do what they are bidden. | 34. My meditation of Him shall be sweet, I will be glad in the Lord. |
| 63. If Allâh were to punish men for their wrong-doing, He would not leave upon the earth a single beast, *etc.* | 35. Let the sinners be consumed out of the earth and let the wicked be no more. Bless thou the Lord, O my soul; praise ye the Lord. |
| 87. Do they not see the birds subjected in the vaults of the sky? none holds them in but Allâh, *verily in that is a Sign unto a people who believe.* | 12. By them the fowls of the heaven have their habitation, which sing among the branches. 17. Where the birds make their nest, [as for] the stork, the fir trees are her house. |

Muhammed almost betrays the imitation in his own words; for he not only mentions the *Zubur* (Psalms) "that had been sent down before" (v. 46),[41] but at the end of the sermon (v. 105) he, apparently without necessity, defends himself against the charge of plagiarism. The traditionists give a number of names as possible sources of this accusation, but it is useless to repeat their extravagant and unreliable tales on the point.[42] To conclude from Muhammed's words ("*We know* that they say: only a mortal man teaches him"), the rumours were only circulated secretly, but he was a match for his foes, and turned his knowledge of their suspicions into a prophetic faculty which made him acquainted with their slanderous whispers.[43]

It is quite in accordance with Muhammed's methods of preaching, that so fine a rhetorical performance should be repeated. Thus some descriptive portions of *S.* xiii.[44] not only recall

[40] صبروا = ישברו in the original which allows a conclusion as to how the Arab Jews pronounced ש and צ; another instance of the same kind is اصرهم, vii. 156 = אסר (*cf.* Ch. V.).

[41] Verse 46 is to be joined to نوحي اليهم (v. 45), whilst the words فاسالوا as far as تعلمون form a parenthesis.

[42] The tratidions are collected by Sprenger, II. 379 *sqq.* *Cf.* xxxvi. 76.

[43] See Ch. II.

[44] The *sûra* is one of those beginning with the "Signs." According to Fihrist p. 251, it is Medinian.

several imitations of verses of Ps. civ. quoted before, but supplement others which he had omitted. To the former belong the verses 2, 3, 4, 18.[45] Of the latter group are:

| *The Sûra.* | *The Psalm.* |
|---|---|
| 13. He it is who shows you the lightning for fear and hope, and He brings up the heavy clouds. | 7. At Thy rebuke they flee, at the voice of Thy thunder they haste away. |
| 14. And the thunder celebrates His praise, and the angels too for fear of Him, and He sends the thunder-clap and overtakes therewith whom He will. | 32. He looketh on the earth and it trembles, He toucheth the hills and they smoke. |

The first part of S. x. (vv. 1 to 57) belongs to those addresses which begin with a reference to the "Signs." A parable inserted here is also of descriptive character.[46] The piece next to it owes its place also to some descriptive verses, but seems to be of Medinian origin.[47]

The best sermon with text on the "Signs" is S. xxxi. (1 to 10, 19 to 34). The descriptions are of the usual style, but there is a piece inserted (vv. 11 to 18),[48] which interrupts the description and is altogether out of place. In v. 22 the speaker is advised not to take the unbelief of the infidels to heart, an advice repeated in the following sermon, S. xxxvi. (v. 76), which is thoroughly descriptive. The homiletic introduction includes a parable[49] of narrative character. After this follows a discourse on the "Signs" (vv. 33, 37, 41). New is the remark on the change of night and day as well as on the stations of the moon, and an observation on the eclipse of the sun.[50]

Now these three paragraphs (v. 33-36, 37-40, 41-44) greatly resemble strophes of four verses each though without metre. This lapse into old habits either revived the reproach that he was a poet, or Muhammed saw the danger in good time, and wished to prevent any misconception. He therefore declared (v. 69) that he had never learnt poetry, nor was it suitable for him. The verse mentioned above, advising him not to be grieved about disbelief, seems to stand in connection with this. Verse 78 has a historical background. Ubeyy b. Khalaf came to Muhammed with a decaying bone and asked who could quicken it. The affair seems to have caused some sensation, as several years later it was made the subject of an attack against the Qoreish by the Medinian poet Ḥassân b. Thâbit.[51]

The descriptive period further includes S. xxvii. 60 to 95—an independent sermon;[52] further S. xxxix., the second part of which is a discourse on death. Some of these verses

---

[45] Verses 22 and 24, صبروا, and صبرتم respectively; see above.

[46] Verse 25, *cf.* Ch. VIII.

[47] Verse 58 [O ye men, now has come to you counsel from your Lord, *etc.*] is spoken in the style of an introduction to a sermon; *cf.* S. ii. 1.—Verse 61, يفترون, *cf.* v. 70.

[48] This is of legislative character and in the form of admonitions addressed by Loqmân to his son (see Ch. VII.). The *sûra* derived its name from this piece which seems to have been placed here on account of the rhyme. *Cf.* Nöldeke, p. 117, who only entertains doubt as to v. 13.

[49] V. 12 *sqq.*, see Ch. VIII.

[50] Verse 39, *cf.* Ch. I. Palmer's translation of the verse is hardly correct. I believe Muhammed wished to express the idea that the movements of the sun and the moon were so well regulated, that it is the latter which "reaches" the former, and not *vice versâ*. The commentators refer to the variety of the sphere. Bagh. وقيل الشمس ينبغي لها ان تدرك القمر لا تجتمع معه في فلك واحد ولا الليل سابق النهار لا يتصل ليل بليل لا يكون بينها نهار فاصل.

[51] Ḥassân b. Thâbit, Diwan, ed. Tunis, p. 81:—

Ubeyy has acquired heresy from his father on the day when the Messenger detached himself from him.
Hast thou come to Muhammed with a rotten bone in order to give him the lie, being ignorant of his condition, *etc.*?

[52] Verse 64 = Ps. civ. 2; v. 72 = S. x. 66, xxxi. 22.

are regarded by Weil as interpolated.[53] The chronology of this *sûra* as well as *S.* xxx. is pretty distinctly fixed by two respective remarks on parables "struck" before (xxxix. 28, xxx. 58). The latter *sûra*, though commencing with an allusion to a defeat which the Byzantine army had suffered at the hand of Persians, is an elaborate homily on the "Sign," as seven verses commence with the words: To his Signs belong, *etc.*[54]

*Sûra* xxii. 1 to 13 and 62 to 71 are two fragments belonging to the descriptive group, whilst all the rest is Medinian. A certain connection between the two pieces is visible in vv. 3, 8, 67 respectively, where those who "wrangle about Allâh" are mentioned. Finally the verses ii. 158 to 162, although placed in a *sûra* commonly regarded as Medinian, has all the marks of the revelations of the descriptive Meccan period.[55]

[53] Verses 31 to 32, 43, see Ch. XIII. Verse 31 is quite out of connection both with the preceding and following verses. The homily coming after it has no marked character, and is therefore difficult to fix. Perhaps vs. 74 to 75, the concluding words in particular, may help to place the portion somewhat nearer to the narrative period.

[54] Verses 19 to 24, 45.

[55] Nöldeke, p. 31, also regards the verses as Meccan.

## CHAPTER VII.

### The Legislative Revelations.

Meaning of the term — Relation of the legislative to previous periods — Loqmân — Laws given to mankind — Character of special laws promulgated in Mecca — Abrogation of Jewish ritual law.

---

The term "legislative" in this chapter applies to those passages in the Meccan portions of the *Qorân*, which are in any way admonitory, and are discussed chiefly with regard to the place they occupy in the book. In the same way as the Old Testament provided laws to meet all the requirements of the Israelites, so the *Qorân* forms the principal source of the moral, ritual and juridical codes[56] of the Faithful. The regulations dictated in Mecca are limited to such as could be given to a religious community which owed allegiance to temporal powers of a different kind. As it was impossible to foretell whether the Prophet would ever be in a position to wield a temporal sceptre, administrative ordinations are entirely excluded from Meccan revelations.[57] As regards ritual laws the Meccan period produced hardly any besides those relating to prayers and other forms of divine worship.

We have seen above that Moslim tradition itself places the descriptive revelations before those of legislative character, but this is not always rigidly adhered to. Some of the former, being mere recommendations, do not aspire to the authority of laws. The belief in Allâh and His Prophet is, of course, an injunction of the earliest date, but it appears in the nature of an axiom meant to carry conviction. Religious observance being of more practical character could not be expected until the former was firmly established in the minds of the believers.

The precepts which Muhammed thought fit to reveal in Mecca had long been under preparation, but it was impossible to promulgate them in anything like a systematic fashion as long as the struggle for the acceptance of the first maxims lasted. After all, the foregoing periods are nothing but a variety of endeavours to end this struggle. During this time the want of a religious code had to be supplied by the example set by the Prophet himself, or by his predecessors with whose stories believers were made acquainted. Nay, Allâh Himself serves as example by imposing mercy upon himself in the style of a commandment as it were (*S.* vi. 12).[58] In the same speech the Prophet is bidden to declare that he was *commanded* to be the first Moslim (v. 17). A second speech (v. 46 to 73) follows the same train of ideas. We hear again "that Allâh has imposed mercy upon Himself."[59] The Prophet is ordered to state that he is forbidden to worship the idols of the Meccans,[60] but that he and his friends are commanded to be Moslims, to recite prayers, and fear Allâh (vv. 70 to 71).

An instance of how legislation was at first given in very small doses, is to be found in three verses attached to *S.* xciii.[61]

> v. 9. But as for the orphan, oppress him not,
>
> 10. And as for the beggar, drive him not away,
>
> 11. And as for the favour of thy Lord, discourse thereof.

The last verse is a reminiscence of the descriptive revelations.

---

[56] See Sachau, *Aeltests Quellen des muhamm., Rechts*. The original meaning of *fiqh* is "tenets of belief."

[57] The passage, vi. 118 to 121, is Medinian.

[58] The speech ends, v. 45, الحمد لله رب العالمين.

[59] *S.* vi. 54. *Cf.* the passage in the Talmud (Berakh. fol. 7vo): God prays. What prays He? R. Zutrâ b. Tôbiyyâh says on behalf of Râb: (He prays:) Be it my will that my mercy overcome mine anger; let my mercy prevail over my (other) attributes, that my conduct with my children be merciful and that I deal with them leniently.

[60] *Ibid.* 55, 67, 69; xvii. 80 to 87.

[61] These three verses do not belong to the preceding part of the *sûra* — from which they differ as to the rhyme — but are placed here on account of v. 6 to 8.

It is indeed most interesting to observe how cautiously Muhammed proceeded to accustom his hearers to regular religious observance. He knew the characters of his friends sufficiently to perceive how dangerous it would be to overwhelm them with religious duties, and the following are instances of his attempts to achieve his object in a somewhat circuitous manner. In one sermon he describes the life of "the servants of Allâh," naturally in order to teach:—

S. xxv. 64. And the servants of the Merciful are those who walk upon the earth lowly and when the ignorant address them, say: Peace!

65. And those who pass the night [adoring] their Lord in prostration and standing.

66. And those who say: O our Lord, turn from us the torment of hell, *etc.*

67. And those who when they spend are neither extravagant nor miserly, but who ever take their stand between the two.

68. And those who call not upon another god with Allâh, and kill not the soul which Allâh has forbidden, save deservedly, and do not commit fornication; for he who does that shall meet with a penalty.

72. And those who do not testify falsely, and when they pass by frivolous discourse, pass by it honourably, *etc., etc.*

The admonition addressed by Loqmân[62] to his son is nothing but a variation of the same endeavour. Being first himself reminded of the gratitude he owed to Allâh, this legendary sage instructs his son — in the fashion of the author of Proverbs, ch. I. to VII. — to believe in the Unity of God, to honour his parents, to lead a virtuous life, and to recite prayers commandments which are all within the scope of religious prescriptions taught in Mecca. The piece which justifies reproduction runs thus:—

xxxi. 11. And we did give unto Loqmân wisdom saying: Be grateful to Allâh; for he who is grateful to Allâh, is duly grateful for his own soul, and he who disbelieves, verily Allâh is independent, worthy of praise.

12. And when Loqmân said to his son while admonishing him: O my son, associate none with Allâh, for, verily, such association is a grave iniquity.

13. And we have commanded[63] man [to honour] his parents; his mother bore him with weakness upon weakness, and his weaning is in two years; be thankful to me and thy parents, for unto me [shall your] journey [be].

14. But if they strive with thee that thou shouldst associate with me that which thou hast no knowledge of, then obey them not, *etc.*[64]

15. O my son, verily if there were the weight of a grain or mustard seed and it were [hidden] in a rock, or in the heaven, or in the earth, Allâh would bring it [forth], *etc.*[65]

16. O my son, be steadfast in prayer, and bid what is proper, prevent what is objectionable,[66] be patient of what befals thee, for this is due of the determined affairs,

[62] Concerning the personality of Loqmân see Sprenger, I. 23 *sqq.* Besides Balaam, with whom he is identified on account of the synonymity of the names, also Job and a negro slave "with thick lips" serve to personate him in the opinion of various commentators. The name seems to me to be a corruption of *Soleimân*, the letter *s* being omitted. The introductory phrase, "we have given to Loqmân wisdom," is in favour of this suggestion as well as the resemblance of the whole speech to the first chapters of the Book of Proverbs. As to the fables ascribed to Loqmân see Derenbourg, *Fables arabe et français.* Berlin, 1850.

[63] This is the only recommendation introduced here by ووصّينا. It is repeated in *S.* xlvi. 14 to 16.

[64] *Cf.* Talmud Yebâm, fol. 5vo (with reference to Lev. xix. 3): It is the duty of *each of you* to honour me, *etc.*

[65] *Cf. S.* x. 62, xxxiv. 3.

[66] This phrase occurs here for the first time, but is very frequent later on, especially in Medinian *sûras.* *Cf.* Mewâqif, p. 331, and Al Ghazâli, *Ihyâ*, II. 207 *sqq.*

17. And twist not thy cheeks proudly, nor walk in the land haughtily: verily. Allâh does not love every arrogant boaster.

18. And be moderate in thy walk and lower thy voice: verily the most disagreeable of voices is the voice of asses.[67]

Another variation is to be found in a series of admonitions given to mankind in general, although there can be no doubt, that Muhammed only had his small Moslim community in view. The sermon in question forms a part of *S.* vii. 28 to 56, and contains rules to be observed in connection with the places of public worship (v. 28 to 30[68]). But fearful, as it were, lest Believers should be discouraged by laws which might only be the forerunners of more arduous ones, Muhammed deemed it expedient to assure his friends that no soul should be burdened with more than it could bear (v. 40).[69] Yet he does not conclude the sermon without a warning to "call on your Lord humbly and secretly, not to do evil on earth, and to invoke Allâh with fear and earnestness" (v. 53 to 54).

There is hardly any group of legislative revelations in which the respect due to parents does not find a place. This forms the nucleus of a short lecture which was placed at the beginning of *S.* xxix. 1 to 12, and xlvi. 1 to 19.

It is not in the least surprising that Muhammed endeavoured to imitate the *Decalogue*, or, rather to adapt it to the requirements of Islâm. This has not only been recognized by European scholars,[70] but also by Muhammedan commentators. Discussing the Decalogue in his *Kitâb AlArâis* AlTha'âlibi[71] concludes with the remark that Allâh had also given it to Muhammed, and quotes the two places in which it is reproduced in the *Qorân*.

Of these two recensions the earlier seems to be that inserted in *S.* xvii., of which it forms the whole middle portion. The following reproduction of the chief part shows that several verses are nearly literally translated from the *Pentateuch:* —[72]

v. 23. Put not with Allâh another god, or thou wilt sit despised and forsaken.

Muhammed was so well versed in the subject, that he altered it freely, substituting for commands which were out of place in Arabia others of more practical value. The prohibition of murder gave him an opportunity of denouncing the burying of female infants alive (v. 33),[73] and it is due to him that that barbarous custom was abolished. He forbade the spoliation of orphans, and ordained that agreements must be kept, true weights and measures must be given (v. 36 to 37), *etc.*

The second and more elaborate reproduction[74] is given, *S.* vi. : —

152. Say, Come! I will recite what your Lord has made inviolable for you (1) that you may not associate with him anything; (2) kindness to your parents; (3) and do not kill your children through poverty; . . . . (4) and draw not nigh to hideous sins, either apparent or concealed; (5) and kill not the soul, which Allâh has made inviolable, save by right; that is what He has *ordained* you, haply you may understand.

153. (6) And draw not nigh unto the wealth of the orphan, save so as to better it, until he reaches full age! (7) and give weight and measure with justice . . . . ; (8) and when ye pronounce, then be just, though it be the case of a relative; (9) and Allâh's compact fufil ye; that is what he has *ordained* you, haply you may be mindful.

[67] See p. 86. [68] See Nöldeke, *Q.* p. 118. [69] *Cf. S.* vi. 153, xxiii. 64.
[70] Sprenger, II. p. 484. [71] Cod. Brit. Mus. Add. 18,508 fol. 139. [72] See *Beitraege*, p. 19 *sqq.*
[73] *Cf. S.* vi. 138 (I. I. p. 58), vv. 118 and 119 containing regulations with respect to killing animals for food are Medinian.

[74] Seems to be an independent piece, and placed here on account of its beginning with قل, like many other paragraphs of the *sûra*.

154. (10) That this is my right way, follow it thou and follow not various paths to separate ourselves from his way; that is what he has *ordained* you, haply you may fear.

The sentences are instructive not only for what they contain, but for what they omit. The omission of Exod. xx. 2 is not surprising, as it implies no commandment, and an allusion to the exodus of Egypt is of still less use for Islâm. The contents of verse 7 are rather against the spirit of Islâm. Frequent enunciations of the name of Allâh formed and still form a powerful means of implanting belief in the hearts of the Faithful. Numerous traditions exist of the benefits derived from frequent repetition of the formula: There is no God beside Allâh. Finally, the law of Sabbath was not required.[75] It is not difficult to discover why Muhammed looked upon the Jewish Sabbath as a punishment for disobedience, and characterized it as being "laid upon those who disputed thereon" (xvi. 125). The reason why a day of rest did not gain ground in Islâm seems to be a social rather than a religious one. Although the creation of the world in six days is frequently mentioned in the *Qorân*, the interruption of work on the seventh day is as regularly omitted. In a country where agriculture is of small account, and hard work altogether unknown, a day of rest has no *raison d'être*. It is possible that some vague notion had reached Muhammed that among Assyrians the seventh day was called an "evil day" on which no work should be done.[76] In a Medinian revelation[77] Muhammed calls those, who celebrate the Sabbath, "cursed." He evidently formed his opinion from seeing that the Jews observed the Sabbath by abstaining from work on that day. While the spiritual side of the celebration remained hidden to him, he saw that it involved great inconvenience in domestic and public life, and impressed him as something very undesirable.[78] By singling out one day in the week, employed from time immemorial for gathering, as the day of public worship, he followed the Jewish and Christian customs to some extent. It is, however, very improbable that he chose Friday in order to eschew either the Saturday or the Sunday. Following the reproduction of the Decalogue, v. 155 seems to be a free rendering of Exod. xxxi. 18. The bounty attached to it formed evidently part of the same speech. V. 160 looks like a rebuke on the multitude of Christian sects, whilst v. 161 again returns to the Decalogue, being a kind of reflex of Exod. xx. 5 to 6.

---

75 Al Beidh. on *S*. xvi. 125: The celebration of the Sabbath and giving oneself up entirely to worship was incumbent upon those who contended with him, *viz*., their prophet. These are the Jews whom Moses had commanded to confine themselves (on this day) to worship, *etc*. Thus Al Beidh. refers فيه not to the Sabbath, but to Moses (see *S*. xli. 45 where فيه refers to الكتاب), and evidently had Exod. xv. 24 in his mind. Rabbinic interpretation, as is well known, refers, *ibid*. v. 25, to the command of the Sabbath, and the words *w'shâm nissâhû* reflect perfectly the idea which Muhammed had conceived on the celebration of that day. *Cf*. Bokh I. 224, a tradition according to Abu Hureira: فاختلفوا فيه فهدانا الله له فالناس لنا فيه تبع اليهود غدا والنصارى بعد غد هذا يومهم الذى فرض عليهم. The puerile character of the tradition speaks for its value. The Moslims, while adopting Friday as a day of public worship, lead both Jews and Christians. On the name يوم الجمعة see Beidh. on *Qor*. lxii. 9 (Medin.). It appears that the day of *alûrûba*, which is the ancient name for Friday, was kept as prayer-day before Islâm. According to Beidh., Ka'b b. Lu'eiyy gave the day that name, because people used *to congregate on it*, probably for mercantile purposes. Muhammed then retained both the ancient custom and the name. I regard *S*. xvi. 152 as Medinian, *cf*. ii. 61 and iv. 50.

76 *Cf*. Schrader K. A. T. 2nd ed. p. 20.

77 See *S*. iv. 50 and below.

78 See Sprenger, II. 482. The Jewish dietary law appeared to Muhammed likewise in the light of a chastisement for frowardness. Abstemiousness from so many articles of food as are tabooed by the Jewish law naturally appeared strange to people whose supply was rather scanty, and who did not despise fallen camels. This latter custom was abrogated by Muhammed in *Qor*. vi. 146, who also did away with several old usages connected with the eating of certain animals (see vi. 143 to 147). He further forbade the eating of animals over which, when being slaughtered, the name of Allâh had not been mentioned (vi. 118 to 121). Nöldeke, p. 119, regards this verse as misplaced. "As to the Jews," Muhammed adds (v. 147), "we have forbidden them to eat everything that has a solid hoof, and of oxen and sheep did we prohibit them to eat the fat, save what the backs of both do bear, or the inwards of what is mixed with bone" (*cf*. *S*. xvi. 119). Muhammed reveals here a close intimacy with details of the Code, which he could not have gained from his own knowledge of the *Pentateuch* alone. I therefore regard all those passages as late Medinian.

## CHAPTER VIII.

### The Parable in the Qorân.

Real poetical element in the *Qorân* — Critical value of the *mathal* in the *Qorân*. — Its development and distribution through the various period — Views of Arab authors on the *mathal* — The shorter aphorisms collected — Parable and dogma — Parables chronologically arranged — Application of *mathals* — Biblical *mathals* in the *Qorân* — Anthropomorphism — Moslim views on the subject — Repetitions of *mathals* in altered forms — *Mathals* in Medinian revelations.

Appendix : The *Mathal* in Tradition.

---

Apart from those few cases already notified, in which Muhammed betrayed his inability to alienate himself completely from certain traditions of the national poetry,[79] we find his sermons embellished to a suprising extent with poetic gems. The *Qorân* is studded with them — to use his own phrase — like "with hidden pearls." The pathos of the declamatory period would hardly bear artistic criticism, but the case is quite different as regards the parables, poetic comparisons, and figures of speech which leapt unsought upon his tongue, and by their simplicity and appositeness give an undeniable charm to many passages otherwise forced and tedious.

When speaking in aphorisms Muhammed introduced no new element into the literature of the Arabs, since proverbs and epigrams are prominent in their oldest productions. His own share is unusually large, and Moslim theologians and literateurs eagerly compiled an enormous number of sayings and parables which they attributed to Muhammed, but with the exception of those occurring in the *Qorân* itself, it is difficult to establish the authenticity of any of them.[80]

The Arabic term for aphorism is *mathal*. The various definitions of this word, given by Moslim authors, commence with the idea of similitude,[81] like the Hebrew *mâshâl*, but the *mathal* also includes fables and short tales which, on account of some peculiar feature, have become proverbial.[82] The *mathal* therefore comprehends every allegory, tale, and sentence containing anything worth remembering. To these the Qorânic *mathal* adds, under certain conditions, the interpretations of description[83] and example.[84] It afforded the Prophet numerous opportunities of alluding to persons and incidents in the guise of a parable or fable of his own invention.

Muhammed's employment of the *mathal* as an element of rhetoric was undoubtedly a concession to the familiarity of his people with this feature of national poetry, although its fictitious character should have placed it in contrast to the reality of the revelations. Indeed, Muhammed limited the fictitious appearance of the *mathal* as much as possible. The aim of his speeches was practical, and the effect of the *mathals* intended to be drastic rather than artistic. Eloquence for its own sake was not the Prophet's chief object, and in using figures of speech he never sought to be poetic.

---

[79] See above Ch. I. To the plays upon words mentioned by Nöldeke, *l. c.* p. 32, should be added *Qor.* vi. 26, وهم ينهون عنه وينأون عنه.

[80] See Appendix to this chapter.

[81] See Al Maidânî, *Arabum Proverbia*, ed. Freytag, III. p. 329. Al Beidh. on *Qor.* ii. 16, and Sprenger, *Dictionary of Technical Terms*, p. 1340. Kashshâf on *Qor.* xvi. 62. Al Ghazâli, in *Kit. almadnûn*, p. 102, *sq.*, establishes the difference between مثال and مثل.

[82] *E. g.*, the sheep and the knife, Ḥariri, *Maqâmas*, introduction, *Z. D. M. G.* xlvi. p. 737, and *Talmud*, Pesaḥ. fol. 66ro.

[83] Kashsh. ii. 16 ; Al Bagh. often.

[84] *Qor.* vii. 176, xvi. 62 ; for further classification *cf. Itqân*, p. 564 *sqq.*

Besides this the *mathals* of the *Qorân* have a literary importance also, as they assist in the critical treatment of the book. In some cases they serve to fix the periods of the addresses of which they form a part, and their dispersion through the book reveals the following interesting facts. In older portions they are extremely rare. None, or hardly any, occur as early as the confirmatory period. It is plain that, when the Prophet was engaged in building up the framework of the new faith, he could not at the same time adorn it, and he may also have feared that *mathals* of any kind would be suggestive of poetry. They, however, gradually crept into the declamatory period in the form of very brief comparisons, whilst real parables could only find a place amidst longer discourses of doctrinal character. The oaths taking as witnesses the sun, moon, stars, dawn, day, night and similar subjects, cannot be regarded as aphoristic expressions, because they are merely high-flown invocations of natural phenomena. Even the appeals, to the "Elevated *Qorân*," the "Book," the "Day of Judgment" in its various descriptions, and other transcendental objects are based on matters which the Prophet taught were real. His pictures of the transformations of Nature, of the Last Day, of the pleasures of paradise and the tortures of hell have also substantial backgrounds. Hence there are considerably more parabolic utterances in the shorter and less pompous period of narrative revelations, whilst the bulk of the Meccan mathals belongs to the periods of the descriptive and legislative addresses. They are still more frequent after the Hijra until the battle of Badr, after which they are not so often met with. We thus see that the *mathal* in the *Qorân* developed gradually. It reached its apogee, when Muhammed's hitherto purely doctrinal mission assumed a political character. Of those which appear later, some are almost repetitions of former ones, some are evolved from personal experiences, others are manifestly borrowed, one is of questionable authenticity,[85] and all of them have little or no fictitious element.

The *mathal* as one of the characteristic features of the *Qorân* has hitherto received no attention from European students; yet its importance did not escape several Moslim writers of repute. Fourteen shorter aphorisms were collected by Abu Manṣûr Al Tha'âlibi.[86] Al Suyûtî in his *Itqân*[87] entered more deeply into the subject proper. According to his statement, based on earlier authorities,[88] Muhammed is said to have given the *mathal* a place among the five ways in which revelations came down, and to have advised believers to reflect on their meaning. He further states that Al Mâverdi, commenting on this, teaches that study on the *mathal* holds the foremost rank among the studies of the *Qorân*, however neglected it may be, and that "a *mathal* without its application is like a horse without bridle and a camel without strap."[89] Of the views of other authors, quoted by Al Suyûtî, on the importance of the *mathal*, I will only mention one, *viz.*, that the *mathals* represent abstract reflections in concrete form, because the human mind grasps by means of the tangible. The purpose of a *mathal* is therefore the comparison of what is hidden to something that is manifest, and comprises the various degrees of approval and disapproval with their consequences. "Therefore," concludes Al Suyûtî his introductory remarks on the topic, "has Allâh inserted in the *Qorân* as well as in His other books many *mathals*, and one of the chapters of the Gospel bears the name: Chapter of the Parables."[90]

The difference between shorter comparisons and figures of speech, and the parable proper has already been pointed out by Al Suyûtî,[91] who treats on both in different chapters of his work, dividing the former into various classes which there is no need to be detailed here.

It is of greater importance to note that the *mathal* had to be submitted to a kind of dogmatic treatment. Some objected to the employment of the *mathals* of the *Qorân* for profane purposes. The poet Ḥarîri was blamed for having interwoven one of the *Qorânic* comparisons in one of his *Maqâmas*,[92] because, according to Al Zarkashi, it is not lawful to transfer *Qorânic mathals* to other works. We conclude from this that Moslim critics had some notion of the poetic element which was hidden in aphorisms and parables, but being accustomed to judge according to the exterior of things, they considered nothing poetic which was not written in verse and rhyme.

85 *Q.* xlviii. 29, see below.
86 *Kitâb alijâz wali'jâz* (Cairo, 1301), p. 4.
87 Page 776.
88 Abû Hureira.
89 *Itq.*, *ibid.*
90 *Cf.* S. Matth. Ch. xiii.
91 *Itq.* 564, Comparisons and Aphorisms.
92 *Qor.* xxix. 40, *cf.* *Itq.* 265. *Cf.* Ḥariri *Maq.* xiii., Schol.

We will now proceed to give a list of the most striking comparisons and aphorisms. Although it does not claim to be exhaustive, it is yet sufficient to show Muhammed's purpose in introducing them. The parable proper will be discussed afterwards. The first group is arranged according to the sequence of *sûras* in our editions, the Medinian passages being marked by an asterisk.

* ii. 9. In their hearts is a sickness.

* 69. They (your hearts) are as stone, or harder still; there are some stones from which streams burst forth, and there are others, when they burst asunder, the water issues out.

* v. 35. We have prescribed to the children of Israel that whoso kills a soul, unless it be for another soul, or for violence [committed] in the land, it is as though he had killed men altogther.[93]

vi. 32. The life of this world is nothing but a game and a sport.[94]

66. To every prophecy is a set time.

125. Whomsoever Allâh wishes to guide, He expands his breast to Islâm; but whomsoever He wishes to lead astray, He makes his breast tight and straight, as though he would mount up into heaven.

164. No soul shall earn aught against itself; nor shall one bearing a burden bear the burden of another.[95]

vii. 38. Until the camel enters the eye of a needle.[96]

* viii. 22 (57). The worst of beasts are in Allâh's sight the deaf, the dumb, those who do not understand.

24. Allâh steps in between man and his heart.

x. 24. Your wilfulness against yourselves is but a provision of this world's life.

28. As though their faces were veiled with the deep darkness of the night.

xiii. 17. Shall the blind and the seeing be held equal? or shall the darkness and the light be held equal?[97]

xvi. 79. Nor is the matter of the Hour aught but as the twinkling of an eye or nigher still.[98]

94. Be not like her who unravels her yarn, fraying out after she has spun it close.

xvii. 86. Everyone acts after his own manner.

xxi. 36. Every soul shall taste of death.[99]

104. As the rolling of the *Sijill* for the books.[100]

* xxii. 32. He who associates aught with Allâh, it is as though he had fallen from heaven, and the birds snatch him up, or the wind blows him away into a far distant place.

xxiii. 55. Each party rejoices in what they have themselves.

---

[93] *Cf.* Mishnah, *Sanh.* iv. 5.

[94] *Cf.* xxix. 64, xlvii. 38, lvii. 19; Hariri, *Maq.* xiii.

[95] This is a very old aphorism and occurs already in liii. 39, xxxv. 19, xxxix. 9, etc. See also Torrey, *The Commercial Theological Terms in the Qoran*, Leyden, 1892.

[96] *Cf.* Geiger, *l. c.* p. 71, and Al Meidâni, II. 498; Hish. 922, l. 16.

[97] *Cf. ibid.* v. 19, xxxv. 20, 21, xx. 124, 125, vi. 50, xl. 60, xxvii. 83, xxx. 52, ii., 166. *Cf.* Isaiah, vi. 10; Ps. cxv 4-7, cxxxv. 15-18.

[98] *Cf.* 1 Cor. xv. 52. The phrase is also common in the Talmud and in Syriac.

[99] *Cf.* xxix. 57; iii. 182.

[100] *Cf.* Ch. IV.

xxix. 40. The weakest of houses is the house of the spider.[1]

xxxi. 18. The most disagreeable of voices is the voice of the asses.

34. No soul knows what it shall earn to-morrow, and no soul knows in what land it shall die.[2]

* xxxiii. 19. Like one fainting with death.

xxxv. 41. The plotting of evil only entangles those who practice it:

xxxvi. 39. Until it (the moon) becomes again like an old dry palm-branch.

xxxvii. 47. As though they (the maidens) were a hidden egg.

63. Its spathe is as it were the heads of devils.

xxxix. 12. Shall those who know be held equal to those who know not?

xli. 34. Good and evil shall not be deemed alike.

xlii. 19. He who wishes for the tilth of the last world — the tilth of this world.

31. The ships that sail like mountains in the sea.

* xlix. 12. Some suspicion is a sin[3] . . . . would one of you like to eat his dead brother's flesh?[4]

l. 15. We are nigher to him than his jugular vein.

lii. 24. . . . . boys of their's as though they were hidden pearls.

liv. 7. As though they were locusts scattered about.

lv. 58. As though they were rubies and pearls.

lvi. 22. Bright and large-eyed maids like hidden pearls.[5]

* lxi. 4. As though they were a compact building.

8. They desire to put out the light of God with their mouths.

* lxiii. 4. Like timber propped up.

lxix. 7. As though they were palm stumps thrown down.[6]

lxx. 8. The heaven shall be like molten brass (9) and the mountains shall be like flocks of wool.

43. As though they flock to standards.

lxxiv. 51. As though they were timid asses which flee from a lion.

lxxvi. 19. Thou wilt think them scattered pearls.

lxxvii. 32. It throws off sparks like towers, (33) as though they were yellow camels.

lxxix. 46. As though they had only tarried an evening or the noon thereof.

ci. 3. Men shall be like scattered moths, (4) and the mountains shall be like flocks of carded wool.[7]

The list is long enough to reveal a poetic element of considerable strength.

We now come to those parables which Muhammed introduced by the term *mathal*. These are more elaborate and contain a moral. I have thought it advisable to discuss them in an approximately chronological order, which will allow us to observe the development of the

[1] *Cf.* Al Meidani, II. 842, and Job, viii. 14. See Al Tha'âlibi, ثمار القلوب في المضاف المنسوب (Cod. Brit. Mus. Or. 9558) fol. 82vo.

[2] *Cf.* Talmud B. Succah, fol. 53vo. R. Jôḥanan says: The feet of man bring him to the place where he is doomed to die.

[3] *Cf.* Ḥariri (p. 28, l. 8), Maq. I. 89.

[4] See Dan. iii. 8.

[5] *Cf.* Ḥassân b. Thâbit, p. 89, l. 6; *Itq.* p. 943.

[6] *Cf.* liv. 20, the same phrase.

[7] *Cf.* lvii. 19, iii. 118; ii. 263, 267, and above Ch. IV.

Qorânic *mathal*. The first does not appear until in the *narrative S.* xviii., in which two occur at once. In the former, the wealthy unbeliever is contrasted with his poor but pious neighbour in the following manner:—

v. 31. Strike out for them a *mathal*: two men[8] for one of whom we made two gardens of grapes, and surrounded them with palms and put corn between the two. Each of the two gardens brought forth its food, and did not fail in aught. (32) And we caused a river to flow between them, and he (the owner) had fruit. He said to his friend, who competed[9] with him: I am wealthier than thou, and mightier of household. (33) And he went in unto his garden having sinned against himself. Said he: I do not think that this will ever come to an end. (34) And I do not think that the Hour is imminent, and surely, if I be sent back unto my Lord, I shall find a better one than it in exchange. (35) His friend — who competed with him — said to him: *Thou hast disbelieved in Him who has created thee from dust, and then from a clot, and then made thee a man*. (36) But He is Allâh, my Lord, and I will not associate anyone with my Lord. (37) Couldst thou not have said, when thou didst go into thy garden: What Allâh pleases! There is no power save in Allâh. If thou lookst at me, I am less than thee in wealth and children. (38) But haply my Lord will give me [something] better than thy garden, and will send upon it a thunderbolt from the sky, so that it shall become bare slippery soil. (39) Or on the morrow its water will be deeply sunk, so that thou canst not reach it. (40) His fruits were encompassed so that on the morrow he wrung his hands for which he had spent thereon, for they (the fruits) had perished on their trellises; and he said: Would that I had never associated anyone with my Lord! (41) Yet he had not any party to help him beside Allâh, nor was he helped.

The second *mathal* consistently teaches the vanity and short duration of earthly pleasures. It is as follows:—

v. 43. Forge for them a *mathal* of the life of this world; [it is] like water which we have sent down from the sky,[10] so that the vegetation of the earth is mingled with it. On the morrow it is dried up, and the winds scatter it. Allâh is powerful over all. (44) Wealth and children are the adornment of the life of this world, but the lasting pious deeds are better with thy Lord as a recompense and better as a hope.

The application of both *mathals* is easily found. The opulent but wicked man represents the stubborn opponent of Islâm, whilst the less wealthy neighbour is the Prophet himself. It is to be noted that, in his censure of his rich rival, the other repeats the chief words of the first proclamation (v. 35 = *S.* xcvi. 1 to 2).[11] Further, the double allusion to the loss of Muhammed's

[8] The fictitious character of parables being objectionable to the Moslim Commentators, they endeavour to explain them as bearing on real persons or accidents. Thus Al Bagh. reproduces a tradition (without Isnâd) according to which this parable refers to two brothers in Mecca of whom the believing one was Abu Salama b. Abd Asad, foster brother to Muhammed, who died A. H. 4, and whose widow Umm Salâma became the wife of the Prophet (see Sprenger, I. 433). Others (Ibn Abbâs) are of opinion, that the *mathal* in question was revealed on account of the Fazâra chief Uyeina b. Ḥiṣn (Sprenger, III. 363 *sq.*) who was converted to Islâm shortly before the conquest of Mecca, and of the Persian Salmân and the friends of both. The subjects of the *mathal* are said to have been two Jewish brothers (see also Kash.). Since all these traditions deserve but little credence, I refrain from entering more fully into them. Biblical parallels to the *mathal* are to be found: Isaiah, xl. 7; Ps. ciii. 15-16.

[9] Palmer: "his next door neighbour," which is hardly correct; he seems to have read يجاوره.

[10] See *Itqân*, p. 566; Al Ghazali, *Kit. Almadn.* p. 101.

[11] *Cf.* lxxx. 17-19.

two sons (v. 37 and 44) in their infancy, as well as that of his former wealth, is too plain to be misunderstood. This melancholy narrative is particularly applicable to his own position a short time after the death of his wife Khadîja, when he also lost his uncle Abû Tâlib, his only protector. The date of the revelation in question could thus be fixed at (the summer 619) about three years before the Hijra.

The comparison of the vicissitudes of human life to the growth and decay in Nature appeared so appropriate to Muhammed, that he not only repeated the last quoted *mathal* in a more elaborate form, but also gave it a didactic tendency. The following instance is particularly interesting:—

> x. 25. Verily the likeness *(mathal)* of this world is like water which we send down from the sky, and with it are mingled the plants of the earth from which men and cattle eat, until when the earth puts on its ornature and becomes garnished, its inhabitants think that they have power over it. Our order[12] comes by night or by day; we make it mown down, as if it had not been rich yesterday — thus do we detail the signs unto people who reflect.

One of the most natural and therefore very common topics in Muhammed's sermons is the contrast between unbelievers and the faithful. This is sometimes expressed in allegorical form, as in the following *mathal*. The infidels are likened to the blind and deaf, while the believers are those who see and hear; shall the two classes be held equal (xi. 26)? The comparison of unbelief with blindness, deafness and dumbness being quite Biblical, is one of the commonest in the *Qorân*.[13] In connection with dumbness alone it occurs again, and in a more developed form, in a *mathal* to be touched upon later.

Unquestionably modelled on Biblical *mâshâls* are the following two contained in the (narrative) xivth *Sûra*. The one (v. 21) represents the works of the infidels as ashes which are blown about on a stormy day.[14] This is clearly a reflex on Ps. I. 4 (Is. xl. 7). The other *mathal*, occurring in the same address (v. 29 to 31) compares a good word to a good tree[15] whose root is firm and whose branches are in the sky. It gives its fruit at every season by the permission of its Lord — Allâh draws parallels for men, haply they may be mindful. The likeness *(mathal)* of a bad word is as a bad tree which is felled down above the earth and has no staying place. — This parable is a free rendering of the verse in Ps. i. preceding the one upon which the foregoing *mathal* is based (see also Abôth, iii. 17; Jer. xvii. 6 to 8). The phrase, *it gives its fruit at every season*, marks the origin without doubt.

Besides the two comparisons mentioned above,[16] *S.* xvi. counts not less than three *mathals*. The first stands in connection with two others placed together in *S.* xliii., of which the second is somewhat earlier, but the first nearly contemporaneous with the one under consideration. It is introduced by a rebuke, directed against the pagan Arabs for their manifest aversion to female children, many of whom they destroyed in infancy. "When any of them," he says (xvi, 60), "is informed [of the birth] of a girl, his face turns black, and he is choked with wrath." In the parallel passage, which also contains a warning against the offence of ascribing daughters to Allâh (*S.* xliii. 15) stands instead of "girl" the phrase:— "that which he (the pagan Arab) employs as a *mathal* for the *Rahmân*" (v. 16).[17] Subsequently Muhammed declares (*S.* xvi. 62) those who do not believe in the "last world" are the *mathal* (prototype) of evil,[18] whilst Allâh is

---

12 *Amrunâ*, *cf.* xvi. 1-2.

13 *Cf.* above, p. 85, where the blind and seeing are compared with one another, but this *mathal* is realistic.

14 *Itq.* 565.

15 Al Qastalâlni, vii. p. 188, كلمة التوحيد او كل كلمة حسنة كالحمد والاستغفار والتهليل; *cf.* Kash.

16 See p. 85.

17 Al Jâhiz (Abstracts from) *Kit. Albayân waltibyân*, Constantinople, 1301, p. 175, says with regard to this verse: Allâh strikes a *mathal* on account of the inadequacy of the language and in order to promote understanding, even going so far as to compare His people to women and children.

18 مثل السوء *cf.* vi. 176, (ساء مثلاً) which I translate: "a bad example;" Kash., صفة السوء; *cf.* Al Bagh.

the highest *mathal*. It would be difficult to understand what Muhammed meant by this vague expression, did he not explain it a few verses later in the distinct prohibition (v. 76): — You shall not forge a *mathal* for Allâh, behold Allâh knows but you do not know.[19] In contrast to this prohibition stands the assertion (*S.* xliii. 57 to 59), that the Son of Maryam was set up as a *mathal*, "he is but a servant upon whom we have bestowed our mercy, and whom we have made a *mathal* for the children of Israel."

Now here is a distinct restriction laid down, which serves not only to emphasize the monotheistic idea, but also to cavil at the anthropomorphistic metaphors used in the Bible. As a sincere convert to monotheism Muhammed disapproved of any attempt to explain divine attributes in the light of human faculties; in other words, he wished to be more monotheistic than the Bible whose anthropomorphistic terms he took literally. In a tradition handed down by Al Shahrastâni[20] Muhammed is said to have declared: — "The *Mushabbiha* (those who personify Allâh) are the Jews of this nation," which means that Moslims who represent Allâh after the fashion of human qualities follow the sinful custom of the Jews. The Prophet, however had only one side of the question in view, and Kremer[21] blames him unjustly for contradicting himself. Though it must be admitted that Muhammed did not investigate the question of anthropomorphism thoroughly, yet all passages in the *Qorân* dealing with the subject are not of one stamp. Muhammed rejected that form of *tashbih* (personification), which in the Bible refers to God individually. Allâh is never spoken of as a "Man of war" (Exod. xv. 3),[22] "the Rock who has borne thee" (Deut. xxxii. 4), or "the Fountain of living waters" (Jer. ii. 13), or as "Father." The last named appellation, so common in both Testaments, appeared to Muhammed as sheer blasphemy. He therefore took an early opportunity of declaring[23] that Allâh had neither a child nor any equal.[24] The title of "Father" is accordingly scrupulously avoided in all the lists of the "Most Comely Names."[25] It seems to me more than accidental that, when Muhammed related his alleged vision, that he did not mention any name of God, but circumscribed it by the epithet of "Mighty of Power."[26] The Commentators refer this expression to the Archangel Gabriel, although at that period Muhammed had not shown any knowledge of him,[27] and in the verse in question evidently alluded to Allâh himself. To prevent misunderstanding, that similitudes of Allâh should not be made, Muhammed cautiously stated that any other title of Allâh used by him was but one of the "Most Comely Names" which belonged to Him, In this way he kept his hand free to employ that other, and rather subordinate, form of anthropomorphism with which he was quite unable to dispense. He certainly tried to do without it, but only succeeded during the first period. Allâh thus speaks and writes, possesses hands, sits on his throne, which is borne by angels, loves, hates, and is even cunning towards the

[19] The Commentators see in this verse only the prohibition to compare Allâh with another being, which in that case would be placed side by side with him. Kash., تمثيل للاشراك بالله والتشبيه به لأن من يضرب الامثال مشبّه حالا بحال وقصّة بقصّة. *Cf.* also Jalalain and Al Beidh. The verse stands in connection with xxxvi. 78.

[20] Ed. Cureton, p. 13; Al Nawawi, v. p. 350, فان مذهب اليهود التجسيم. *Cf.* Goldziher in *Monatschrift f. Gesch. u. W. d. Jdth.* xxviii. p. 309.

[21] *Geschichte der herrschenden Ideen, etc.* p. 17.

[22] In the first part of his *Kitâb al Milal wilniḥal* (fol. 30vo) Ibn Hazm, in his criticism of the O. T., gives a translation of Exod. Ch. xv., and remarks that to describe Allâh as a "strong man" is heresy. He professes to have urged this point to a Jew of his acquaintance, who replied that in *Qor.* xxiv. 35. Allâh is styled "the Light of heaven and earth." While admitting this, Ibn Ḥazm referred the Rabbi to a tradition, according to which Abu Ḏarr asked Muhammed if he had ever seen Allâh? The answer was "yes," but this "light" did not mean a visible light, but an invisible one. Ibn Ḥazm therefore explains the "light" in question as guidance for the inhabitants of the earth, but "light" is to be counted among the names of Allâh. It is, however, not difficult to see that in the expression "light" there is an inconsistency which even embarrassed Mu'tazilite interpretation. Al Beidh. endeavours to show that, in this passage, "light" virtually applies to Allâh only and stands for "he gives light." *Cf.* also Mawâqif, p. 169. In several Meccan (xx. 113, xxiii. 117) and Medinian (lix. 23) revelations Allâh is styled "King," but this offers less difficulty for abstract interpretation; *cf.* Al Beidh. on lix. 23, Mewâq. p. 161, and Al Qastalâni (ed. Bûl'q. x. p. 316) who explains: "Possessor of government." See also on this subject my article "Mohammedan Criticism of the Bible," *J. Q. R.* XIII. p. 222 *sqq.*

[23] *Cf. Qor.* cxii. 3; *cf.* xxiii. 93, vi. 101, *etc.*

[24] *Cf.* Deut. iv. 35, 39.

[25] See Redhouse, *J. R. A. S.* 1880.

[26] See Ch. IV.

[27] The name occurs only in Medinian *sûras*.

wicked.[28] All this is quite in harmony with the Biblical style. Traditions of a more sensual character are to be received with scepticism as to their authenticity.[29] The famous tradition according to which Muhammed said: — The heart of a believer is between the two fingers of the Merciful[30] is by no means more realistic than the verse (*S.* xxxviii. 75): "I have created with *my hand*," or any of the numerous passages in which Allâh sees, hears and speaks.[31]

The Qoranic anthropomorphism is but a variety of that in the Bible, which Muhammed considered he had improved on, but which otherwise he accepted without much reflection during the time of his training. Later Moslim theologians, who had gone through a similar course of studies, naturally looked upon anthropomorphistic revelations with a different eye, and endeavoured to explain, that they were inbred doctrines. Inconsistency was the result. The punctilious Zahirite school did not allow the "Ninety-nine most comely names" to be surpassed,[32] and put up a long list of names *not* suitable for Allâh.[33] Schools of more liberal ideas took no heed of this restriction, but observed a certain restraint in names which Allâh did not attribute to himself either in the *Qorân* or in tradition.[34] On the other hand the Zahirites follow the more free thinking theologians to some extent in the allegorical explanation of human faculties with which Allâh is endowed,[35] and only one class goes so far as to take even those literally.[36]

The warning that Allâh must not be made the object of *mathals* is at once illustrated by a parable set up by Himself in the following manner: —

> v. 77. A bond slave who is quite unable to do any work, and another whom Allâh has provided with every good provision, and who gives alms from it secretly and openly; are these two equal?
>
> 78. And Allâh has forged a *mathal:* two men, of whom one is dumb and able to do nothing, a burden to his master, wherever he turns, he does no good; is he to be held equal with him who bids what is just and who is on the right way?

The parable of the servant was very popular both among Jews and Christians. I only mention those of Abôth, I. 3,[37] and St. Matth. xxiv. 45 and xxv. 14 *sqq.* Both *mathals* in question have the same object in view, *viz.*, to show that man, whilst dependent[38] on Allâh, should be charitable and righteous. In both parables also allusions to practical religion are not wanting, *viz.*, in *yunfiqu* (give alms), *ya'muru bil'adli* (bids what is just) and *ṣirâṭin mustâqîmin* (right way), through which the general character of the *mathals* is considerably limited.

The last *mathal* in *S.* xvi. (v. 113) furnishes an instance of the manner in which it developed in a later repetition. It speaks of a city which was safe and happy, whilst its provisions were flowing in from all sides; but it would not acknowledge, that all these had been sent by

---

[28] Ps. xviii. 27; *Qor.* viii. 30; *cf.* Al Beidhâwi: It is not lawful to use this term without restriction.

[29] Kremer, *Gesch.* p. 18 *sq.*, places reliance in some traditions on that matter, which are fictitious, but even if they had been authentic, Muhammed would not have referred them to Allâh.

[30] *Cf.* Al Shahrastani, p. 77.

[31] Al Qastal. امتثالا لامرى اى خلقته بنفسي من غير توسّط كاب وامّ والتّانية لما فى خلقة
من مزيد القدرة واختلاف الفعل و قيل المرادُ باليَد القدرة

[32] I. Ḥ. fol. 153vo *sq.* See also Al Beidh. on xxxix. 67.

[33] Reproduced by Goldziher, *die Zahiriten, etc.* p. 149.

[34] *Ibid.*

[35] *Ibid*, p. 164. The original passage of I. Ḥ.'s work is given there after the Leyden MS., to which the London Codex offers several variations.

[36] The school of Aḥmad b. Hanbal.

[37] The *Mishnâh* in question is re-echoed in the numerous assertions of Muhammed that he expected no recompense for his ministry. See p. 60.

[38] *Cf.* Iḥyâ, I. p. 249, l. 8. Al Suyûti in *Mufḥimât alqrân* refers the two men (v. 78) to Useid b. Abil 'Îs and 'Othmân b. 'Affân. Al Beidh. sees no allusion to any individual in either *mathal*.

Allâh. He therefore affected the inhabitants with hunger and fear for their wickedness. Then one of their town-fellows approached them in the character of a divine messenger, but was not believed. Thereupon the city was overtaken by heavy punishment.

The parable is, of course, perfectly clear. The happy and wealthy city is no other than Mecca[39] whose merchants traded in all directions. The messenger out of their midst is Muhammed whom they called an impostor, but dire punishment is in store for them. The threatened famine will also become clear presently.

Now this parable is repeated in a later and considerably altered form. The alteration was necessary, probably because the threatened punishment had not taken place, whilst the situation of the Prophet had meanwhile become much more difficult and dangerous. I give the translation of the *mathal* in full:—

*Sûra* xxxvi. 12. Forge for them a *mathal:* the inhabitants of *the* city, when *the* messengers came to them, (13) when we sent to them those two, but they called them both liars; so we strengthened them with a third, then they said: verily, we are sent to you. (14) They replied: You are only mortals like ourselves, and the Merciful has revealed nothing [to you], you are naught but liars. (15) They said: Our Lord knows that we are sent to you; (16) we are only charged to clearly convince you. (17) They answered: We have augured concerning you; if you do not desist, we will surely stone you, and painful punishment shall be inflicted on you by us. (18) Said they: your augury is with you, what if you have been warned? but you are a sinful people! (19) And there came hastily from the remotest parts of the town a man who said: O my people! follow the messengers. (20) Follow those who do not ask for reward from you, whilst being guided. (21) What ails me that I should not worship Him who created me, and to whom you will be made to return? (22) Shall I take other gods beside Him? If the *Merciful desires harm for me*, their intercession will not avail me at all, neither can they save me. (23) I should then be in manifest error. (24) I believe in your Lord, therefore hearken unto me! (25) [When they had killed him] it was said [to him]: Enter thou into paradise; said he: O, would that my people did but know, (26) that Allâh has forgiven me and made me one of the honoured ones . . . . (27) it was but a single noise, and lo! they were extinct.

Although this parable is told in the usual legendary style of prophetic messengers, it is a variation of the preceding one with a historical background. It speaks about *the* city and *the* messengers who at first number only two, and are later on supported by a third. The *mathal* seems to be of Christian origin, but Muhammed made the mistake of putting the attribute of *AlRahmân* into the mouth of the heathenish townspeople.[40] He had evidently the tale (Acts xi. 22 to 30) in his mind, and some Commentators rightly declare the city to be Antioch,[41] whose pagan population forms the exact parallel to Mecca. The application of the *mathal* is given in v. 29: Alas for the men, there comes to them no messenger, but they mock at him!

---

[39] Ibn 'Abbâs in *Mufḥ. alaqr*; Al Beidh. and Jal. A tradition by Ibn Sihab on behalf of Ḥafṣa refers it to Medina.

[40] The heathenish character of the populace may be gathered from the expression تطيّرنا (v. 17) which means: we have augured from the flight of birds.

[41] Kash. and Jal. Al Beidh. gives a different story which, however, does not suit the case. "The man" mentioned (v. 19) is called Ḥabîb, the carpenter (Kash.: Hab. b. Israîl). This name is evidently a translation of Agabos. His prophecy of a coming famine links this *mathal* to Q. xvi. 113-114 ("a messenger out of their midst"). As to the famine see Josephus, *Ant.* xx. 2.

A couple of rather forcible *mathals* taken from the social life of the infidel Meccan citizens are the following (*S.* xxx. 27): The Prophet asks the people, if they would feel inclined to regard their slaves as their equals, and allow them to share their property. The meaning is that Allâh cannot be expected to look upon the idols, which are made by man's hand, as His equals! In one more complicated, or rather confused, form the *mathal* re-appears in a later revelation as follows (*S.* xxxix. 30): One man has partners who disagree with each other, whilst another is entirely subservient to one who is his master; are these two men (the one who has partners and the slave) to be considered equal? By no means[42] — The first man represents Allâh to whom the heathen Meccans attribute associates. The last figure in the parable is evidently also meant for Allâh. The hostility prevailing between the various idols very appropriately expresses the narrowness and diversity of the powers with which they are endowed.

A fine parable, connected with a descriptive passage, is the following (*S.* xiii. 18): Allâh sends down rain from the sky, the water-courses flow according to their bulk, the torrent carries along with it foam that swells up. A similar foam arises from the fire kindled by men [when melting metals and] craving ornaments and utensils. Thus does Allâh hit the truth and the falsehood, *vis.*, the foam disappears in nought, whilst that [solid part], which profits man remains on earth. This is Allâh's way of forging parables.[43]

It appears that Muhammed's opponents responded to his parables with similar ones, particularly with reference to resurrection.[44] To such remarks he had a kind of constant reply which appears twice in the same form, *viz.* (*Ss.* xvii. 51 and xxv. 10): Look how they forge for thee parables,[45] but they err, neither can they find a way [to refute thee]. — On the other hand Muhammed boasts (*S.* xxv. 35): They bring thee no *mathal*, unless we (Allâh) brought thee the truth and the best explanation. — As a demonstration he reminds his audience of the cities and peoples which had been annihilated, and adds (v. 41): For each have we forged the *mathals*,[46] and each we have crumbled to pieces.—Such general references to *mathals* mentioned previously in detail confirm the comparative lateness of the passages just quoted, and one of the latest must therefore be the following summing up (*S.* xxxix. 28): Now we have forged for men in this *Qorân* all kinds of *mathals*, haply they are mindful.[47]

With this the series of *mathals* in the Meccan part of the *Qorân* concludes. The comparatively large number found in the last two periods is still surpassed in the first year after the Hijra, when they suddenly became extremely numerous. This is certainly not a mere coincidence, and shows the critical value of the *mathal* in general for researches on the composition of the *Qorân*. The Medinian *mathal*, moreover, stands in close connection with Muhammed's altered position and the new tone of his speeches. He soon became aware how much more critical and analyzing this new audience was. His addresses now being calculated to win the Jews of Medina as well as its pagan inhabitants, he dared not offer them hollow declamations which, even for the Meccan world, had only served for a certain time. He himself had also become riper, and his aim lay clearer before his eyes. The moral success won by the invitation of the Medinians, his own personal safety and daily increasing authority gave his word a power hitherto unknown. Above all, he had had more than ten years' practice in preaching,

---

42 See above.

43 V. 19 contrasts him who knows the truth with the blind man; v. 35 of the same *sûra* contains a "*mathal* of the garden promised to the pious," which is but a description; *cf.* Kash. صفة الجنة.

44 See *Q.* xvii. 52, xxxvi. 78.

45 Al Beidh. refers it to the various titles of poet, soothsayer, sorcerer and madman given to Muhammed by the Meccans.

46 Al Beidh. بيّنا له القصص العجيبة من قصص الأوّلين انذارا و اعذارا

47 *Ibid* v. 30, a *mathal* discussed above, but evidently misplaced on account of v. 28; v. 29 does not suit the context either and the same is the case with v. 31. The arrangement of the verses is here visibly in confusion. See also xxx. 38 in somewhat modified form.

whilst his own knowledge augmented continually. It is of no small moment that the space of time between the Hijra and the battle of Badr, that is to say, the time before Muhammed became an important political factor, should be richest in mathals. *Sûra* ii., which consists of the oldest Medinian sermons, counts no less than eight parables, six of which are of indisputable originality. The language also, if not poetic, is yet fluent, and abounds in allegories. The first Medinian *mathal* is taken from the daily occupation, and is as follows (v. 15): Those who buy error for guidance — their commerce brings no profit, neither are they guided — (16) their *mathal* is like him who kindles a fire, but when it lights up his surroundings, Allâh carries his light away, and leaves them in darkness, so that they cannot see. (17) They are deaf, dumb and blind,[48] so that they cannot turn round. — To this *mathal* is immediately joined the following (v. 18): Or[49] they are like a stormcloud from the sky in which is darkness and thunder and lightning; they put their fingers in their ears[50] because of the noise of the thunder for fear of death; Allâh encompasses the unbelievers. (v. 19) The lightning all but takes away their sight; as often as it shines for them, they walk therein, but when it becomes dark around them, they stand still; and if Allâh so pleased, He would surely deprive them of their hearing and their sight; Allâh is almighty.

It seems that some Medinian critics had taken exception to Allâh's employment of animals, particularly insignificant ones like spiders and flies as the subjects of *mathals*.[51] Muhammed shows how undeserved is their censure in the dignified manner (ii. 24): Behold Allâh is not ashamed to forge a *mathal* on a gnat or what is above it [in size];[52] those who believe know that it is the truth from their Lord; but the unbelievers say: what means Allâh with such a parable? He leads many astray with it, and guides others, but he only leads astray the wicked.

Muhammed was so little prepared to cease composing parables about animals, that he invented several more of the same kind. In *S.* ii. 161 the infidels are compared to a man who shouts to that which hears naught but a noise and a cry, they are deaf, dumb and blind[53] and without sense. The Commentators[54] have already seen that the metaphor stands for the word "cattle."

The fly re-appears in a revelation of somewhat later date. "O men," he says (*S.* xxii. 72) "a parable is forged for you, so listen to it. Verily, those whom they adore beside Allâh could never create a fly, if they all united together to do it, and if the fly should despoil them aught they could not recover it from it — weak are both the seekers and the sought."

Several of Muhammed's Medinian opponents, Jews in particular, when hearing one of the above mentioned mathals (*S.* ii. 24) enquired what its meaning was. They also questioned him about one of the earlier revelations (*S.* lxxiv. 33) in which it is stated that *nineteen* angels were appointed to watch over the hell fire. "Those in whose hearts there is sickness"[55] and the infidels ask: What does Allâh mean by this as a *mathal*[56] (v. 33)? Muhammed's answer is rather unsatisfactory, as the number *nineteen* seems to have been chosen at random, a fact which he dared not admit. But thus much is clear that both questions as well as the answers to them date from about the same time, *viz.*, the first year after the Hijra, although the one was placed by the compilers next to the revelation which it was meant to explain.

---

[48] See p. 85. [49] Second *mathal*, although the term is omitted. [50] *Cf.* 1 Sam. iii. 11; 2 K. xxi. 12.

[51] The animals mentioned in *mathals* are birds, camel (twice), spider, ass (twice), locusts, moth, dog, fly.

[52] فما فوقها, 'much more so.' Al Beidh. فضلا عماهو اكبر منة; *cf. Itq.* 256. [53] *Cf.* verse 17 and above.

[54] Al Beidh.; Nöldeke, *Q.* p. 132, regards vv. 163-6 as Meccan, but this cannot be concluded from ما ألفينا عليه ابا ءنا, since this is also a common Jewish phrase.

[55] *Viz.*, the Jews; *cf.* Ch. IX.

[56] *Lit.*, what means Allâh with this as a *mathal*? The Commentators are at a loss to explain the construction of the phrase. Kash. takes مثلا a *tamyîz* to *hâdâ* or as a *Ḥâl*. Vv. 31-34 are undoubtedly Medinian, and were only placed here on account of their reference to v. 30.

Many of those who rallied round the Prophet in Medina, particularly emigrants from Mecca, were extremely poor. Although liberally supported by the more wealthy inhabitants of the town who had joined Islâm, they looked forward to raids on Meccan caravans as a means of gaining some property of their own. Robbery was so little regarded as anything illegal or immoral, that Muhammed not only sanctioned raids by participating in them himself, but did not hesitate to violate the sacred month in order to makeb elievers "walk in the path of Allâh." There were plenty of people anxious to enrich themselves by plunder in honour of Allâh, but they lacked the means to carry out their plans. Muhammed, therefore, continually urged the wealthy to raise funds for this purpose, with promises of ample reward hereafter. The admonition sometimes took the form of a parable as follows:—

(*S.* ii. 263) The likeness of those who spend their fortune in *the path of Allâh* is like a grain which produces seven ears, in every ear a hundred grains, Allâh gives twofold to whom He pleases; Allâh is bounteous and omniscient. But those, he continues, who give alms while taunting and annoying the receiver — as a man would do who only gives for appearance's sake — are compared (v. 266) to a rock covered with dust which a shower washes away, leaving the stone bare.

This fine parable which seems in part to be built on St. Mark iv. 5 *sqq*, is followed by a third not less striking, on the same topic in the following manner:—

(v. 267) Those who lay out their wealth merely to obtain the grace of Allâh, and as an insurance for their souls, are like a garden on elevated ground. Rain waters it richly, and its crops grow twofold. Should rain fail, dew irrigates them.

These *mathals*, intended to encourage believers to spend their fortune to increase the Prophet's worldly power, contrast strangely with two others which gave little comfort after the defeat at Uhud. As for unbelievers, he says (*S.* iii. 112), their wealth shall not profit them, neither their children, against Allâh, they shall be the companions of hell fire, and they shall dwell therein for ever. (113) The likeness of what they lay out in this present life is as a wind wherein there is a cold blast; it affects the corn-fields belonging to people who have injured their own souls and destroyed them.[57]

Still more pessimistic is the following[58] (*S.* lvii. 19): Know ye that this present life is but a toy and vain amusement and pomp and affectation of glory among ye,[59] and multiplying of wealth and children — like rain which astonishes the husbandman[60] by its fertility, but then the vegetation withers until thou seest it turn yellow, and become dry stubble — but in the last world there is heavy punishment.

Here we have to notice several *mathals*, which show how bitter Muhammed felt against Jews and Christians. "The *mathal* of Jesus is in the eye of Allâh like the *mathal* of Adam, whom he has created from dust" (*S.* iii. 52). Still more spiteful is an epigram hurled against the Jews, whose power was considerably weakened after the expulsion of the tribe of the B. Qainoqâ. "They are burdened, he says, with the Torâh, which they do not observe, they are likened to the ass which carries books" (*S.* lxii. 5).[61]

To this period belongs a *mathal* which contains an attack against a certain individual not mentioned by name, and is so densely veiled that even the Moslim Commentators are at a loss to establish the identity of the person in question. It is evident that Muhammed pointed

---

[57] *Cf. Itqân*, p. 565.

[58] See v. 22, lxiv. 11, and Nöldeke, *Q.* p. 145.

[59] See p. 85. Al Qastal. ix. p. 237, كلعب الصبيان ولهو كلهو الفتايا وزينة كزينة النسوان وتفاخر كتفاخر الاقران .وتكاثر كتكاثر الرهبان

[60] الكفار, see Al Beidh.

[61] See Geiger, *ibid*, p. 9?.

at a man of high station and education, otherwise he would hardly have described him as one "whom we have given our *signs*, but he stepped away from them; had we wished we would have exalted him thereby, but he crouched[62] upon the earth and followed his lust. He is likened unto a dog, whom if thou shouldst attack, he hangs out his tongue, and if thou shouldst leave him, hangs out his tongue too" (*S.* vii. 174 to 175).

From the text of the *mathal* it is clear that the person to whom it refers, had been given opportunities of embracing Islâm, but had not made use of them, and thereby set "a bad example to the people who declare our *signs* to be lies" (v. 176).

Following Arab Commentators, Sprenger suggests that the *mathal* refers to the poet *Omayya b. Abi Ṣalt* of Ṭâ'if,[63] who was a gifted and well educated man. According to Arabic tradition he was an apostate from paganism, but refused to follow Muhammed from jealousy. It is, however, clear that Muhammed did not refer to him. He admired his poems,[64] and would not have used such offensive language about him. The words "whom we have given our Signs," and "they declare our Signs to be lies," can only refer either to a Jew or a Christian, but since the passage belongs undoubtedly to a Medinian revelation, very probably a Jew is meant, which would agree with the remarks of Al Beidhâwî, that he was one of "the learned of the Jews."

It seems to me that this man was no other than the poet Ka'b b. Al Ashraf, the chief of the B. Al Nadhîr, who was very active in stirring up Muhammed's enemies. After the battle of Badr he went to Mecca to incite the Qoreish to take revenge on those who had slain their kinsmen, and composed songs in which he denounced Muhammed and Islâm.[65] I see an allusion to Ka'b's poems in the simile of the dog that hangs out his tongue. Moreover the alliteration of the name *Ka'b* with *kalb* (dog) appears to be intentional rather than accidental. Finally we must bear in mind that Ka'b was assassinatad shortly afterwards by order of the Prophet.

The expulsion of Ka'b's tribe[66] which was to follow, had to be abandoned for the moment owing to the defeat of the Moslims at Uḥud. It was carried out shortly afterwards as being conducive to the prestige of Muhammed who celebrated it in the following two *mathals*. In the first (*S.* lix. 15) the expelled are compared to people "who had shortly before tasted the evil consequences of their conduct," which means that the B. Al Nadhîr had to share the fate of their brethren of the Banû Qainoqâ. In the second *mathal* (*ibid.* v. 16) they are likened to Satan, who first entices men from the faith, but then withdraws and pretends to fear Allâh.

This *mathal* misrepresents the facts. The expulsion of the two Jewish tribes, and the subsequent slaughter of the B. Koreiza were acts of treachery, for which Muhammed wanted an excuse. Although the Jews refused to acknowledge his mission, still they were monotheists; but we shall see later on, how Muhammed tried to impute pagan doctrines to them. The weakness of his arguments is perceptible in his comment on the foregoing *mathals*. "Had we, he says (v. 21), revealed the *Qorân* on a mountain, one would have seen this mountain humble itself and split for fear of Allâh,[67] such are the *mathals* which we forge for men, haply they may consider." — This verse reads like the fable of the fox and the grapes. Muhammed was ill satisfied that revelation did not come to him like that on Mount Sinai; but we must remember, that according to a tradition originating from his own statement, the received the first revelation on mount Ḥirâ.

62 أَخْلَدَ

63 I. I. 279 has other persons in view; other interpreters infer Baleam; *cf.* Al Beidh. Al Ghazâli in *Jawâhir al Qoran* also refers the *mathal* to Baleam (f. 42vo).

64 *Kit. Al Aghâni*, III. p. 187 *sqq.* (*cf.* Sprenger, I. p. 110, *sqq.*). According to Al Zobeir he had read the Bible, did not believe in idols and forbade the drinking of wine. The last item is evidently added from religious tendency

65 *Cf.* R. E. J. x. p. 19. The hanging tongue is also made a symbol of poetic satire (*Hijâ*) in the traditions on Ḥassân b. Thâbit, Aghâni, iv. 3-4.

66 *Q.* lix. 11 *sqq.*

67 Confusion of Mount Sinai with Zach. xiv. 4; *cf.* Ps. cxiv. 4.

Muhammed liked to compare unbelievers, and Jews in particular, to people who walk in darkness. When inculcating the precept, which makes it unlawful to eat flesh from an animal "over which the name of Allâh has not been pronounced," he asks (*S.* vi. 122): Is he who was dead, and we have quickened and made for him a light that he may walk therein amongst men, like him who finds himself in darkness which he cannot emerge from? — It seems that the material of this *mathal* is derived from Isaiah ix. 1.

The more the Prophet of Allâh became merged into a worldly potentate, the more his speeches assumed the tone of manifestor. It seems all the more strange to find a group of three rather fine *mathals* attached to Muhammed's endeavour to vindicate the honour of his wife 'Âisha, whom public opinion had accused of infidelity. The verses in question (*S.* xxiv. 34 to 40) may not, indeed, have been revealed on this occasion at all, but it appears, as if Muhammed, after having gone through that disagreeable affair, was anxious to change the subject.[68] The first of these *mathals* (which are all taken from scenes met with in travelling, and with the exception of third probably recollections of his own journeys) has already been discussed above,[69] and gives an impressive, but not very detailed account of incidents of bygone days. This is followed (v. 39) by a neat comparison of the unbelievers to "a mirage in a plain (desert) which looks like water to the thirsty traveller, until he approaches it, when he finds nothing."[70] The infidels are further (v. 40) compared to darkness in a deep sea,[71] in which one wave covers another; dark clouds rise above it increasing the darkness to such an extent, that we cannot see one's outstretched hand. They are again likened (*S.* lxvi. 10) to the disobedient wives of Noah,[72] and Lot to whom (v. 11 to 12) are opposed the wife of Pharaoh and Maryam as models of piety and chastity. Here Muhammed's Biblical recollections became rather confused. Instead of Noah's he seems to have had Job's wife in his mind. For Pharaoh's wife Geiger has already rightly substituted his daughter.

There only remains one more *mathal* occuring in a verse the authenticity of which as an original Qoranic revelation is doubtful to me. It has, however, been embodied in the official text of the *Qorân;* we must, therefore, discuss it here, whilst reserving the investigation of its authenticity for later on.[73] The verse in question (*S.* xlviii. 29) forms an appendix to a *sûra* which was revealed concerning various events of the seventh year of the Hijra, and is entirely out of connection with the context. It is easy to see why the compilers of the *Qorân* placed the verse here, from the preceding one, which states that "Allâh has dispatched His messengers with the right guidance and the true faith, in order to exalt the same above every other creed, and Allâh is sufficient as witness." This verse evidently formed the conclusion of an address, and quite unexpectedly we read the following announcement (v. 29): Muhammed is the messenger of Allâh, and those who are with him, are fierce against the unbelievers, but merciful towards one another. Thou seest their bowing down and adoring, seeking favour and good will from Allâh. The Sign [they wear] upon their faces is an emblem of the worship; such is their *mathal* in the Torâh. Their *mathal* in the Gospel is as a seed which puts forth its stalk, makes it grow and strong, so that it rises upon its stem, and astounds the sower, *etc.*

Now only the second part of the verse, bearing on the New Testament, is a real parable, and is taken from S. Mark iv. 8, whilst the first part belongs to those cases in which *mathal* is to be taken in a wider sense, as is also done by the Commentators. The words evidently describe some external adjustment of the Jews during worship, which would not have remained unknown either to Muhammed, or to any one who visited a Jewish house of prayer. I can refer the words in question to nothing else but to the phylacteries derived from *Deut.* vi. 8,

---

[68] Nöldeke, *Q.* p. 157, leaves the question undecided.

[69] *Cf.* p. 28. The parable is explained in a scholastic manner in Ibn Sinâs *Risâla*, فى اثبات النبوّة وتاويل رموزهم و امثالهم, ed. Constant. 1298 H. pp. 85-86. See also Al Ghaz. *Kit. Almaḍnûn; Itq.* 566.

[70] Not expressly styled *mathal*, but introduced by *ka; cf. Itq.* 565.

[71] *Itq* p. 567. [72] Geiger, p. 111. [73] Ch. XIII.

xi. 18,[74] and styled "Sign." Although our verse only mentioned the one worn on the forehead — the other placed on the arm probably being covered by the garment — the term "sign" was applied[75] to both by the person whom Muhammed might have been asked about their character. The Commentators explain this *mathal* as a description, which it undoubtedly is, and it seems to me that its proper place should be among the traditions appended to this chapter.

## APPENDIX TO CHAPTER VIII.

### The mathal in Tradition.

Apart from the *mathals* in the *Qorân* a large mass of sayings and parables supposed to have originated with Muhammed lived in the recollections of the first generations of Believers. This increased marvellously as the sacred and polite literatures of the Arabs developed. To endeavour to establish or refute the authenticity of these would be a hopeless task, the means of testing them being much smaller than those we have for traditions on religious and historical matters. Muhammed was obviously fond of speaking in parables and metaphors when pronouncing revelations, and from this we may conclude that he employed the same method of instruction when discoursing with his friends, or addressing Believers from the pulpit. Although many of the sayings attributed to him may be authentic, only a few can be substantiated with any certainty.

The apocryphal sayings of Muhammed may be divided into two classes, *viz.*, those embodied in the *Ḥadîth* or religious tradition, and those registered by secular writers. This division is, however, superficial only, and does not touch the greater or lesser veracity of either class. In the following pages I have collected as many as I could find, but have only mentioned such works as I have been able to examine. I do not therefore claim to have exhausted the subject.

A series of "Speeches and Table Talk" of Muhammed, containing proverbs and general remarks, has been compiled by Mr. Stanley Lane Poole, London, 1882.

At the head of my collection I place two comparisons which are chronicled in all standard works on Moslim tradition. Both of these are connected with the manner, in which revelations came down to Muhammed. In the one he stated that he heard the voice of revelation "as the chiming of bells," in the other the first revelation came down to him as "the dawn of the morning" (Bokhâri beginning, *Mu'atta*, p. 86, *etc.*). Although a large number of these sayings are dispersed in the *Ḥadîth* works of Al Bokhâri (died 256 H.) and Muslim (died 260 H.), these authors did not devote much attention to them. Al Tirmidi (died 279) however in his collection of traditions has a special chapter on fourteen *mathals* which I reproduce here (after the edition of Bulâq, 1875, Vol. II. p. 143 *sqq.*).

1. [From Jubeir b. Nufeir from Al Nuwâs b. Sinân Al Kilâbi:] Fantastic description of the "Right Path" (*Qor.* I. 5).

2. [Jâbir b. Abd Allâh Al Ansâri:] The Prophet once heard in a dream a discussion between the Archangels Michael and Gabriel on the following parable: Thou [O Muhammed] and thy people are compared to a king who chose a city of residence, where he built a palace. In this he placed a table and then he sent messengers to invite the people to partake of the repast he had spread thereon. Some of them accepted the invitation, but others refused. The King is Allâh, the residence Islâm, the palace is Paradise, and thou, O Muhammed, art the messenger. Whosoever accepts thee, enters Islâm, and is received into Paradise where he enjoys all that affords him pleasure.

It is possible that this parable is modelled on a Talmudical one (*Sanhedrin*, fol. 38vo) of great popularity, in which an explanation is given why in the creation of the component parts

[74] *Cf.* Exod. xiii. 13.

[75] אות is in this instance rendered by آية, because the latter has its fixed Moslim terminology.

of the world, the earth, stars, and animals preceded man, who, being the noblest creature, found a *garden* prepared for abode, and food ready, when he appeared on the earth. The moral of both parables is nearly the same.

3. [Muh. b. Bishâr from Muh. b. Abi Adiy from Ja'far b. Maimûn from Abû Tamim Al Hujaimi from Abû Othmân from Ibn Mas'ûd:] Muhammed said: My eyes are asleep, but my heart is awake (see I. Hish. p. 375, *Kâmil* of Al Mubarrad, ed. Wright, p. 77 and 741). This saying is evidently a mistranslation of Cantic. v. 2 caused by mis-hearing *'êni* "my eye" instead of *anî* "I" (see my article: Historical and legendary controversies, *etc.* J. Q. R. x. p. 105). A *mathal* following this sentence deals with the same subject.

4. Another and shorter repetition in a somewhat modified form, also on the authority of Jâbir b. Abd Allâh.

5. [Muh. b. Ism'âil from Mûsâ b. Ism'âil from Abân b. Yazîd b. Abi Kathîr from Zeid b. Abi Salâm from Al Ḥârith Al Ashâri:] The infidel is compared to a man who buys a slave. He brings him to his house, and instructs him in the work he has to do, but the slave [instead of following his instructions] works for somebody else. Which of you wishes to be Allâh's servant? Allâh has commanded you to *pray*, so do not turn away from him, since he turns his face towards that of his servant, while the latter is engaged in praying. Allâh has further commanded you to *fast*. He who fasts is compared to a man in a turban, who has in his possession a bag with musk, the odour of which makes everybody wonder. The odour of the breath of a fasting man is pleasanter to Allâh than the smell of musk. Giving *alms* is further illustrated by the parable of a man who was taken prisoner. He is loaded with chains and ill treated, but afterwards ransomed for a small sum. The *saying of the Dikr* is finally compared to a strong castle, which gives refuge to a fugitive, who is surrounded by his foes. Man can guard himself against Satan only through the *Dikr*.— This group of *mathals* seems to betray Christian influence. For the author of *Silâḥ Al Mûmin* (Brit. Mus. Or. 3855, fol. 12) has the following version: Muhammed said: Allâh commanded John to teach the Israelites five sentences; among them is the *Dikr*. This is compared to a man who is persecuted by his enemies, but finds refuge in a fortress.

6. [Anas from Abu Mûsâ from Muhammed:] A Moslim who reads the *Qorân*, is likened to a citron, whose fragrance and taste are both good, but a Moslim, who does not read the *Qorân* is likened to a fruit which has no fragrance, though its taste is pleasant. The hypocrite who reads the *Qorân*, is likened to a fragrant plant of bitter taste, but the hypocrite who does not read the *Qorân* is likened to the coloquinth which smells as badly as it tastes bitter.—This parable is to be found in nearly all works of *Ḥadith*; *cf.* Bokh (ed. Krehl, III. 401; Moslim, (Bulâq 1304,) IV. p. 81; Mishkât, 276). The sundry recensions show slight variations. See also Lane Poole, *l. c.* p. 154.

7. [Al Ḥasan b. Aliy Al Khilâl and several others from Abd Allâh b. Razzâq from Muhammed from Al Zohri from Sa'îd b. Al Musayyab from Abu Hureira:] Muhammed said: The believer is likened to the sapling, which the winds incessantly try to upset. The believer is also continually exposed to trials, but the hypocrite is as the cedar which is not shaken untill the time of the harvest comes. In Muslim (x. p. 267) this tradition is reproduced with the same (very unreliable) Isnâd, but is twice repeated on the authority of Ka'b b. Mâlik, the "tree" being replaced by an "ear of corn." Since this *mathal* seems to be, at least in part, modelled on that in *Abôth*, III. 17, the version with the tree seems to be the more authentic one.

8. [Isḥâq b. Manṣûr from Ma'n from Mâlik from Abd Allâh b. Dinar from Ibn Omar:] Muhammed said: The Believer is likened to a tree whose foliage does not fall off.—This tradition, which is badly authenticated, is followed by a discussion of the species of that tree.

9. [Quteiba from Al Laith from Ibn Al Ḥâdi from Muhammed b. Ibrahim from Abu Salama from Abdal Raḥmân from Abu Hureira:] Muhammed said: If anyone had a river

passing by his gate, he would bathe five times a day; could, then, any uncleanness remain on his body? No! This is the likeness of the five daily prayers, with which Allâh washes away the sins.

10. [Quteiba from Ḥâmid b. Yaḥyâ from Thâbit al Banâni from Anas:] Muhammed said: My people is likened to the rain, no one knows whether its beginning is more pleasant or its ending.

11. [Muhammed b. Ismâ'îl from Khilâd b. Yaḥyâ from Bashîr b. Al Muhâjir from Abd Allâh b. Boreida from his father:] Muhammed threw down two dates and asked: "What does this mean?" No one knew. "The one," he said, "is hope, the other fulfilment."

12. [Al Ḥasan from Al Khilâl from Abdal Razzâq from Mu'ammar from Al Zuhr from Salâm from Ibn Omar:] Muhammed said: Men are likened to camels; among a hundred thou findest but one fit to ride on (see Muslim II. p. 275; Al Tha'âlibi, *Syntagma* ed. Valeton, p. 7).

13. [Quteiba b. Sa'îd from Al Mughîra b. Abdal Raḥmân from Abu Zinâd from Ala'raj from Abu Hureira:] Muhammed said: I and my people are likened to a man who kindles a fire in which flies and butterflies are caught. Thus I seize your race, and you are thrown into the fire (see Muslim, II. p. 206).

14. [Musaddad from Yaḥyâ from Sufyân from Abd Allâh b. Dinâr from Ibn Omar from Muhammed, who said:] You, O Moslims, the Jews and Christians are symbolised in the following parable: A man hired labourers to whom he said: "Who will work for me until noon for one carat?" The Jews did it. Then he asked: "Who will work for me until the afternoon (prayer time)?" The Christians did it. "Then you, O Moslims, shall work for me from the afternoon till evening for two carats." They answered: "We give the most work for smallest pay." "Have I," asked he, "wronged you?" "No." "Thus," he replied, "do I bestow my favour upon whom I choose." — The reader will have no difficulty in recognizing in this parable an adaptation of the Parable of the Householder (St. Matthew xx. 2) as far as it suited the situation. (See also Mishkât, Engl. transl. II. p. 814.)

To these *mathals* I attach a few more which are dispersed in the collections of traditions. One of the best known of these, which is also mentioned in most modern works, is the comparison of a reader of the *Qorân* to a man who owns a camel. If he keeps it fastened, it remains with him, but if he loosens it, it runs away (*Mu'aṭṭâ*, 88, Al Nawawi, *Kit. Al Tibyân* p. 81; *cf.* Sprenger, III. p. xxxv.).

Ibn Abbâs handed down the tradition that Muhammed said: He who has in his inside nothing of the *Qorân* is compared to a desolate house (*Tibyân*, p. 14).

[Mûsâ from Wahîb from Ibn Tâ'ûs from his father from Abu Hureira:] The Prophet said: The niggard and the almsgiver are compared to two men clad in coats of mail from their breast to their collar-bone. On the almsgiver it grows until it covers the tips of his fingers and obliterates his guilt. On the niggard, however, every buckle keeps firm in its place, so that he cannot loosen it (Bokh. ii. 158, iii. 21). — For أثره which gives no sense, I read إثمه "guilt." The text of this parable shows several corruptions, which may be taken as a sign of its old age, and probable genuineness. Al Nawawi's corrections (*ibid*) are of little assistance — The same tradition with a different Isnâd, likewise going back to Abu Hureira, Bokh. *ibid*. The *mathal* is an imitation of *Qor*. ii. 263, 267: see above, p. 172.

The worshipper of idols is likened to a thirsty traveller, who sees a mirage in the deserts, but cannot reach it (*cf.* Qastalâni, viii. p. 183). This *mathal* is fashioned after *Qor*. xxiv. 39 (see above, p. 174).

[Abu Bakr b. Abi Shaiba and Abu Âmir Ash'arî and Muhammed b. Al 'Alâ (the wording being that of Abu Âmir) from Abu Usâma from Boreid from Abu Borda from Abu Mûsâ from Muhammed:] My mission to guide to knowledge is likened to the rain which reaches the earth. Part of the latter, which is good, absorbs the water, and produces herbs and other vegetation in abundance. Some parts of the earth are hard, and therefore retain the water, which serves for man to drink therefrom, and to water their flocks and herbs. Another part is [barren] level ground, which neither holds the water nor allows anything to grow. This is typical of those who accept the Law of Allâh. He allows them to benefit by my mission, to learn and to teach. It is also likeness of him, who does not raise his head and does not accept the guidance of Allâh, which was entrusted to me (Muslim, II. 206).

In connection with *Qor.* lvii. 19 Al Qastalânî (ix. 237) quotes a comparison, handed down by Muslim as follows: Muhammed said: If one of you dips his hand in the sea, let him see what remains on it, when he takes it out again. — [Abu Hureira:] Muhammed said: I and the prophets before me are likened to a building which a man has erected and beautified. People surround it, and say: We have never seen a finer building, except one brick [which is Muhammed], Moslim, *ibid.*

[Abu Borda from Abu Mûsa:] Muhammed said: I and my people are likened to a man who said to his people: "I beheld an army, and I warn you to escape; and now you may depart in ease." One portion obeyed and was saved, but the other which refused to believe him, was surprised by the enemy and destroyed. — Follows application [Muslim, *ibid.*].

Of other authors who have embodied larger and smaller collections of alleged sayings of Muhammed I have quoted the following:

The famous Amr b. Baḥr Al Jâḥiz of Baṣra (died 255 H.) in his *Kitâb Al Maḥâsin wal'a ḍhdâd* (ed. van Vloten, Leyden, 1898) quotes many dicta ascribed to Muhammed on liberality, niggardliness, and other subjects. More sayings are to be found in Abstracts of the same author's work, *Kit. Al Bayân wal Tibyân* (Constantinople, 1883).

A small collection of dicta is contained in Al Belâḍorî's *Kit. futuḥ albuldân* (ed. de Goeje) p. 537, but much more are dispersed thoughout the *Kâmil* of Al Mubarrad (ed. W. Wright).

In the *Kit. Al Mujtani* of Ibn Doreid (died 321) sayings attributed to a number of persons, beginning with Muhammed (pp. 2 to 4) are collected. The sayings are accompanied by annotations.

The works of Abd Al Malik Al Tha'âlibi (died 429) are very rich in alleged sayings attributed to Muhammed, *viz.*: —

1. *Kit. al'ijâz wal 'ijâz* (ed. Valeton, 1894, and Cairo, 1301). The same work is recorded under the title, *Kitâb nawâdir al ḥukm* (Brit. Mus. Add. 9569).

2. *Al Laṭâif wal 'arâif fi-l aḍdâd* and *Al yawâqît fi baiḍâ-e-mawâqît* prepared by Abu Naṣr Al Muqaddasi (Cairo, 1883). Sayings in praise or blame of all sorts of things.

3. *Thimâr alqulûb* (Add. 9558), a volume which contains a large amount of interesting information on every imaginable subject, concerning anecdotes, folk-lore, proverbs, etc. The author draws largely on the writings of Al Jâhiẓ, and is therefore of great importance for the literary study of the latter.

4. *Muntakhabât al tamthîl*, Constantinople, 1884.

5. *Bard al Akbâd*, Cairo, 1883, arranged according to the number of subjects mentioned in each saying.

Abu Abd Allâh Muhammed b. Salama Al Qudâî Al Shafa'i (died 454) wrote a work titled *Kit. Al Shihâb*, which contains a thousand dicta supposed to belong to Muhammed (Add. 9692).

Abul Qâsim Husein b. Aḥmad Al Râghib Al Isfahâni (died 500) wrote *Kit. Muḥâḍarat aludbâ' wa muḥâwarat al shuarâ walbulaghâ* (Add. 7305; *cf.* H. Kh. v. p. 414).

Al Ghazâli reproduces in his *Iḥyâ 'ulûm aldîn* a very elaborate parable attributed to Muhammed on the life of this world. This parable has been translated into German in Kremer's, *Geschichte der herrschenden Ideen, etc.* p. 158. Shorter sayings to be found in the same work are the following (I. p. 279):

1. Anyone who speaks the *D̲ikr* amongst those who neglect it, is like a green tree in the midst of barren ground.

2. Anyone who speaks the *D̲ikr* amongst those who neglect is, is like one who fights in the midst of those who run away.

3. The *D̲ikr* of Allâh in the morning and evening is better than the clashing of swords in the war path of Allâh, or spending one's fortune in lavish expenditure.

The same author's work *Jawâhir Al Qorân* (Add. 9483; *cf. Itqân*, p. 843) contains many *mathals* on behalf of Muhammed. The work was composed after the *Iḥyâ* which is quoted fol. 11vo, l. 11, and forms a very important supplement to the author's theological treatises.

The best known of all collections of sentences attributed to Muhammed is undoubtedly to be found in Al Maidâni's famous work *Amthâl Al Arab* (ed. Freytag, III. pp. 607 to 617. The same chapter has been reproduced by Aḥmad Al Damanhûrî in his *Kit. sabîl alrishâd* (Alexandria, 1871), pp. 62-66.

The *Kit. Al muwashshâ* by Al Washshâ (ed. Brünnow) is likewise to be mentioned among the works concerned in this subject. The same is the case with the *Taṣḥîfât al muḥaddithîn* by Al Askari Al Lughawi (Br. M. Or. 3062), who endeavours to be critical with regard to the authenticity of the sayings handed down.

Some *mathals* attributed to Muhammed are to be found in Ḥarîri's *Mâqâmas*, ed. J. Derenbourg, p. 48, l. 16.

There are still to be recorded an abridgment of Al Farâbis' *Khulâṣat Al Khâliṣa* by Al. Badakhshâni (Kazan, 1851). Forty sayings attributed to Muhammed are also collected with a Persian commentary in a richly illuminated MS. of the Brit. Mus. Or. 5081. The work is printed under the title *Jâmi*, Firozpûr, 1887. (To this my attention was kindly called by Mr. A. G. Ellis of the British Museum.)

## CHAPTER IX.

### Medinian Revelations up till the Battle of Badr.

Features common to Meccan and Medinian revelations — Differences of both classes — Muhammed's attitude towards the Jews — Revelations of the period.

---

The features common to Meccan and Medinian revelations are few but important. They comprise — similarity of diction and form, the same aggressiveness of tone, the tenets of the religion and the doctrines of its ethical code. If we had no other critical aid, it would frequently be quite impossible to distinguish between Medinian and later Meccan revelations. Moslim authors on the subject are unreliable, if not directly misleading, and the anecdotes which they relate in connection with many revelations must be received with caution. Medinian addresses, like the Meccan ones, abound in declamatory, narrative, and parabolical passages. Many of these have been handed down as Medinian, though it is doubtful if they should so be classified, and there is not sufficient evidence to justify their removal from their present position in the official text. The legislative revelations are less difficult to place, as those bearing on ritual (except some on prayer and almsgiving), or legal matters, are of distinctly Medinian origin.

The Medinian portions of the *Qorân* must not be criticised from the same standpoint as the Meccan ones, on account of the altered circumstances under which they appeared. It is impossible to get a clear insight into the events connected with the Meccan sermons; therefore so far as they are concerned, we have no satisfactory background to work upon. The case is different as regards the Medinian revelations, which are illustrated by facts recorded in exegetical and historical works. Unfortunately the authors of these works were remarkable for religious zeal, rather than for their capacity for distinguishing between truth and fiction, whilst many of the authorities on whom they relied were not always veracious. Thus, a large number of Medinian revelations have been linked with persons and affairs with which, in reality, they had no connection, whilst the resemblance between various military expeditions is responsible for a certain confusion which defies all attempts at disentanglement. We may hope to be more successful in matters exegetical, and it must be conceded that the better a passage is understood the greater is the chance of ascertaining to what it refers, and the place to which it belongs in the order of revelations.

Another difference between the two chief portions of the *Qorân* is due to the change which had taken place in the author himself. His aims were not precisely the same as they had been. Whilst the teachings promulgated in Mecca affected the church exclusively, many of the Medinian ones were devoted to the organisation of the State. Without the Hijra Islâm would probably never have outstepped the limits of a religious sect, and might at best have lingered on in an insignificant and powerless minority. Muhammed's merit as founder of the State is not less than as the creator of the faith. The most powerful ethical idea cannot be effective for any length of time, unless it is established on a material basis, because those who are called upon to uphold and propagate it are in most cases actuated by personal interests and inclinations. The people who will accept the true and the ideal for its own intrinsic value alone are rare, but many will receive it when tendered in a gilded casing, or when they are compelled to do so. In Medina, Islâm was fortunate enough to be able to employ both methods in the furtherance of its objects, and this is the secret of its rapid progress all along the line.

Finally, in contradistinction to the Meccan revelations, the Medinian ones unfold the network of the hierarchic constitution, comprising religious as well as administrative measures. Under the care of Moslim theologians it developed into a minutely worked out code of laws which, similarly to the Jewish one, holds the whole life of the believer under its sway, drawing purely legal matters within the province of religious decision. The first impulse towards this course of action in Islâm was, however, given by Muhammed himself. For, without it he would not have been able to achieve the most urgent reforms. By intermixing juridical expositions with pastoral admonitions[76] he placed the former above the ancient customs of his country.

There are, however, other circumstances, which could not fail to affect the general tone of Muhammed's utterances as soon as he entered the precincts of his new abode. Having been invited to come by many of the leading citizens, his life was not only safe, but he became possessed of a worldly power which was absolute, within the circle of his admirers. His wish was a command, his censure condemnation. Speaking with the authority of a man who was blindly obeyed, his eloquence lost its excited character, and assumed the calm tone of a legislator. "Obedience to Allâh and His Messenger" is the *Leitmotiv* of nearly all Medinian speeches.

As for the new adversaries of Islâm, they were divided into two large groups of very different nature. Those Arabs who adhered to the old pagan belief were not such fanatic opponents as the Meccans, because Islâm endangered no institution which was a source of wealth or influence to them. Only sundry chiefs, who feared that the spread of Islâm might deprive them of their power, offered, individually, an obstinate resistance. Many antagonists belonging to this class, not having the courage to resist the growth of Islâm openly, agitated against it secretly, whilst showing outward submission, but even they saw the power slip gradually out of their hands. It did not take the Prophet long to recognise the real attitude of the "Hypocrites," as he styled them, and the trouble they gave him during the whole remainder of his life is faithfully reflected in the virulent rebuffs he administered to them from time to time.

The foes Muhammed feared most, were the three Jewish clans, which had settled in and around Medina. Circumstances had not only favoured the spread of their faith among the Arabs, but had also drawn the ties of kinship closer through intermarriage with their pagan compatriots. By keeping in touch with their religious literature they had gradually acquired the leadership in spiritual matters, and they still maintained it, although their temporal influence had received a severe check shortly before Muhammed crossed their path.[77]

Wherever the Jews wandered, in the *Diaspora*, they took with them at least those portions of the Old Testament, which form part of the liturgy. These not only comprise the Pentateuch, but also such sections of the Prophets, as were selected for Haftârôth, the Psalms[78] and the Five Scrolls.[79] One of the consequences of this practice was the preservation of the Hebrew language both for prayer and study, and however much most Jews of the Ḥijâz may have adopted manners and customs of the Arabs, and although many lived in great ignorance,[80] Hebrew was never forgotten among them. Of this unmistakeable evidence exists. From a tradition repeated on various occasions by AlBokhârî[81] we gather, that the Jews in Arabia read the Tôrâh in Hebrew, but interpreted the same to the Moslims in Arabic. — From this, first of all, we may conclude, that the Pentateuch — probably the whole of the Old Testament — was studied and publicly interpreted in the [Bêth] "Midrâs."[82] When Muhammed heard of this, he was so perplexed, that he did not know, at first, what policy to pursue. He therefore simply forbade his followers either to confirm or to refute the Jewish interpretation, giving as his reason that the Jews had altered the law, written the Tôrâh with their own hânds, and stamped the same as God's original work.[83] The less discreet Abu Bakr, however, could not abstain from entering the schoool-house by force and assaulting the Rabbi engaged in teaching.[84] From these traditions which receive confirmation from yet another one,[85] we gather, that the Jews in

[76] *Cf. Qor.* ii. 282 *sqq.* and often. [77] *Beitraege*, p. 47 *sqq.*

[78] The Tôrâh and Psalms are further mentioned in the verses of the Jewish poet AlSammâk in his dirge on Ka'b b. al Ashraf who had been assassinated by order of Muhammed. *Cf.* R. E. J. VIII. p. 23.

[79] As to Canticles *cf.* Ch. II. [80] *Qoran*, ii. 73. [81] IV. pp. 221, 250.

[82] Hish. p. 362. Through misunderstanding on the part of some traditionists the term *midrâs* is applied to the lecturing Rabbi, Hish. pp. 354 and 378; *cf. Beitr.* p. 52.

[83] Bokh. *ibid.*; according to *Qor.* ii. 73. [84] Hish. *ibid.*; R. E. J. *ibid.* p. 13.

[85] Hish. p. 393. The Jews made Muhammed umpire in an adultery case, but opinions disagreeing, Abd Allâh b. Salâm (see below) had a copy of the Tôrâh brought, and pointed the verse out which commanded the culprit to be stoned; *Beitr.* p. 54. Although this tradition must be taken with caution, because of its tendency to make Abd Allâh prominent, the kernel seems to be genuine.

Medina not only practiced writing, but made copies of the Tôrâh, and endeavoured to work upon the Moslims in private and public discussions. From the concluding words of the tradition mentioned above, as well as from many verses of the *Qorân*, it is certain that they also had at their disposal the Mishnâh, which is traced back by Rabbinical teaching to oral communication given to Moses on Sinai as a supplement to the written Law."[86]

From several almost literal quotations from the O. T. in the *Qorân* the question arose, whether an Arabic translation of the former existed in Arabia. Whilst Sprenger[87] is convinced that this was the case, or that at any rate certains portions of it had been translated, Prof. De Goeje, in a recent article,[88] arrives at a negative result. The latter theory is undoubtedly correct. Had such a version existed, Muhammed would have certainly succeeded in procuring one, and his renditions of Biblical passages would consequently have been more verbal, and less intermixed with *agâdic* ornamentation. Since this was not the case, we must assume that he gained the bulk of his Biblical knowledge from intercourse with the people. In his earlier years he may have had opportunities of seeing Hebrew books, but, not being a skilled reader, misread several words.[89] These he subsequently rendered in a corrupt fashion. He had scarcely set foot in Medina, when he took pains to display before the Jews a grand knowledge of the Bible and later Jewish writings, which he had picked up secretly.

It is almost certain that the Jews in Arabia were acquainted with an Aramaic version — either Targûm or P'shîttâ — of the Pentateuch. Through Talmudical channels Aramaic elements penetrated their religious terminology, and even their name Yahûd is an Aramaic form.[90] We may gather from this that the Arab Jews possibly exercised a certain indirect influence on the construction of the Talmud. Some paragraphs in the Mishnâh refer exclusively to the Jews of the Peninsula. It was considered lawful for them to live in Bedouin tents,[91] and their women were permitted to go out on Sabbath wearing a veil.[92] The Talmud also alludes to the custom of circumcision among Arabs,[93] and twice mentions Arab foot gear.[94]

The maintenance of the spiritual — and probably also commercial — intercourse with the centres of Jewish culture in Palestine and Babylon prevented the process of assimilation extending beyond the external conditions of life, although as far as these were concerned it was complete. At this period the Jewish standard prayers had long been settled, and it is certain that they also constituted the prayers of the Arab Jews, probably in the original Hebrew. These Jews, however, did not produce any liturgical compositions of their own, at least none survive either in Hebrew or in Arabic. But they have left a large number of poems in pure Arabic, containing a few allusions to Biblical books.[95] Otherwise these poems do not differ in style and tone from those of the pagan Arabs, and are of about the same stamp. Finally it is to be remarked that they preferred Arab names to Hebrew ones, and in a list handed down by Ibn Isḥâq only few specifically Jewish names are to be found.[96] This corresponds to a custom found among Jews everywhere in the diaspora, but in Arabia it was more prevalent, because they numbered among themselves many proselytes who did not change their names or those of their children when converted.

There is a good deal of evidence that the art of writing was practised to some extent among the Jews of North Arabia, and that not only they themselves wrote Arabic in Hebrew square characters

---

[86] Abôth, I. 1. [87] *L. c.* I. p. 132.

[88] *Semitic Studies* in memory of Dr. A. Kohut, p. 180 *sq.* The quotations given in this article as well as in that of M. Schreiner, *ibid.* p. 495 *sqq.*, only give a small fraction of the material existing on this question. — Ps. cxi. 10; *cf.* AlMaidâni, *Ar. Prov.* iii. p. 29 بدء الحكمة خوف الرب Prov. i. 7; Cantic. v. 2; *cf.* Hish. p. 375, *Kâmil* ed. Wright, pp. 77, 741; AlShahr. p. 165 *l.* 2 fr. b. = Deutr. xxxiii. 2. The same verse, differently translated, see Schreiner, *ibid.* p. 503, accoording to Almâverdi. *Cf.* Ibn Ḥazm, Pt. I., who gives numerous translations from the Pentateuch, and J. Q. R. xiii. p. 222 *sqq.*

[89] See Ch. I. [90] See Ch. II.; also *sabt* (Sabbath) represents the Aramaic form.

[91] Ohol. xviii. 10. [92] Sabb. vi. 4.

[93] Abôd. Zar. 27vo; Yeb. 11ro. Arabs called "Tayyittes" because the tribe of Tayy was the one nearest to Babylon (*cf. Beitr.* p. 49).

[94] Yeb am. 102ro; Sabb. 112vo. [95] *Cf. Beitr.* p. 61. [96] *Cf.* R. E. J. VIII. p. 11.

but also several Christian Arab tribes who lived near Syria.[97] Other Arab reports trace the invention of the Arab alphabet back to the same origin.[98] A tradition handed down in the name of Zeid b. Thâbit, Muhammed's secretary, informs us that the latter ordered him to learn the *kitâb*[99] of the Jews, which he did in two weeks so satisfactorily, that he wrote to the Jews [letters dictated to him by Muhammed] and read the letters they wrote to him. From this we can safely conclude that in North Arabia Arabic was written in square characters long before any other form was used, and it is only in continuance of this custom that Jewish authors of Arabic works during the Middle Ages used the same. The majority of Jews living at present in Arabic-speaking countries have little or no notion of the Arabic alphabet.

In spite of the wealth and influence ascribed to the Arab Jews, they could never forget that they were living in exile; for before the rise of Islâm they were frequently reminded of this fact by buffets and petty tyrannies.[100] This position must have been anything but pleasant, because they were always longing for Messianic deliverance. The two Arab tribes of AlAus and AlKhazraj, their fellow-citizens in Medina, were perpetually at loggerheads, and the various Jewish inhabitants were distributed on both sides. Being rather inclined to peaceful handicraft, palm-culture, and trade, these everlasting feuds and occasional raids on their property were not to their taste, and they used to say: "The time is near, when a prophet is to come, whom we will follow, and with his help we will defeat you."[1] Moslim tradition connects this word of hope somewhat remotely with Muhammed, and it is possible, that the rumours of the new prophet, which had reached the ears of the inhabitants of Medina, were looked upon by some Jews as the culmination of their hopes. But the essence of the tradition is probably only an echo of some paragraphs in the Jewish prayer-book which refer to a Messianic future. However, as soon as the Medinian Jews heard of the Meccan prophet, they considered it worth while to make enquiries concerning his person and mission, but the accounts of these enquiries and their results as given by tradition are so eccentric that they deserve little credence,[2] at least as regards many of the details. Now if the Medinian Jews were interested in Muhammed, he was at least equally concerned about them, and sought to win them over either by persuasion or force. Shortly before the Hijra six Medinian Arabs made a pilgrimage to Mecca. Muhammed at once questioned them whether they were friends of the Jews.[3] When invited in the following year to emigrate to Medina, it appears that one of the conditions made by Muhammed was that the alliances with the Jews should be dissolved.[4] From the resistance which Muhammed experienced from the Meccans who were ignorant in religious matters, he could easily gauge what a struggle was in store for him with the "People of the Book." The friendly sentiment he expressed towards the Jews in some of the earliest Medinian revelations[5] seems to have been an attempt to soothe a dangerous rival, rather than a desire to show sympathy for a cognate faith. The Jews also, on their part, are said to have made enquiries about the new Messias, but what they had learnt on this occasion, as well as what they found out later on personal observation, showed that a struggle was imminent. Muhammed's having come to Medina by invitation must have led him to believe that the pagan population of that city would be won over with comparative ease. He was aware that the Jews lived in exile, and languished under the wrath of Allâh. This conviction furnished him the cue for remonstrances, and he was not loth to remind them as often as possible that they were "cursed." The alleged friendly attitude Muhammed assumed towards the Jews is peculiarly illustrated in the following list of abusive titles which he hurled at them during the Medinian period:—

*Sûra* ii. 6.[6] Allâh has sealed their hearts.
8. They try to deceive Allâh.
9.[7] In their hearts is sickness.

[97] *Cf.* Renan, *Hist. des lang. Sém.* I. p. 348; Sprenger, *l. c.* I. p. 131.

[98] *Fihrist*, p. 4, where groups of Hebrew (or Syriac) letters are mistaken for names of persons.

[99] Evidently not "book," but "writing." The tradition is given Khamîs, I. p. 434.

[100] *E. g.*, by the Ghassanide prince Abu Jubeila (about 500) and by AlḤârith b. Abi Shamir who pillaged Kheibar (about 530); *cf.* R. E. J. VII. pp. 172-5.

[1] Hish. 286 and 374.

[2] *Cf.* R. E. J. *ib.* p. 191 *sq.*

[3] Hish. 286-8; 293.

[4] *Ibid.* 297.

[5] *Q.* ii. 49; *cf.* v. 73.

[6] Already in Meccan revelations, *e. g.*, vi. 46; *cf.* xlii. 23 with the variation: "sealed his hearing," xlv. 22.

[7] Only in Medinian passages. This confirms the verses lxxiv. 31-34 to be *Medinian*. *Cf.* Isaiah i. 5.

11.[8] Doers of evil.
13.[9] Satans.
15.[10] Those who buy error for guidance.
17.[11] Deaf, dumb and blind.
82.[12] Allâh has cursed them.
259. Their patrons are Ṭâgût.[13]
iii. 177. They have murdered the prophets undeservedly.[14]
iv. 53. They devise lies against Allâh.[15]
v. 85. The bitterest foes of the Believers.
xlvii. 27. Those who turn their backs, after guidance has been manifested to them.
lvii. 15. Allâh is wrath with them.

In addition to these unflattering epithets we have to mention others of a more general character such as: "Those who disbelieve," which refers to Jews and Christians indiscriminately, or "the Possessors of the Book," those to whom the Book (or the "Knowledge") was given, and finally: "The worst of beasts in the eyes of Allâh are the unbelievers" (viii. 57)."[16]

One of the most frequent invectives against the Jews is that "Allâh has cursed them." With this Muhammed evidently wished to show off his acquaintance whith those passages of the Pentateuch which deal with the subject,[17] in order to impress upon them the feeling that they were forsaken by God, but had now an opportunity of being redeemed if they acknowledged his mission.

After these preliminary remarks we now enter upon the discussion of the Medinian revelations, and begin with those which form *Sûra* ii., and which, according to both ancient and modern authors, represent the oldest speeches held in Medina. As to the first section (vv. 1-19*a*) the Moslim Commentators leave undecided whether it refers to the Jews or "Hypocrites,"[18] but since the latter are not mentioned in the whole of the *sûra* at all, it is probable that in the section in question the former are alluded to.[19] It is hardly likely that these "Hypocrites" were prominent at that time. Cant is always difficult to detect. Those Medinians who, from political motives, had embraced Islâm whilst waiting an opportunity to shake it off again, were careful to appear as good Moslims in Muhammed's eyes, and we cannot wonder if he was somewhat credulous. A positive evidence, however, also exists that the verses in question refer to the Jews.[20] Verse 6 is a reproduction of Isaiah vi. 6, and vv. 10-11 repeat the old reproach launched against the "Sons of Israel" in a Meccan revelation (xvii. 4). Finally the phrase (v. 12), "shall we believe as fools believe?," evidently reproduces words actually spoken by some Jews who ridiculed Muhammed, whilst the "Satans" (v. 13) represent the Rabbis who abetted such behaviour. The two parables, with which the address concludes, are similar in tendency to that which precedes.

The portion following (vv. 19*b*-37) is in no way connected with the address just discussed, since v. 24 in which the use of the minutest animals in illustration of parables[21] is justified, cannot refer to *mathals* mentioned in the verses 16-19*a* which deal with fire and lightning. Nöldeke is inclined to reckon this address as belonging to the Meccan period, but the renewed challenge (v. 21), to produce anything like the *Qorân*, is evidently directed against the Jews. In v. 25 Muhammed denounced certain practices of the Jews, it having appeared to him that they had broken laws laid down in the Tôrâh.[22] This was

[8] *Cf.* V. 201; v. 69 and xvii. 4, altogether about 30 times in the *Qorân*.

[9] See Goldziher, *Abhandlungen*, p. 106 *sq*.

[10] With the variation: "they barter my signs away for a little price," ii. 38, 73, 159; v. 48, 105; ix. 97, *cf.* Romans i. 25.

[11] *Cf.* V. 166, xlvii. 25. Ḥassân b. Thâbit, *Dîw.* p. 45, l. 8, فهم عمي من التورية بور

[12] With the variation: "the curse of Allâh is upon the infidels," ii. 83 and often, *cf.* iv. 55, xlvii. 25.

[13] *Cf.* V. 65.

[14] *Cf.* ii. 85, iii., 77; Lam. ii. 20; Matth. xxiii. 34.

[15] *Cf.* iii. 88; also vi. 21, 93, 145 (Meccan), *etc.*

[16] Refers also to the Jews; *cf.* iv. 54-5 and below.

[17] Levit. xxvi. 14-43; Deut. xxvii. 15-26; xxviii. 15-63.

[18] V. 13 permits a reference to the "Hypocrites," but see v. 71.

[19] Nöldeke, *Q.*, p. 128, refers v. 1-19*a* (قدير) to the "Hypocrites" and therefore place the address in the earlier part of the year 2 H. — V. 8-9 and 13 need not be referred to the *munâfiqûn*, because they can just as well aim at the Jews.

[20] *Cf.* V. 17 and vi. 46.

[21] *Cf.* Ch. VIII.

[22] *Cf.* Ch. VIII.

the old reproach of having altered the Law, and it gave Muhammed an opportunity of saying that they "did evil on earth."[23] After this the story of Adam[24] is repeated with such details as could only be appreciated by a Jewish audience. The words: "We celebrate Thy praise and hallow Thee" (v. 28), recall the words of the "santification" in the Jewish prayer-book.[25] To this speech another is joined in which the Banû Isrâil are addressed (vv. 38-58), but where the Jews are meant. They are told that they "recite the Book." This probably refers to the custom of reading portions of the Bible during public worship. They are also reminded of the miraculous delivery of their ancestors from Pharaoh's bondage (vv. 46-47), of Moses' forty days' stay on the mountain, of the making of the golden calf (v. 48),[26] and the grant of the protecting clouds, the Manna and the quails. Then follows a verse (55) which has puzzled all interpreters, and has not even yet been satisfactorily explained.[27] I now believe that the Commentators are right in considering that the 'city' mentioned in the verse refers to Jerusalem, whilst the words, "enter ye the gate worshipping, and say *ḥiṭṭa*, we might forgive you your sins," describe the moment when the High Priest on the Day of Atonement entered the "Holy of Holies" in the Temple.[28] The word *ḥitta* is probably taken from the formula of confession of sins recorded in the Mishnâh (Yômâ iii. 8; iv. 2; vi. 2). The "alteration"[29] for which Jews are again blamed in connection with this matter is probably of liturgical character, since the formula just alluded to has a different text in the ordinary prayer-book, but Muhammed lost no opportunity of repeating the hackneyed reproach as often as possible.

The compilers of the *Qorân* have placed between this address and the following one a verse (59) which stands detached, and represents an attempt to bring Jews,[30] Christians and "Sabaeans" on a line with Believers. The same verse, though shorter by a few words, occurs again in a longer speech (*S.* v. 73), where it has equally little connection with the text. The verse can only be explained as a casual remark made at a moment when Muhammed relaxed his hostile attitude, and hoped to win dissenting monotheists by kindness. It is very improbable that Muhammed spoke in this way more than once, or later than the second year. The verse is, therefore, instructive to show the way in which the *Qorân* was compiled. It was kept in memory, and communicated to the compilers in two slightly varying versions, which both had places allotted to them in Medinian speeches. There can be no doubt that the verses v. 71-88[31] also belong here, containing, as they do, a call to the prophet to preach which resembles that in the earlier Meccan period. There was ample reason for the repetition of that call. In Mecca Muhammed had preached only to his own people. The Medinian audience, however, was less homogeneous, and included numerous Jews and Judaeo-Arabs. Lest these should imagine that his ministry was addressed exclusively to the pagan inhabitants of Medina, the "Messenger" is commanded to preach (v. 17); for if he did not do so, Allâh would not hold him free from men. The next verse shows that these words were also meant for the "Possessors of the Writ," who were sadly in want of a new message, since they neglected to "stand fast by the Tôrâh and the Gospel and what had been revealed to them by their Lord." The preacher is quite aware that his appeal will only increase their rebellion and unbelief, but must not feel annoyed at it *(ibid.)*. As to the Jews, they had, in spite of the covenant made with them, either disbelieved, or murdered their prophets[32] (v. 74), being struck with blindness and deafness (75). In a similar manner the Christians fell into disbelief by identifying Allâh with the Masiḥ, whilst the latter had only taught them to worship Allâh, his and their Lord (v. 76). Allâh cannot be One of Three, but only One (v. 77), and the Son of Mary is but a Messenger like those before him (v. 79). One sees clearly that v. 78 forms a complete contrast to all verses just discussed, and

[23] This expression probably caused the address to receive its place in the *sûra*.

[24] *Cf.* vii. 10-18, xv. 28-44, xvii. 63-68, xx. 115, xxxviii. 71, 86.

[25] So called *Qedûshâ*.

[26] See Geiger, *l. c.* pp. 154-5; *cf.* vii. 147-155. V. 52 was misunderstood by Geiger. In the *Qorân* it is the people who desire to see God, whilst Muhammed confounded Exod. xx. 19 with xxxiii. 18 and Numb. xvi. 33-35.

[27] My own previous endeavour (*Beitraege*, p. 54) included.

[28] Levit. xvi. 12; Mishnâ, *Yômâ*, v. 1. *Qor.* iv. 153: the same command is given in connection with the words "we held over them the mountain at their compact."

[29] The Commentaries endeavour to explain the "alteration" in a different way.

[30] As to the term الذين هادوا see Ch. II.; *Beitraege*, p. 16.

[31] V. 73 on account of v. 72, "Possessors of the Writ."

[32] *Cf.* ii. 85, iii. 177, and above.

owes its place among them only to some accident. The rest of the speech is in the same tone, except that in the last verse (85) the Jews are styled the bitterest foes of the Believers, whilst the Christians stand as "nearest in love to the Believers." This spark of kind feeling towards the Christians is undoubtedly due to the gratitude Muhammed felt for the King of Abyssinia for having protected a number of early Meccan Believers in Islâm. Muhammed perhaps flattered himself that this hospitality was only the beginning of still closer relations, and possibly an ultimate acceptance of Islâm. It is further probable that the words in question were also meant for the Christian Arabs, some of whom had been moved to tears when hearing recitations from the *Qorân* (v. 86). This assertion was probably based on a real incident out of which Muhammed made as much capital as possible (v. 87-88).

The address (*S.* ii. 60-77) which seems to come next consists of various sections, each of which begins with the phrase: We "took" a covenant with you (vv. 60, 77, 78, 87).[33] The whole sermon records laws given to the Israelites, but the speaker first recalls their transgression which brought about the transformation of the desecrators of the Sabbath into apes (v. 61). The interpretation of this verse has caused considerable embarrassment both to the traditionists and modern authors. Geiger has remarked that in Jewish writings no trace is to be found of such transformation.[34] The Talmud speaks of the transformation of a class of sinners into apes and evil spirits,[35] but I doubt whether Muhammed knew of this legend. The matter seems to me to rest on a misunderstanding on the part of the compilers, or those who copied the revelations from the original notes. The word in question, *qiradatan* [قِرَدَةً], is recorded in the dictionaries as plural of *qird*, meaning an ape. If we read *qirdân* [قِرْدَانٍ], "vermin" (and in the archtype of that passage the difference between these two readings was probably difficult to distinguish), the verse would be a mistaken rendition of Exod. xvi. 20, 24. The mistake was probably caused by the circumstance that the transformation of living human beings into apes seemed much more fitting than into worms. Now the reason of the transformation is, in the *Qorân*, disobedience in connection with Sabbath, which is the same cause as mentioned in the Pentateuch. Instead of the food left over night, Muhammed has the disobedient persons transformed. The words, "those who go too far," are perhaps a rendering of Exod. xvi. 29, and refer to a given space of ground in the sense of the Rabbinical interpretation (*Mishnâh, Erûbhin,* ii. 3). The tales invented by the Moslim traditionists for the purpose of explaining the verse do not concern us now any further.

It is rather surprising to observe the knowledge which Muhammed suddenly betrayed regarding the ordinance of the "red heifer" (v. 63-68), as this practice had fallen into desuetude long before his time. Whoever taught him about it probably also explained the purpose of that ritual. Muhammed, however, seems to have forgotten this, and confounded the cow of Numb. ch. xix. with the calf of Deut. xxi. 1-9. The reason for reproducing this law in a very broad dialogue seems to be that it left an impression, that even Moses himself had occasionally to ask information from God (Numb. ix. 8 and ch. xxvii.). — Attached to this passage is the reproach (v. 69) that the people had "hardened their heart so that it was like a stone or even harder for verily of stones are some from which streams burst forth, *etc.*," which comparison is but a reflex of Exod. xvii. 6; Numb. xx. 10.[36]

"Some of you," Muhammed continued (v. 70), "hear the speech of Allâh, then they alter the same." This verse stands in connection with another (v. 87) which probably belongs to the same sermon, and contain the following words: "They say 'we have heard,' but disobey *(sami'nâ wa-'aṣainâ).*" On a somewhat later occasion (*S.* iv. 48) we read the same reproach, *viz.*, some Jews *(min alladina hâdû)* alter the words from their places[37] and say: *we have heard but disobey*, and

[33] V. 77 has "the children of Israel;" v. 87 repeats: "and we held the mountain over you" (*cf.* iv. 153), which is taken from the Midrâsh that God when giving the law on Sinai took the children as a pledge (*Shir Hashirîm R.*)

[34] *L. c.* p. 184. [35] Sanhedrin, fol. 109vo. [36] *Cf.* v. 16.

[37] عن مواضعه. The word الكَلِمَ is according to AlDâni one of those in which the *Alif prolongationis* is omitted. AlBeidhâvi also records the reading الكَلْمِ; see v 16.

hear! that which cannot be heard,[38] *etc.* (49). But had they said: *We have heard and obey,*[39] and hear! and look upon us! it would have been better for them and more upright, *etc.*

The verses just quoted throw a flood of light upon the way which Muhammed had pursued to gain his knowledge of the Pentateuch. The reproach that the Jews had altered the Law becomes a standing phrase, but the strange rebuke that they should have bluntly admitted sbriving disobedience to the divine command is much more than a reminiscence of the frequent murmurings of the people of Israel in the desert, and the censures passed upon them in consequence. We have here a most interesting misinterpretation of the words of the Pentateuch (Deut. v. 27) *weshâma'nû we'âsînu*[40] "and we will hear and do [it]." Muhammed had, on some previous occasion, heard, or possibly read, these words, and from their resemblance to Arabic thought that he understood them. He therefore identified *'âsînû* with Arabic *aṣainâ*[41] which gives the opposite sense. Now it appears that some years later Muhammed became aware of his mistake. To correct it was, however, impossible, since the true version did not suit his purposes at all. He therefore replaced the faulty word by "we obey," placing this avowal into the mouth of the Believers "who believe in Allâh, His angels, His Books, and His Messengers (we make no difference between any of His Messengers) and they say: We hear and obey" (*S.* ii. 285), *etc.* The Commentators see in this verse an allusion to those Medinian pilgrims who had an interview with Muhammed shortly before the Hijra,[42] and invited him to exchange his place of abode with theirs. It is, however, clear that Muhammed owed the correction of his mistake to some converted Jew. The verse in question can not therefore have been revealed till the year 8 or 9 of the Hijra, or shortly before Muhammed's death.

The next address (vv. 98-115) contains the verse on which the principle of Abrogation[43] is based, and touches also upon a subject which formed an important factor in Muhammed's subsequent conduct towards the Jews, *viz.*, his discussions with the Rabbis. These controversies have been preserved in a large number of traditions, but many of them were made in order to serve as explanations for verses in the *Qorân* not accounted for otherwise. By comparing himself to Moses (v. 102), who had also had to listen to questions asked in a rebellious spirit,[44] Muhammed removed the chance of any disrespect which might have resulted from such questions, and turned the affair into another proof of his prophetship. "Do you," he asked, "wish to question your Messenger, as Moses was questioned in former times?" The Jewish custom of restricting the use of the name of God,[45] alluded to above, led the Prophet to make a grave charge of irreverence (v. 108). He represented this self-imposed restriction as a law forbidding the name of God in places of worship, and took the same opportunity of intimating the necessity of changing the Qibla from Jerusalem to Mecca (v. 109).[46] In another address delivered for a similar purpose, corrupted Christianity and Judaism are contrasted with Abraham's pure monotheism.[47] On the ground of this supposition, and in spite of the anticipated objection of "the fools among men" (v. 130), the alteration of the *Qibla* was made law (vv. 138-147).[48]

With v. 163 commences a series of ritual prescriptions[49] which comprise things lawful or unlawful for food, the law of retaliation or the acceptance of a fine instead, the rules concerning the

---

[38] غير مسمع Palmer: "Do thou listen without hearing" does not render the original accurately.

[39] *Cf.* ii. 285, see below; *cf.* v. 10; xxiv. 50.

[40] Likewise instructive for the pronunciation of sibilants; see Ch. VI.

[41] *Cf.* V. 247 where Moses says to the Israelites هل عسيتم, and xlvii. 24.

[42] See I. Hish. pp. 286-288. *S.* v. 11 seems to refer to the same persons.

[43] See Ch. I. p. 509.

[44] Probably alluding to Exod. v. 12-21; Numb. xiv. 3; Ch. XVI., *etc.*

[45] It is hardly justifiable to refer the verse to the Ka'ba and the endeavours of the Qoreish to prevent Muhammed from holding a service there in the sixth year after the Hijra. The text speaks of "places of worship." The phrase, أن يذكر فيها اسمه, recalls Exod. xx. 24.

[46] See Nöldeke, p. 131.

[47] V. 128-135; V. 129, *cf.* 134.

[48] Vv. 148-157 are justly placed by Nöldeke after the battle of Uhud, but v. 153 belongs to a much later revelation on pilgrimage (see also vv. 185-199). Muhammed not only performed the ceremonies himself when he made the pilgrimage in the year 7, but encouraged others to follow his example. See Moslim quoted by Sprenger, III. 522, rem. As to V. 154 see I. Hish. p. 382.

[49] Nöldeke only mentions three, but there are four.

will of a dying person, and the regulations for the fast of Ramadhân. The prohibition of "eating" solid food during this month concludes with a metaphorical admonition not to "eat your wealth among you vainly" (v. 187).[50]

There can be no doubt about the date of the group of regulations (introduced by the phrase: "They will ask thee"),[51] which now follows, because one of them refers to the raid which Abd Allâh b. Jaḥsh undertook at the behest of Muhammed two months before the battle of Badr, towards the end of the month of Rajab. Muhammed saw himself obliged to condone the violation of the sacred month as best he could. It is more difficult to fix the right date of the regulations contained in the vv. 224-243,[52] as it seems that they were placed here solely on account of their legislative character.

The next address (vv. 274-268) was, like the preceding one, delivered with a view to teach contempt of death in the struggle with the Meccans whom Muhammed had now resolved to attack. Believers must devote their lives as well as their fortunes to the holy cause. The various paragraphs of the sermon are illustrated with instances from the records of the past. Verse 244 evidently stands in connection with 261, both containing recollections of the vision of Ezek. ch. xxxvii.,[53] and teaching the revival of the dead by the will of Allâh. The sketch of the election of Saul which is confounded with the story of Gideon, and of David's combat with Goliath, have a similar tendency. A set off against the rather feeble tone of the exhortation is the fervent style of verse 256 which, under the name "Verse of the Throne," is held as one of the holiest revelations of the *Qorân*.[54] The speaker reminds his hearers of Abraham who informed his aggressor without fear, that it was Allâh who revived the dead, and was therefore favoured with the vision related in Gen. ch. xv. This tale, however, is in so far modified, as "the two birds," although divided in many pieces, are brought to life again. The importance of spending one's fortune for the purposes of the holy war is finally illustrated by two parables.[55]

The section vv. 269-281 hardly offers any clue as to its date. The repeated admonition to give alms only explains the reason of its place after a speech of similar tendency. V. 271 seems to be an answer to some Jewish scoffer who had told the fugitives that Islâm would keep them in poverty for ever. "The devil" is one of those mentioned in v. 13. The allusion that the evil-doers have no helpers (*anṣâr*, v. 273) is evidently an attempt to draw the Medinian Moslims, who had received the honouring title of Anṣâr, away from their Jewish allies. The latter Muhammed was not bound to guide (v. 274). These words perhaps belong to the period following the battle of Badr when affairs already began to assume a more settled aspect. The regulations with regard to money transactions mentioned in the same speech seem to belong to a time, when the spoils of victory had increased the wealth of the Believers.

[50] Nöldeke regards V. 184 as a fragment of a long revelation, but this is not necessary.

[51] See AlBeidh., *etc.* Sprenger, III. 107 *sq*. Nöldeke detaches vv. 212-3 but without valid reason, as they form an introduction to v. 214. The subtlety of the discussion is characteristic of the situation.

[52] V. 241, see Nöldeke, p. 134.

[53] See Palmer, and *Beitraege*, p. 80.

[54] V. 257 should be compared with Abôth, II. 23: Make not thy prayer compulsion.

[55] Vv. 263, 265, 267, see Ch. VIII.

## CHAPTER X.

### POLITICAL SPEECHES.

CONSEQUENCES of the battle of Badr — Regulations on the distribution of the booty — Revelations on the events of the period — Charges against Jews and Christians — Battle of Uḥud — Disposition of conquered property forms an important precedent — Revelations on the Event — Composition of *Sûra* iv.

---

The defeat of the Qoreish forces at Badr was not only a personal triumph for Muhammed, but also of the greatest importance for the further development of the Moslim Commonwealth. Muhammed's position was improved in every way, yet he did not, as might have been anticipated, break forth into hymns of thanksgiving, or even deliver a triumphant address. It is true that he immediately attributed the victory to Allâh, but it is characteristic that his first address dealt prosaically with the distribution of the spoils.[56] This was, however, due to the force of circumstances, as many believers were thus relieved from extreme poverty and repaid for the sacrifices they had made for the faith before the Hijra The expedition had been undertaken with a view to acquire wealth, and this having been achieved, other thoughts were, for the moment, banished from the minds of the victors. This is significant for the condition of Islâm at that juncture, as it proved that everything was considered lawful which helped to injure or frighten the enemies of the Prophet.

On the other hand it must be admitted that the financial side of the matter had to be settled at once, and perhaps Muhammed did not act entirely in accordance with his own inclinations when taking this in hand first. Many of the conquerors cared much more for a large share in the spoil than for the glory of the faith. Quarrels seemed inevitable. From the opening words of the first speech dealing with the affair, we gather that questions on the subject of the distribution had actually been addressed to Muhammed, who alludes to them in the following words (*Sûra* viii. 1*a*): "They ask thee about the spoil; say: the spoils are Allâh's and His Messenger's."

This was a most important decision to make. If the spoils remained the property of "Allâh and His Prophet," the latter was free to dispose of them according to his own judgment, and to grant rewards to such persons as he thought proper. The decree was exceedingly statesmanlike, as it not only prevented quarrels, but also created a precedent for lines of conduct in future cases of conquest by Moslims of movable or landed property. Thus the consequences of the battle of Badr form an important factor in the development of Muhammedan law of property.[57]

The chief cause of the Qoreish defeat was the lack of discipline in their army. This seems to have been noticed by Muhammed, who lost no time in calling the attention of the Believers to the duty of strict obedience to Allâh and His Messenger (v. 1*b*-3). He could not refrain from remarking on those Medinians who, in spite of their faith, had refused to join the expedition (v. 5), and blamed those also who were satisfied with making a raid against a caravan, whilst endeavouring to escape a meeting with its armed escort.[58] Such timidity was all the more unexpected, as Allâh had promised to assist the believing corps with a thousand angels (v. 9) to cast dread in the hearts of the infidels (vv. 10-12). At a critical moment during the battle, when Muhammed's sharp eyes detected that the enemy was

---

[56] See I. I. p. 476.—Muhammed chose the expression أنفال (pl. of نَفَل) on purpose. The Commentators explain it as a *grant* from Allâh (عطيّة من الله وفضل), see Al Beidhâwi.

[57] See Sachau, *Aelteste Quellen des mohammedan Rechts*. Ac. Vienna, 1870, p. 699 *sqq.*; Yaḥyâ b. Adam, *Kitâb Al Kharâj*, ed. Juynboll, p. 5.

[58] Wellhausen, *Mohammed in Medina* (Al Wâqidi), p. 77, incorrect.

on the point of retreating, he took up a handful of sand, and threw it at them. The victory must have seemed a real miracle to those who witnessed it, and one of Muhammed's dearest wishes was thus fulfilled. He had been favoured with a miracle! Muhammed had no desire to pass for a great general, and was better served by ascribing the victory to Allâh. The handful of gravel which he had thrown at the enemy[59] would not have decided the skirmish "had Allâh not thrown (v. 17)". It is not difficult to perceive that the superstitious Meccans, discouraged by having lost many of their leaders in single combat, turned their backs on what they feared to be witchcraft. They found themselves once more opposed to the man who, a few years previously, could be insulted with impunity, but who now commanded a well disciplined army (vv. 15-26).

It is but natural that after such a miraculous turn of events Muhammed recalled to his mind the humble and perilous position he and his friends were in before the emigration to Medina. He now took an opportunity of admonishing Believers to be grateful to Allâh, and faithful to His Apostle (v. 26-27). One of his most dangerous enemies, Al Nadr b. Al Ḥârith, who had repeatedly ridiculed his tales by imitating him, had been taken prisoner. I believe it was for his and his fellow-captive Oqba b. Moeit's special benefit that Muhammad revealed vv. 30-31: "And when the infidels were crafty with thee to detain thee a *prisoner*, or to kill thee, or to drive thee forth, they were crafty; but Allâh was crafty too, and Allâh is the best of the crafty. And when our Signs were rehearsed to them, they said: We have heard [it] already; if it pleased us, we could tell the like, *verily these are nothing but old folks' tales.*"[60] — The fate that awaited the two prisoners seems to be predicted in v. 35: "Now taste the punishment for your disbelief."[61] They were executed during the return to Medina.

The next piece (v. 42-46) is the fragment of an address also on the topic of the battle. His first regulation with regard to the spoil Muhammed now amended, so that in future one fifth should be assigned to the church.[62] The statement that Allâh had shown the Prophet in a dream before the battle the number of the enemies smaller than it was in reality, was evidently an afterthought. Another speech devoted to the same subject draws lessons for the guidance of believers on future occasions (vv. 47-49), and warns the "Hypocrites" (v. 51), the Jews,[63] and the Meccan army, which Muhammed very effectfully compared to Pharaoh and his host (vv. 52-56).

Then follows a short address (vv. 57-70) which, I believe, does not refer to the battle of Badr, but to the expedition against the Banû Qainoqâ. These were among the signatories of the treaty which was concluded between Muhammed on one side, and the pagan inhabitants of Medina and the Jews on the other, but a pretext was easily found for charging a section of the latter with having violated the compact (vv. 57-58).[64] The war preparations alluded to in v. 62 cannot refer to the Qoreish, because they were to be made against "unknown infidels," and such who endeavoured to betray the Prophet (v. 64). The enemies Muhammed here had in mind were only to be found in Medina in the ranks of the Jews and those Arabs who, from political motives, assumed outwardly a friendly attitude towards Islâm. The stout resistance the Jews offered to all his endeavours to convert them,[65] is portrayed in the same verse: "Didst thou spend all that is on earth, thou couldst not reconcile their hearts, *etc.*" The invitation to the Moslim warriors to fight the Jews is then expressed in a slightly modified reproduction of Lev. xxvi. 8 (v. 67). When the Banû Qainoqâ had surrendered, Muhammed intended to have them all massacred (v. 68), but yielding to the demand of Abd

---

[59] I. I. p. 445 with a curse; Vâqidi, p. 58.

[60] Sprenger. II. p. 290, seems to regard the passage as Meccan, but without reason.

[61] We should expect the Dual, but Muhammed did not address them direct, expressing himself in a more general way.

[62] These verses are referred by some authorities to the expulsion of the Banû Qainoqâ (*cf.* Nöldeke, p. 188), but v. 43 seems to be against it; see also Yahyâ b. Adam, p. 3.

[63] "Those in whose hearts is sickness" (v. 51).

[64] Al Beidhâwi wrongly refers the verses to the Banû Koreiza. The phrase فأمّا تثقفنّ is reproduced by Ḥassân b. Thâbit. p. 6.

[65] Muhammed met them on their market place.

Allah b. Ubeyy, the recognised chief of the Medinian Arabs, whom he did not care to provoke unnecessarily, he merely expelled the vanquished tribe (v. 69),[66] and confiscated their property for the benefit of those who had taken part in the raid (v. 70).

The proceedings which Muhammed had taken against the Banû Qainoqâ were so plainly illegal, that he felt himself compelled to justify them by means of a divine revelation. Their punishment, he explained, was due solely to their treacherous conduct (vv. 71-72). Having thus weakened the hostile forces, the Prophet now took an opportunity of surveying the general situation in Medina, and of criticising the fraternal alliance which had, at his own instigation, been formed immediately after entering Medina between the believing inhabitants of the town and his fellow-fugitives. For some reason, probably in order to be able to deal with the Jews as he thought best, he suddenly dissolved their alliances (v. 74). He apparently felt strong enough also to make a slight distinction between the Medinian citizens and his aristocratic Meccan compatriots.[67]

The first portion of *Sûra* iii. must have been revealed soon after *Sûra* viii. The former statement, that Allâh had shown Muhammed in a dream the enemy to be smaller in number, is now changed into a "Sign" that the Moslim army appeared to the infidels twice its strength.[68] I believe also that a large portion of this *sûra* was delivered chiefly for the benefit of the Jews, or, at least, those Judæo-Arabs whom Muhammed hoped to win through persuasion. I would, therefore, date it prior to the expulsion of the Banû Qainoqâ. The leading ideas of the address seem to be that Islâm so nearly approached Judaism that the Jews should feel no scruples in recognising Muhammed as a true prophet. The conspicuous accumulation of formulas of Unification in a small compass (vv. 1,[69] 4, 16 *bis*) with *Huwa* instead of *Allâh*,[70] and with a supplement so familiar to Jewish ears as "the Living and Self-subsistent" is anything but accidental. In the same speech Muhammed mentions the Tôrah (vv. 2, 43, 44, 58) and the Gospel (vv. 2, 43, 58) for the first time. The allusion to Pharaoh and his nation, standing as they do as the prototypes of wicked people, was calculated to resound nowhere more powerfully than in the minds of the Jews. When Muhammed says (v. 17) that in the eyes of Allâh the *Dîn*[71] is Islâm, "and those to whom the Book was given disagreed not until after that there was given to them knowledge," it is clear that he refers to the Rabbinical interpretation of the Law, on the basis of which the Jews used to argue with him (v. 18).[72] The verses 25-26 are rather out of place here, but they are so closely related to Jewish formulas of prayer, that it is not improbable that Muhammed inserted them in this speech intentionally. Whether the censure of the friendly intercourse between Moslims and Jews (v. 27) was originally inserted here, it is difficult to say, as it would have been more in place at the beginning of the open hostilities against the latter.

What was Muhammed's purpose in introducing the stories of the births of John and Jesus in a speech not addressed to Christians (vv. 30-43)? I believe his intention was the same as in the previous sermon, *viz.*, to show that in vital religious questions he stood on the same ground as the Jews, but had authority to "abrogate" part of what had been made unlawful for them (v. 44). "Jesus was a created being like Adam, whilst there is no God beside Allâh"[73] (vv. 52, 55). The pleonastic form of v. 57: "That we (Muhammed and the Jews) serve no other God than Allâh, and associate no one with Him," makes it manifest that Muhammed, when it suited him, was not loth to side with the Jews against Christians. Later on he also found an opportunity of doing the opposite.

---

[66] The verse is regarded as abrogating the preceding one. Nöldeke refers it to the spoils of the battle of Badr, but I cannot share his opinion.

[67] Nöldeke denies that v. 73 is abrogated by v. 76; *cf.* ix. 101.

[68] Refers either to viii. 9, 12 or to 45-46. See also الفرقان (iii. 2 and viii. 42); iii. 23 وغرّهم في دينهم *cf.* viii. 51; iii. 47 *cf.* viii. 30.

[69] V. 1 *cf.* ii. 256. الحيّ alone xl. 67.

[70] This again v. 55.

[71] See Ch. III. at the end.

[72] From v. 23 it appears that they answered Muhammed's hell fire threats with the Talmudical symbolism that the sojourn of the wicked in Gehenna only lasts twelve months: see *Rôsh Hash.* fol. 17vo.

[73] See xxxvii. 34.

On the basis of the strict monotheistic view common to Moslims and Jews he invites the latter to return to pure Abrahamism (v. 58), which was identical neither with [Rabbinic] Judaism nor with Christianity (v. 60) The purport of verse 65 is not quite clear to me, although the Commentators try to explain it. Whom should the Jews style "Believers" but their own people? The Commentators naturally think of the Moslims, and Muhammed may perhaps have meant that also, but the sentence seems to be the result of a misunderstanding on his part. It is not likely that one section of Jews should have encouraged another to profess the Islamic cult in the morning and to abjure it again in the evening.

"Those who barter away the covenant of Allâh and His faith for a small price" (v. 71) is one of the derogatory appellations given to the Jews by the Prophet. The threat that the persons thus described "shall have no share in the final world"[74] can only have been calculated to impress Jewish hearers, since the phrase is but the Muhammedan adaptation of a well known Rabbinical one. What Muhammed really aimed at in those remarks was an onslaught against the authority of the Rabbinical code, which he represents as claiming equal authority with the "Book." Some Jews, he says, pervert the Book in order to reckon to it what does not belong to it (v. 72). Whether, or not, Muhammed was convinced of this he at any rate wished to convey to the minds of Moslims, that the Jewish Rabbis, by making laws,[75] placed themselves on a level with God (v. 73), and desired to be worshipped. Allâh, however, never commanded men to take angels and prophets as Lords (v. 74). The point of this criticism lies in the terms *Rabbâniyyûn* and *arbâban* which are both to be interpreted as indicating the supremacy of Rabbinism.

It is not difficult to see how Muhammed imbibed the notion that Jews paid their Rabbis greater homage than was due to mortals. Not only was he aware that they performed many rites solely on Rabbinical authority, but he seems to have seen them pray at the supposed graves of Biblical prophets and pious men in general. In a tradition handed down by Al Bokhâri,[76] Muhammed is said to have remarked that Allâh had cursed the Jews because they used the graves of their prophets as places of worship. If this be true, he could not have foreseen to what extent such a custom was destined to prevail in the Moslim world.

Some scholars regard v. 79 as very late,[77] but there is no reason to place it much later than v. 17. Since the words are addressed to the Jews (see v. 81), their number and influence in Medina must still have been great enough to make it worth the Prophet's while to try and convert them (v. 85).[78] Verse 87 is supposed to have been the reply to a query addressed to Muhammed by some Jews. The authenticity of this question, with which I have dealt elsewhere,[79] is very doubtful. It is, therefore, not quite clear what Muhammed meant by this remark, except that he wished to parade his intimate acquaintance with the Pentateuch, and the passages in Gen. ix. 4 and xxxii. 33 in particular. By bringing one of their scrolls and reciting the verses in question they could convince themselves of the truth of his allegation. The next verse, which concludes the address, brands again post-Biblical prohibitions as "forging a lie against Allâh."

At about the same time as the first half of *Sûra* iii., *Sûra* xlvii. must have been revealed. V. 2, however, is out of connection with the verses 1 and 3, and altogether out of place here.[80] The compilers did not, perhaps, care to commence a *sûra* with a condemnation of the wicked. The victories gained hitherto are made the basis for admonitions and a censure of the Jews.[81] In v. 21 Muhammed

---

74 חלק לעולם הבא = خلاق

75 A distinct allusion to the Jewish oral law is to be found in تدرسون (Geiger, p. 51), see also *J. Q. R.* Vol. XIII. p. 223.

76 Ed. Krehl, I. p. 118.

77 Nöldeke, p. 141. His remark, that Muhammed regarded "true Christians" as believers, is incompatible with v. 52.

78 *Cf.* Numb. xxii. 18, and Al Beidhâwi.

79 *J. Q. R.* Vol. X. p. 105.

80 ذلك v. 3 refers to أضل أعمالهم v. i. *cf.* vv. 9 and 10. As to v. 2 see Ch. XIII.

81 Palmer wrongly refers the words "those to whom has been given the knowledge" to Ibn Abbas, who cannot be meant by this verse.

settled the formula of the *Dikr* finally, and gave it for the first time with the introductory command: Know![83] It is possibly modelled on verses like Exod. viii. 6, 18, ix. 14, or Deut. vi. 4. Verse 22 in so far differs from the similar one S. ii. 21, that in the former it is the Moslims,[83] who expect a special revelation with regard to the oppression of the Jews. From this we may gather, that the verse was revealed after the expulsion of the Banû Qainoqâ. It shows distinctly that Muhammed was resolved to exterminate all the Jews as soon as circumstances permitted. That the Jews were meant, is to be seen from the expression "those in whose heart there is sickness." In v. 23 we see the war against the remaining Jewish tribes decided upon, and their only escape from slaughter speedy conversion to Islâm. Their obstinacy is, then, described (vv. 25-29) in the usual phrases.[84] V. 32 refers to certain emblems[85] (probably connected with the Jewish ritual). The term *lahni-lqawli* probably alludes to the *chanting* of prayers and portions of the Pentateuch and Prophets read during service. The prayer-books of the Jews in Arabic-speaking countries show the word *lahn* at the headings of *Piyyûtim* (hymns), in order to intimate the tunes to which they are to be sung. The Jewish custom of chanting prayers is as old as it is universal, and there is no reason to doubt that it also existed in Arabia at the time of Muhammed. The words in question may also refer to a habit of the Medinian Jews of intermixing the vernacular with Hebrew words, especially in discussions on matters religious. — Those Moslims, Muhammed continues, who might hesitate to take up arms against their former allies, are warned that their first duty is to obey Allâh and His Messenger (v. 35). Since success is certain (v. 36), there is no reason for any Moslim to be behind hand in contributing towards the cost of the expedition against the Jews (vv. 39-40).

The defeat which the Moslim army suffered at Uhud in the third year after the Hijra, caused a momentary diversion in the constant denunciations of the Jews who, in their turn, were not loth to prejudice Medinians, Moslims and pagans alike, against Muhammed. The latter, seeing that his prestige was at stake, took pains to restore the same in a speech which fills out the rest of *Sûra* iii. He warned Believers against intimate relations with the enemies of Islâm (v. 114), and admonished them not to lose their faith in the revelations, which had assured them of final victory (v. 115). The misfortune over which their enemies rejoiced (v. 116) was chiefly due to the cowardice of two companies of the Moslim army (v. 118). In order to raise the spirits of his friends Muhammed reminded them again of the victory of Badr, even introducing this name into the revelations in questions (v. 119). The thousand angels who had assisted the Moslims on that occasion (*S.* viii. 9) is in this speech trebled (v. 120), but they would in the next emergency increase to five thousand (v. 121). Some of the following verses insinuate that the disaster may have been a punishment for "usury doubly doubled" exercised by Moslims (v. 125), and those who felt themselves guilty of this or other crimes (v. 129), must at once invoke Allâh's forgiveness (v. 127), and give alms (v. 128) Accidents had happened before (v. 131). Moslims were, therefore, not to give way to grief, and would be victorious in the end (v. 133).

The next group of verses (134-137) reminds Moslims to be always as ready to die for the cause of Islâm as they had been once before; and that no soul died save by permission of Allâh, and at its appointed time (v. 139). Before the last mentioned verse one is interpolated (v. 138) which has caused much comment among Moslim theologians.[86] The verse, which will occupy our attention later on, is nothing but a copy of *S.* v. 79*a*,[87] and not only disturbs the connection between vv. 137-139, but forms a complete contrast to v. 140, which speaks of prophets who did not show themselves weak even in the face of myriads of enemies. The reproach of cowardice is then repeated (v. 145). In order to make similar faintheartedness impossible for the future, Muhammed lays it down here as a principle that, had they all been in their houses, those who were fated to die, had gone forth to meet

[82] See Ch. II.

[83] Palmer read الذين كفروا which is not in the text; he also translated "a decisive *sûra*," but the text has مُحْكَمَةٌ.

[84] See ii. 10, 11, 17, 247.

[85] See xlviii. 29 and Ch. VIII. end.

[86] *Cf.* Al Shahrastani, *Milal*, p. 11; *cf. Beitraege*, p. 67, and Ch. XIII.

[87] See also iii. 150, 152.

their doom (v. 148). This verse gives manifest evidence that any fatalistic notions occurring in the Qorân are not the result of theological speculations, but were grown on purely political soil. It was necessary to render another defeat impossible, because Islâm could not afford it. The demoralisation after Uhud was so great that the Moslims made Muhammed responsible, and charged him with having deceived his friends. He was obliged to defend himself against this accusation[88] (v. 155), but reminded his accusers that Allâh had sent a messenger to them out of their own midst (v. 158), and that their misfortune was their own fault. He described the situation very accurately in saying that "on that day they were far nigher to disbelief than to faith" (v. 160), but those who had suffered martyrdom, were not dead but alive, and enjoyed the pleasures of paradise by the grace of Allâh (vv. 163-168).

In close connection with this speech stands the next which is less severe and rather more hopeful in tone. To turn the general attention from the cheerless subject of the defeat, he makes use of a well worn device in launching another rebuke against the Hypocrites and Jews. In answer to the Prophet's request for funds to continue the war against the Meccans, they asked sneeringly whether Allâh was poor (v. 177). The question originated, according to tradition, with Finhâş, a member of the expelled Banû Qainoqâ, and is evidently only a reflex of Numb. xi. 23.[89] Muhammed, however, taking the sarcasm seriously, placed this alleged blasphemy on a par with the old reproach that the Jews had "killed their prophets undeservedly" *(ibid.)*. Not less sinful, he adds, is the assertion that Allâh had covenanted with them not to believe in a prophet until he had brought a sacrifice which the fire devoured[90] (v. 178). A remark of this kind, whether spoken in jest or earnest, was not founded on any condition laid down in the Old Testament, but entails an allusion to such passages as Jud vi. 21, xiii. 20; 1 K. xviii. 31. Probably this fire *(alnâr)* is purposely contrasted in one of the following verses with the illuminating *(almunîr)* Book (v. 181) and those who are removed from hell fire and brought into paradise (v. 182). — Further warnings addressed to the scoffing Jews (vv. 183-186), a fervent prayer, and admonitions to bear the situation patiently, conclude the *sûra*.

A more powerful lever than speeches was now applied to the drooping spirits of the Moslims by the expulsion of the second Jewish tribe, the Banû Al Naḍîr, after Muhammed had caused their chief, Ka'b b. Al Ashraf, to be assassinated.[91] The Moslim bards hastened to celebrate these two events in various songs, and Muhammed himself was so rejoiced, that he composed a series of Hallelujâh-Psalms. It is as such — and as imitations of Biblical ones, and Pss. cxlvi.-cl. in particular — that I regard the *Sûras*, lvii.,[92] lix., lxi., lxii., lxiv., all of which begin with the words; Praise Allâh whatever is in the heavens and in the earth." It is rather difficult to fix the order of succession of these five *sûras*, but this is of little account, as they were all composed at this period. Their poetic element is almost entirely confined to the superscription mentioned, the rest being prose, and in one of them we read the demand to give alms from the conquered treasuries (lvii. 7). The victory alluded to in v. 10 is no other than the expulsion of the B. Al Naḍîr.[93] The reverse previously sustained was still fresh enough in his mind to cause him to warn his friends not to exaggerate their joy (v. 22-23). The verses 24-28[94] refer to Muhammed's failure to get the Jews to contribute towards the fine to be paid for the slaying of two men of the Banû Âmir. The phrase (v. 24) "those who are niggardly, and bid men be niggardly" runs parallel to Abôth, v. 13, though only by accident. The verses seem to have been placed here because they form a contrast to several of the preceding ones (*e. g.*, 10, 11, 17), in which the topic of giving alms is discussed.

*Sûra* lix. begins with a reference to the expulsion of the Banû Al Naḍîr.[95] The verses 2 and 3 look like an attempt to justify that act by stating that Allâh was responsible for it. If the banishment of those Jews had not been pre-ordained, their fate might have been much worse. So here Muhammed

[88] Nöldeke, p. 143, quotes the reasons given by traditionists.

[89] Perhaps also 2 K. vii. 2; *cf.* *S.* v. 69.

[90] See xvii. 92, and *J. Q. R.* Vol. X. p. 106.

[91] See the dirges of the Jewish poet Samamâk, *I. Hish.* pp. 657, 659.

[92] Nöldeke, p. 144 *sq.*, rightly does not refer the *sûra* to the conquest of Mecca.

[93] iii. 147, lxiv. 11.

[94] See *I. Hish.* p. 652; Vâkidi, p. 250.

[95] Nöldeke, p. 153; *I. Hish.* p. 654 ونزل فى بني النضير سورة الحشر بأسرها.

makes use again of the fatalistic principle, but this time to exculpate an act of open violence. More than this, he had caused the palm groves of the Jews to be cut down and burned.[96] This appeared to them a flagrant violation of the law in Deut. xx. 19, and seems also to have been condemned by public opinion. Muhammed was so conscious of the outrage he had committed, that he found it necessary to shelter those who had executed his will behind the command of Allâh (v. 5).

The consequences of this bloodless victory were even greater for the economy of the future State than the preceding ones. The estate of the Banû Al Naḍir had not been taken by "pressing forward with horse and camel, but Allâh authorised His apostle to give it to whom he pleased" (v. 6). In other words, whatever spoil was not taken in open warfare, but by surrender, became the property of Allâh and His Prophet. This furnished a very important precedent for future enlargement of Moslim territory by pact or cession. The new lands were the property of the realm.[97] The old inhabitants were left unmolested, but their produce filled the coffers of the state.

This new manner of distributing the spoil placed at Muhammed's immediate disposal large means to reward the poor and lowly, who had cast in their lot with him in Mecca. He declared that they had the first claim to a share in the booty (v. 8), in which the Anṣâr were not to participate at all (v. 9). It is but natural that Muhammed now taunted the Hypocrites, who, after having encouraged the Jews to offer resistance, had left them in the lurch, so that they had to retire to their castles, and finally surrender (vv. 11-14). Such conduct subjected them to some very unflattering comparisons.

The middle part of the *sûra* being somewhat poor for a Hallelujâh-Psalm, Muhammed endeavoured to make at least the end as thrilling as the commencement. Now verse 21 shows clearly that the author had Ps. cxiv. in his mind which, though not being a Hallelujâh-Psalm itself, belongs to a group of Psalms which are known in the *Mishnah* under the name of *Hallêl*, and which occupy an important place in the prayer-book. Through the pathos of this verse a faint regret is observable that the *Qorân* was *not* revealed upon a mountain which "would have humbled itself and been split for fear of Allâh."[98] Lest, however, any man should think that such a sight had ever presented itself to the eyes of man, Muhammed adds that he had only spoken in metaphor. Very impressive appear the two *tawḥîds* and the profusion of divine epithets, many of which are borrowed from Jewish terminology,[99] whilst the "Hallelujâh" repeated in the last verse, leaves no doubt that the whole *sûra* forms a continuous sermon.

*Sûra* lxi. begins with a severe reprimand addressed to Believers "who say what they do not do," a thing which is very hateful to Allâh. The purport of this reproach, repeated twice, is not quite clear, although the Commentators connect it with a declaration on the part of the Moslims, that they were prepared to sacrifice both wealth and life for the sake of the faith. It appears, however, that Muhammed again alluded to the spiritless conduct of a part of the Moslim army at Uḥud.[100] At any rate the recommendation given in v. 4, *viz.*, to fight in future "in closed ranks, as though they were a compact building,"[1] throws some light on the meaning of the two preceding verses. The chief function of v. 5 is to introduce v. 6, memorable on account of the new title Aḥmad, under which Muhammed states that he was announced by Jesus. I take this name as an attempt at an Arabic rendering of Messias, and to find that formation of the root HMD, which would most appropriately express the character under which Muhammed wished to be known to the following generations. From this we may conclude that he was not called Muhammed, at least not till several years after the Hijra.[2] V. 7 refers again to the Jews who try to extinguish "the light of Allâh with their mouth." The certainty Muhammed expresses in the verses 9 and 13,

---

[96] See Bokhari, iii. 13.

[97] Sprenger, III. p. 164, regards the first portion of v. 7 as interpolated. Moslim authorities declare the verse to refer to other places than the territory of the B. Al Naḍir.

[98] *Cf.* Zach. xiv. 5; Ps. lxviii. 9, xcviii. 5.

[99] *E. g.*, *almalik, alquddûs, almuhaimin, aljabbâr, etc.*

[100] *Cf.* iii. 118 and above; v. 3 "most hateful in the eyes of Allâh;" v. 4 "Allâh loves those who fight in His cause."

[1] See Ch. VIII.

[2] See also the Baḥîra legend in Ch. II.

that Islâm would be victorious in the end "in spite of the objection of the infidels," proves the address to have been spoken after the banishment of the Banû Al Naḍîr, when Muhammed was entitled to hope that, at least in Medina, no one would be able to withstand his rule. V. 14, being a re-echo of *S.* iii. 45, stands detached, and seems to have been placed at the end of this *sûra* on account of v. 6.

It is not difficult to recognise that the beginning of *Sûra* lxii. is closely connected with the conclusion of *Sûra* lix. The strenuous efforts Muhammed had to make, in order to find material for the psalmody is plainly visible. The *sûra* consists of two parts of unequal length, which are not in connection with each other. The first portion contains another of the well worn onslaughts against the remaining Jews, as bearers of the Rabbinical law in the shape of an insulting comparison.[3] The verses 6 and 7 are a repetition of *S.* ii. 88. The latter portion of the *sûra*, which discussed the duties of the "Day of Congregation,"[4] is said to owe its origin to the indignation of the Prophet who saw a caravan, led by unbelieving Medinian citizens, enter the city with great noise on Friday, and cause great disturbance among the worshippers.[5]

The descriptive element in the first portion of *Sûra* lxiv. is not indicative of Meccan origin, but of a feeble effort to revive the spark of enthusiasm proper for a psalm. The reminiscences of the defeat of Uḥud[6] (v. 11) and the double admonition to be obedient (vv. 12 and 16) leave no doubt as to the place to which the *sûra* belongs.

It appears that *Sûra* iv. originally only consisted of the pieces vv. 1-45, 126-129 and 175[7] which treat of legal matters in connection with the rights of women and orphans, and the regulations of wills and bequests. The promulgation of these regulations could not have been undertaken without very careful preparation. It was dictated by the necessity for arranging the rights and duties of a growing community, many members of which had suddenly become wealthy, and which, owing to the various battles, numbered many widows and orphans, who had to be provided for by the commonwealth in whose service their natural supporters had lost their lives. It is therefore probable that the revelations in question cannot be dated earlier than the year five.[8]

Between the portions of the *sûra* under consideration the compilers have inserted a mass of revelations mostly belonging to the same period for which they could not find more suitable places. To this category belong the ritual precepts in v. 46, being reflexes of Levit. x. 9, xv. 16-18 increased by Rabbinical interpretations.[9] Then follows a vigorous attack against the Jews (vv. 47-72), which appears like an attempt at stamping the banishment of the Banû Al Naḍîr as a religious duty. Muhammed endeavoured to demonstrate that the Jews had so far deviated from the teachings of the Tôrah by altering the same (vv. 48-49),[10] that they were no better than heathens. This, he said, might be deduced from the nearly divine homage they paid to their sages. The point is of importance. "Behold," he says (v. 53), "how they devise a lie against Allâh, and that is manifest sin enough (54). Do ye not see those to whom a portion of the Book was given believe in the *Jibt* and *Tâghût*,[11] and say to the infidels : these are better guided in the way than those who believe [in Allâh and His messenger] (55)? These are *those whom Allâh has cursed*, and whom Allâh has cursed shall find no helper." — Nöldeke ascribes the words placed in the mouth of the people accused in this verse to some of the expelled Jews who betook themselves to Mecca, and tried to stir the Qoreish up to renew their hostilities against Muhammed.[12] This is, however, utterly improbable. Whence did Muhammed gain the knowledge that they had done so ? "The infidels" of v. 54 are none others than the Jews

[3] See Ch. VIII.

[4] See Beidhâwi and Bokh. i. 224 according to Abu Hureira. It is alleged that Ka'b b. Loeyy gave Friday the name *'Arûbâ*, because the people used to congregate on that day. This tradition, which is given on uncertain authority, deserves no credit. *Ârûbâ* or *Ârûb'thâ* is, in the Talmud, a name of Friday (*Jerush. Terûma*, viii. 10). It almost appears that Muhammed at first intended to use this term for Friday, but discarded it as he did with *'Âshûra*. Later tradition, then, gave the word a pagan origin.

[5] See Al Beidhâwi.

[6] See lvii. 22, iii. 147.

[7] ويستفتونك vv. 125 and 175.

[8] See also Nöldeke, p. 145 *sq.*

[9] See Geiger, p. 88; Nöldeke, p. 147, is not convincing.

[10] *Cf.* ii. 87, 98.

[11] Geiger, p. 55, not quite correct.

[12] Nöldeke, p. 149.

as a whole. The practice of the Rabbinical prescriptions, which went far beyond the bare laws of the Pentateuch, is termed by Muhammed *Tâghût* in the Aramaic meaning of this word. Exactly the same idea is again expressed in v. 63, *viz.*, that "they (the Jews) wish to refer their judgment to *Tâghût*,[13] *i. e.*, they follow the decisions of the latter rather than that of the Tôrah. The word *Jibt* (which does not occur again) has evidently a similar meaning, and belongs to those terms which Muhammed misread from his notes, and distorted beyond recognition. — It is unfortunately not clear whether Muhammed, at any time, met Jews who entertained ideas propagated later on by the Karaites, but as a believer in the Tôrah he is so unmistakeably Karaitic, that this is not improbable.

The verses 73-86 were revealed shortly after the catastrophe at Uḥud. Again Muhammed reminded Moslims that the disaster (v. 74) should by no means discourage them (vv. 78, 86), since death could occur at any time, but for this misfortune they had only themselves to blame (v. 81). The pieces 87-95 and *Sûra* v. 56-63[14] show Muhammed in possession of considerable power (v. 91),[15] and seem, therefore, somewhat later, *viz.*, dating from the time of the siege of the Banû Koreiza (end of A. 4), and, according to the Commentators, the section iv. 96-105[16] is contemporaneous with them. The group of verses 106-115 is said to owe its origin to a theft committed by a Medinian, who eventually fled to Mecca. If this be true, the date of the revelation in question can be approximately fixed as having taken place after the conversion of the poet Ḥassân b. Thâbit (A. H. 4), who in some verses,[17] alludes to this incident as well as to Muhammed's prophetic faculties. Greater difficulties are offered by the verses 116-125. It is, however, hardly justifiable to regard them with Nöldeke[18] as Meccan, because the "People of the Book" are mentioned in them (v. 122), without disparaging epithet or as "friends." The verses 130-133 are of quite uncertain date, and evidently placed here on account of v. 125. Just as uncertain is the date of v. 134, unless, as Nöldeke suggests,[19] it also refers to the affair of the theft, since the friends of the culprit gave false evidence in his favour. V. 139 forms the repetition of an old Meccan revelation,[20] and is now revealed evidently for a similar reason. The words that "Allâh deceives the Hypocrites"[21] (v. 141) are, to say the least, drastic. The sermon to which this remark belongs only goes as far as v. 145. The verses that follow up to v. 151 are quite uncertain as to date, although v. 147 might be brought in connection with the adventure of Âisha, which took place in the year 4.[22] The furious onslaught against the Jews (vv. 152-168) must be somewhat older, because it contains many reminiscences of similar orations of the first year.[23] The same holds good for the remarks applied to the Christians (vv. 169-173).[24] Verse 174 stands detached, and is of controversional character. Some Commentators regard it as the last of the whole *Qorân*.

---

13 Palmer: *to them* misprint.

14 Nöldeke, p. 172, refers vv. 57-63 to the battle of Uhud, but in reality they refer to the "War of the Trench," A. H. 4, and the alliance with the B. Koreiza.

15 See Nöldeke, p. 150, with slight differences.

16 *Cf. ibid.*

17 *Diwân*, ed. Tunis, p. 64 *sq.*; *cf. I. Hish.* p. 359, and Nöldeke, p. 151.

18 *Ibid.*

19 P. 152.

20 *S.* vi. 67.

21 See Ch. VIII.

22 Treated more in detail in *S.* xxiv.

23 *Cf.* ii. 52, 55, 60.

24 Nöldeke, p. 152.

## CHAPTER XI.

### Revelations on Muhammed's Domestic Affairs.

Revelations beginning "O thou Prophet" — Marriage with Zeinab — Sermon on the *amr* — Refutation of the charge against *'Áisha* — Regulations concerning women.

---

Every work on Moslim Tradition, or on the life of Muhammed, contains special chapters on his personal appearance and characteristics. These works, however, being written more with a view to promote the religious fervour of the reader than to chronicle facts, obscure this point rather than throw light upon it. The *Qorán* portrays the man Muhammed more faithfully than any Moslim biography. His real individuality, as well as the transformation of his character during an eventful career may be clearly traced from his own utterances. There we see how great qualities may be marred by grave faults.

Muhammed was undoubtedly conscious of his own weaknesses, and did what other men in prominent positions have done. He surrounded them with a halo. Among Muhammed's passions, an ever increasing love of the gentle sex was the greatest. Yet, in spite of his ideal calling, he did not endeavour to master it, but allowed it to increase with his years. What clearer sign is needed for the absolute sway he held over the minds of the Believers than his boldness in canonising his passion for women, declaring it to be under the special protection of Allâh *(amr)*? Muhammed's domestic affairs form the substrata of a series of revelations dating from the fifth year after the Hijra. They are externally distinguished by the introduction: *O thou Prophet!*[25] With very few exceptions[26] they refer to matrimonial matters, and form the least edifying chapter in the history of Islâm.

The Prophet of Allâh coveted Zeinab, the wife of his freedman Zeid b. Ḥâritha whom he had adopted, and wished to marry her. The two obstacles of her being a married woman and the wife of his adopted son (whom Arab custom made as near a relative as if he had been his real son) had to be removed, if the wish of Muhammed was to be fulfilled. This was, however, easy enough, if in the place of a personal desire, he gave expression to a divine command. Under these circumstances there was no choice left. Zeid had to divorce his wife, and Muhammed had to dissolve the paternal tie which connected him with his adopted son, and to marry Zeinab. The history of this interesting marriage is laid down in *S.* xxxiii. 1-62. Out of five sections of this sermon beginning with the words: *O thou Prophet*, four (vv. 1-8, 28-39, 49-52, 59[27]) treat on matters of Muhammed's Harem. The spirit of the revelations will be best demonstrated by translating one of them literally:—

> (v. 7) Allâh has not made for any man two hearts in his inside, nor has He made your wives, whom you desire to repudiate, your [real] mothers,[28] nor has He made your adopted sons your [real] sons. Such is only your way of expressing it, but Allâh speaks the truth, and He guides in the right path."

He thus abolished the old formula of divorce. After this declaration Muhammed was free to marry Zeinab who, on this occasion, with all the present and future wives of the Prophet, received the honorary title "Mother of the Believers" (v. 6). The marriage having taken place in the year 5 of the Hijra, there is no doubt about the date of the address in question.

*Sûra* xxxiii. shows some traces of artistic arrangement for which, however, the compilers are alone responsible. The first and largest portion (v. 1-59) is so arranged that addresses to "the Prophet" alternate with those to "the Believers." Since the different sections of both classes belong to various periods, it is best to discuss them in the order of the events to which they relate.

---

[25] xxxiii. 1, 28 (44). 49, 59; lxv. 1; lxvi. 1, 9. Lx. 12 also treats of women. [26] viii. 65, 66, 71; ix. 74.

[27] As to v. 44 see below. [28] The words were used in the old formula of divorce.

Section vv. 28-39 also refers to the incident of the marriage of Zeinab. Muhammed now pretended to have advised her former husband not to part with his wife, but Allâh had decreed otherwise, and Zeid was rewarded for his compliance by having his name coupled with that of the Prophet in a special revelation (v. 37).[29]

If Muhammed had merely wished to obtain Zeinab for her own sake, he could probably have achieved this without invoking the aid of Allâh, but I believe that the incident was also meant to increase his prestige by placing him again on a par with one of the Biblical prophets. The marriage of a prophet by special divine command had a befitting precedent in the [symbolical] marriages of the prophet Hosea (i. 2, iii. 1-2), which Muhammed interpreted literally. Both cases have several points of resemblance. The wives chosen were not virgins, and the marriages had to serve as object lessons for the populace. The only redeeming feature in Muhammed's proceeding was his insisting on a proper divorce instead of the objectionable practice of pre-Islamic times. Now the short address which follows (vv. 44-47), being the only one superscribed: "O thou Prophet," and yet not referring to anything matrimonial, seems nevertheless to bear upon the same incident, and to teach that Muhammed is the herald of glad tidings and a warner, *etc.* It is unexpected, at this juncture, to see Muhammed again accredited as a prophet, but his words were apparently designed to pacify those supercilious Believers, who considered his behaviour in the affair of Zeinab a sign of human weakness where prophetic self-abnegation should have been. He, therefore, thought it proper to convince his people that in this case also he had acted as Messenger of Allâh. To this he attached a regulation regarding the provisions to be made for a Moslim woman married to a Believer, who wished to divorce her before consummating the marriage (v. 48).[30]

The lessons to be deduced from this marriage were not even then exhausted. According to tradition several guests at the wedding feast, having given offence by their conduct, Muhammed forbade Believers to enter his houses in future without special invitation, to leave as soon as the meal was finished, and not to speak to his wives unless they were veiled (vv. 53-58). The command to be veiled was subsequently given to all believing women (v. 59),

The last address contains the sentence (v. 56) that "Allâh and His angels pray for the Prophet." These words seem to be modelled on a Talmudic homily.[31] In v. 41 the same phrase is repeated, but with reference to the Moslims. I believe this verse and v. 42, from which no clue can be gathered as to date, were inserted in this *sûra* merely on account of v. 56.

The piece vv. 9-27 is of later date. It describes the siege of Medina by the "Confederates," consisting of the Qoreish and Ghatafân, assisted by the Banû Kureiza, the remaining Jewish tribe in the environs of Medina (A. H. 5). From verse 27 we gather that the piece was revealed after the annihilation of the B. Koreiza.

The twofold success found an adequate expression in this triumphant address which is somewhat elated and almost dramatic in style (v. 19). — The last section headed "O thou Prophet" (v. 49-51)" makes it lawful for him to marry women who were among the captives or slaves. The first of this class was the Jewess Reihâna, widow of one of the B. Kureiza, whom Muhammed married A. H. 6. The verse placed next to this must, however, be much later, because the speaker takes upon himself not to increase his Harem any further except by concubines. The verse can therefore not have been revealed until the year 7 or 8.[32]

To these speeches the compilers have added three more which form the concluding part of the *sûra*. Verses 60-62 announce the speedy extirpation of the rest of the Jews of Medina. They are declared outlaws and free to be murdered wherever found.[33] The partial concordance

[29] The words فلما قضي زيد منها وطرا have been utilised by Hassân b. Thâbit (Diwân, p. 41, l. 11) in a dirge on Othmân, but the words refer to Zeid, brother of the poet.

[30] *Cf.* ii. 237. [31] See p. 79, rem. 59. [32] As to v. 52 see Weil, Mohammed, p. 358.

[33] *Cf.* ii. 187 referring to all unbelievers, Meccans included.

of v. 62 with v. 38 explains why the little piece was placed in this *sûra*. The short discourse on the "Hour" which then follows (vv. 63-68) is quite uncertain as to date, but from v. 68[34] it would appear that the words were spoken, when the Jews in Medina were still a factor to be reckoned with. The concluding speech (vv. 69-73) seems to stand in connection with that in which Muhammed reproved those Moslims who had caused annoyance at the wedding feast. Moses also had to bear annoyance, "but Allâh cleared him of what they said."[35] The Commentators refer this remark to charges brought against Moses by Korah, or other people who suspected Moses of having murdered Aaron.[36] It seems, however, that Muhammed had the incident of Numb. ch. xii. in his mind, because the accusation referred to in this chapter also bears on a woman. — Muhammed then cautions Believers always to speak in a straightforward manner! Verse 72 seems to be built on the framework of a Rabbinical homily.

In spite of Muhammed's strenuous efforts to convince Medinians that the marriage of Zeinab was performed in fulfilment of a divine command, he seems to have been afraid that some sceptics would regard the remarks he had attached to the affair as spoken *pro domo*. He, therefore, once more took up the subject of divorce in a special series of revelations, and had these also addressed to him personally. It was further necessary to show that matters of marriage and divorce of Moslims altogether stood under the direct providence of Allâh. The address in question is that of *S.* lxv., also headed by the phrase: *O thou Prophet.* This short sermon is also a perfect lecture on the *amr*, which is mentioned not less than *eight times* in it (vv. 1, 3, 4, 5, 8, 9 *bis*, 12), being the created Will of Allâh and His Providence over mankind.[37] The little homily appended which repeats hackneyed phrases, only serves to round off the sermon, and there can be no doubt as to the date of the same.

To the group of *sûras* dealing with Muhammed's personal affairs also belongs *S.* xxiv. although the customary allocation is omitted. Nearly the whole of the *sûra* is an endeavour to prove the innocence of Muhammed's favourite wife Âisha who was suspected of having committed adultery during the expedition against the B. Muṣṭaliq. The date of the event is not beyond doubt. It is, however, hardly advisable to place it, as Sprenger seems inclined, in the year 4.[38] I believe the incident did not occur till A. 6. The efforts Muhammed made to convince his hearers of his wife's innocence are visible in the beginning of the *sûra* which, in Medinian speeches, is quite unique. The severity with which he wished adultery to be punished, is calculated to make the impression that it was quite impossible that any person of his household could be capable of such a crime (v. 1-3). It is, however, noteworthy that the punishment of those who charge "chaste" women with adultery, but are unable to bring four witnesses, is not much less severe, beside disqualifying the informer for ever from giving evidence before a judge (v. 4-5).

Of the speeches forming *S.* xxiv., the first (vv. 1-33) and the last (vv. 57-64) evidently belong together, and are perhaps but parts of the same sermon.[39] Their chief object being the defence of Âisha, they begin with regulations concerning immorality and false charges brought against virtuous women in general, or against one's own wife. The latter case is obviously modelled on Numb. v. 11 *sqq.*[40] Now the first section (vv. 1-21) has a kind of ornamental phrase: "And were it not for Allâh's grace upon you," which divides the section into *four* paragraphs ending in the verses 10, 14, 20, 21.[41] The verses 27 to 29 repeat the warnings of *S.* xxxiii. 53, while extending it to all Moslims, and are therefore probably later. This is not the first case where an ordination which had arisen out of a special incident, was generalised for the benefit of the whole community. The verses 30 to 33[42] and 57 to 64 containing rules for decorous and respectful beha-

34 "Give them double torment." *Cf.* Isaiah xl. 2, a verse very popular in Jewish liturgy.

35 As to آذوا see v. 53 ان تؤذوا.

36 *Cf.* Numb. xx. 29, and Midrâsh Rabbâh, ch. xix.

37 See Ch. I., Appendix, Note II.

38 iii. 192; *cf.* Nöldeke, p. 156.

39 V. 57 resumes the rhyme of v. 33.

40 V. 7, "the curse;" *cf.* Numb. v. 18-21.

41 V. 21 consists of two verses, the second beginning ولولا.

42 V. 31, *cf.* Isaiah iii. 16 *sqq.* As to ولا يضربن بارجلهن see Jacob, *Das Leben der vorislam, Beduiner.*, p. 51.

viour towards the Prophet, as well as other Moslims, form too natural an appendix to the subject proper of the sermon to require special discussion.

Between the two portions of the sermon the compilers have inserted a discourse, quite alien to the character of the former, and probably later. The piece vv. 34 to 40 consists of a set of parables,[43] which are all borrowed from travels on land or on sea. It appears that the piece was given this place in order to divert the attention of the reader from an unedifying subject. As to its date, only so much may be said with certainty that it was revealed after several places of worship and regular hours of prayer had been fixed (vv. 36-37). Verse 41 reflects the Rabbinical metaphor that heaven, earth, and the creatures thereof sing the praise of God.[44] This verse, as well as the descriptive ones which follow (vv. 42-44) suit verses 39 to 40 very well. Verse 46 *sqq.* contain another attack against the Jews.[45] To judge from the repeated admonitions to obey (vv. 46, 50, 52, 53) it appears that this piece is later than corresponding verses in *S.* iv.,[46] as the phrase "we are disobedient" is dropped.

Similar in character to the preceding addresses, though of later date, is *Sûra* lxvi. It commences with the characteristic *O thou Prophet!* and was due to Muhammed's wife Ḥafṣa having discovered his relations with Maria, a Coptic slave girl, in the year 7. In *S.* xxxiii. 52 Muhammed had reserved for himself the right of adding concubines to his Harem. If in a moment of perplexity he swore to his irate spouse to forsake Maria, he believed himself entitled to cancel this oath[47] (vv. 1-2). Since attack is the best defence, he now in his turn reproved Ḥafṣa severely by exposing her as a tale-bearer, because she had promised him to keep the matter secret, but had nevertheless confided in Âisha (v. 3). He expected them to repent, because he was supported by Allâh, Gabriel, the true believers, and the angels" (v. 4). He was free to divorce his wives and take other, better, and more believing women in their stead (v. 5). In three verses which follow Muhammed extends his admonitions to Believers, as well as infidels. The words that "on the Day [of Resurrection] Allâh shall not disgrace the Prophet and the Believers" sound like an allusion to the disrespectful treatment he had been subjected to on the part of his wives.

The second portion of the *sûra*, commencing likewise with *O thou Prophet*, evidently stands in connection with the first. There is certainly a hidden meaning in Muhammed's reference to the *two women* who stand as prototypes of misbelief, *viz.*, the wives of Noah and Lot, who were themselves devout servants of Allâh. In contrast to these are two pious ones, *viz.*, the wife of Pharaoh and Mary (daughter of Amrân). It is possible that the last name was an allusion to the other Mary, the Coptic slave. As she changed her Christian faith for Islâm, she was likewise stamped as a model of piety.

The expedition against the B. Muṣṭaliḳ mentioned above, also gave rise to *Sûra* lxiii. In consequence of a quarrel between some Meccan fugitives and Medinians, Abd Allâh b. Ubeiyy, the chief of the latter is said to have exclaimed: "When we return to Medina, the mightiest will surely drive out the meanest therefrom." These words were reported to Muhammed who now took an opportunity of lancing a severe philippic against the "Hypocrites," and criticising the treasonable utterances ascribed to their leader[48] (vv. 7-8).

This was not the only incident, however, which showed Muhammed that the old spirit of freedom was far from being crushed in Medina. He has further to experience that it was easier to denounce heathen practices than to stamp them out by a revelation. He would, perhaps, have been more successful in abolishing the old custom of divorcing wives, had his first attempt in this direction not been suggestive of personal motives. It occurred that a woman appealed to Muhammed against her husband who had divorced her in the manner judged unlawful by the Prophet. The latter is said to have declared the divorce valid nevertheless. The woman, having little children to provide for, complained to Allâh, who then revealed *Sûra* lviii. 1-4,[49] in which the objectionable formula is definitely abolished. Now although the date given to this incident by the traditionists, *viz.*, A. 7, is not very reliable, the revelation in question seems to be posterior to that of xxxiii. 4. It is hardly credible

[43] See Ch. VIII. [44] See *Beiträge*, p. 84. [45] V. 49. "In their hearts is sickness." [46] Verses 48-49.
[47] *Cf. S.* v. 9. [48] See Ibn Hishâm, p. 725. [49] See AlBeidhâwi.

that Muhammed should have forgotten that he had once given a decision in this manner. I therefore doubt the authenticity of the tradition in question, and believe that Muhammed seized this opportunity of denouncing the old formula of divorce over again in a case with which he was not personally connected. He did this in a form which made it appear that, whilst he personally might acquiesce in the preservation of the old custom, it was Allâh who insisted on its abrogation. "Allah," he said, "has heard the speech of her who wrangled with thee about her husband, and complained to Allâh; Allâh has heard your conversation, behold Allâh hears and sees" (v. 1).

In connection with the final decision of the question of divorce Muhammed repeated his warnings against disobedience (vv. 9, 10, 14). Remonstrance with the Jews fills up nearly the whole of the remaining part of the *sûra*. From v. 6 we may conclude that it was revealed shortly before the fight against the B. Kureiza, who were to share the fate of those who had been destroyed before them. Of other details in the *sûra* we note the following: Verse 8 being directed against the secret plots of the enemies of Islâm, is a kind of reproduction of Abôth iii. 2-3. The verses 9 *sqq.* are lanced against the Jews whom, according to tradition, Muhammed exposed for turning the phrase of greeting into a curse. Believers are cautioned against rebellion, and warned against friendly intercourse with "people who suffer the wrath of Allâh" (v. 15), *viz.*, the Jews. Although Muhammed still feared the influence of the latter to some extent, he expressed his confidence that Islâm would ultmately prevail; yet he was cautious enough to phrase it that "Allâh has written, I will surely prevail, and my messengers" (v. 21). Allâh has likewise "written" faith in the hearts of the Believers (v. 22), a phrase which recalls sentences as Jer. xxxi. 33; Prov. iii. 3, vii. 3.

## CHAPTER XII.

### Preparations for the Pilgrimage to Mecca. Renewal of Allegiance.

Pilgrimage preached — Treaty of Ḥudeibiya — Conquest of Mecca — Messages from Arab Tribes — Conversions — Expedition against the Greek army — Tabûk — Renunciation of treaties *(barâ'a)* — Deuteronomic revelations.

---

The successes gained in the last few years had obliterated the shame of the Uḥud disaster. The enemies of Islâm in and around Medina had been vanquished, and the joint attack of the Qoreish and their allies against the town had been repelled. Muhammed's power was fast approaching its apogee, and he felt himself strong enough to venture pushing his authority right into the very heart of his enemies. To enter as conqueror into the city, in which he had for many years lived the life of an outcast, appeared like a bold dream. Muhammed was, therefore, careful to disguise his intention by suggesting a peaceful pilgrimage to the Ka'ba. Even this idea had to be broached with great caution, and he endeavoured to suggest it in an address, which forms the largest portion of *Sûra* xxii. This sermon is introduced by some general remarks touching upon the difference between believers and infidels, and the expectations of both classes hereafter.[50] The compromise made with the heterodox of various types in two previous Medinian revelations,[51] *viz.*, that the Jews, Baptists, Christians and Magicians could be regarded under certain circumstances as believers, is now abandoned, and they are ranked among the infidels (v. 17), whom Allâh shall place in contrast to true believers on the Day of Resurrection. The topic of the Ḥajj is then introduced in a rebuke lanced against the Meccans for preventing Moslims from visiting the sacred spot, which was established "for all mankind (*i.e.*, Arabs) alike, and *the sojourner and the stranger*" (v. 25). Those who might eye the proposal of worshipping at the shrine of Hobal with religious scruples are reminded that the place was originally established for Abraham with the injunction to shun idolatry, to keep "my house" pure for those making the prescribed circuits, to promote pilgrimage, and to "proclaim the name of Allâh therein" (26-29). With these words Muhammed not only boldly claimed the Ka'ba, but also the heathen ritual[52] for Islâm — a masterpiece of diplomacy. Another noteworthy feature of this speech is that Allâh, to whose service the ritual is to be transferred, officially takes the place of Rabbika. That this is not a mere accident will be shown by the following instances. In verse 31 we find the "sacred things of Allâh," in the verses 33 and 37 "the rites of Allâh." In the verses 35, 36, 37, 41 the proclamation of the name of Allâh (see verse 29) is again touched upon either in the form of a statement or an admonition. In verse 41 Muhammed places in the mouth of those who had fled with him from Mecca the words: *Our Lord is Allâh.* One cannot fail to see in this speech the efforts made to transplant the Meccan shrine and the ceremonies belonging to it into the bosom of the Moslim church. It is now easily intelligible why, in the treaty concluded with the Qoreish at Ḥudeibiyah (A. 6),[53] which precluded Muhammed from entering Mecca that year, he raised no objection to the demand of the pagan plenipotentiary to have the document initiated by the formula: *In thy name, O Allâh,* instead of the usual *In the name of Allâh.* Any difference between these two formulas had now ceased to exist, and far from losing prestige, he had gained considerably. It is, therefore, wrong to place the verses 39-42 before the battle of Badr. A special divine permission to fight the infidels, as Weil and Nöldeke assume,[54] is not to be found in this revelation. This question had already been settled in *Sûra* ii. 214-215 on the occasion of the illegal[55] expedition of Nakhla, when the *jihâd* was laid down as a command.

---

[50] Nöldeke, Q. 158, regards vv. 1-24 as Meccan, v. 17 is, however, Medinian on account of الذين هادوا.

[51] ii. 59; v. 73.

[52] See Snouck Hurgronje, *Het Mekkaansche Feest*, p. 28.

[53] As to the text of the treaty see Sprenger, III. p. 246.

[54] Weil, *Einleit.* p. 80; Nöld. p. 160; see *Hish.* 313 with doubtful authority.

[55] See Ch. IX.

Somewhat older than this is the address contained in the verses 48 to 59, but it cannot be of Meccan origin,[56] because in v. 52 "those in whose heart is sickness and whose hearts are hardened (the Jews)" are mentioned. Verse 51 is generally explained by Moslim teachers as replacing the objectionable verses liii. 19-20 which Muhammed was, according to tradition, obliged to expunge owing to their semi-pagan character.[57] The verse is, however, nothing but a reflex of Zach. iii, 1, very popular in Jewish liturgy, and which Muhammed found wonderfully adaptable to his own career. Now verse 55 re-echoes Zach. xiv. 9 of even greater liturgical popularity, and therefore also speaks for the Medinian origin of the group in question, which probably dates from shortly after the battle of Uḥud (v. 57).

With regard to the last portion (vv. 72-78) of the *sûra* we can only assume that it was placed here for the sake of the beginning, which is the same as in the verses 1 and 48. The *mathal* of verse 72 probably taunts the Meccans with their alleged success obtained at Ḥudeibiya. As the verses 76-78 point to a well arranged divine service, they can hardly be older than the group 48-59.

To an incident which happened shortly before the conquest of Mecca the traditionists refer the verses *Surâ* v. 39-44, dealing with the punishment meeted out to a thief. There is hardly anything better to be said about the origin of these verses.

An interesting retrospect on the allegiance sworn by the Believers at Ḥudeibiyah is given in *Sûra* xlviii. 18-28. The phrase *under the tree* is, as we have seen on a previous occasion,[58] more than a mere historical recollection. Neither is it accidental that the *Shekinah* is mentioned in the same verse.[59] The following verses are justly considered to refer to the rich spoil made during the raids on the Jews of Khaibar (v. 20), Fadak, Teimâ, and Wâdil Qorâ (v. 21). Muhammed cannot help expressing some discontent at having allowed himself to be persuaded to rest satisfied with so incomplete a pilgrimage, or, what is still more probable, he tried to weaken the treaty concluded with the Meccans by charging them with having hindered the Moslims from sacrificing at the Ka'ba (v. 25). This intention is more clearly expressed in verse 27,[60] where he tells the world of a vision in which he is assured of entering Mecca "if Allâh please" in safety, and of performing all rites connected therewith without fear "and He has appointed, besides this, a victory nigh at hand." This victory does not refer to Khaibar, as Palmer thinks, but to Muhammed's firm resolution to conquer Mecca at any price.

The conquest which took place in the following year was accompanied by the address *Sûra* ii. 185[61]-196, which cannot have been revealed prior to this event.[62] Muhammed was only now strong enough to include those who still refused to embrace Islâm in the proscription uttered some time since against the Jews and Hypocrites, *viz.*, to kill them wherever found,[63] "and to drive them on whence they drove you out" (v. 187). The last words in particular are unmistakeable. Muhammed had made up his mind to treat Mecca as a conquered city irrespective of the treaty which only granted him permission to enter it as a pilgrim. Possibly the defeat which the Moslim warriors had suffered in the Jumâda (September) of the same year at Mûta made a retrieval necessary. The expression "drive them out who drove you out" allows of a literal explanation in so far as the treaty of Hodeibiyah stipulated that the Qoreish were to leave the city, while the Moslims performed their devotions within its walls. It seems that Muhammed was waiting for the retirement of the Qoreish from the town in order to prevent the re-entrance of all those who still refused to embrace Islâm. For it must be observed that he forbade fighting only in the immediate surroundings of the sanctuary

[56] Nöldeke, *ibid.* p. 158, regards v. 43-56 as Meccan, but v. 57 cannot have opened a new address.

[57] See *Hish.* 370, and Nöldeke, p. 150.

[58] Ch. II.

[59] Verse 18. *cf.* 26.

[60] As to the spurious character of v. 29 see Ch. XIII.

[61] The address begins with a remark on the new moons which are called "indications of time." This is a translation of Ps. civ. 19.

[62] Nöldeke, p. 133, rightly places the verse after the treaty of Ḥudeibiya. I do not believe that Muhammed was afraid of a violation of the treaty on the part of the Meccans. It is more probable that he looked for a pretext to defy them, and for this very reason accepted conditions apparently so unfavourable to him.

[63] See Ch. X. and *Sûra* xxxiii. 61.

except in self-defence, or to quell a revolt (v. 187). This, however, is a meaningless phrase, since no enemy was expected to be present. Why should Muhammed suddenly recommend his warriors "to fight them that there be no sedition" (v. 189)?[64] This does not look as if he wished the Qoreish to become masters of their town once more. In connection with these instructions Muhammed then describes in detail the ritual to be observed during the Ḥajj (vv. 190-196b).[65]

How little Muhammed felt himself bound by the treaty mentioned before, will appear from the circumstance that he actually placed himself at the head of an army in order to take Mecca by surprise. His plan was, however, betrayed by a Moslim who informed the Meccans of the Prophet's arrival, the letter which was carried by a female slave being intercepted. Muhammed rebuked the deed in a warning which fills out the beginning of *Sûra* lx.[66] Thus far tradition. According to our judgment there could not have been any betrayal in the matter, as the visit of the Moslim army was to take place by agreement and in open daylight. The only person to be charged with perfidy is Muhammed himself. — The verses 10-13 of this *sûra* are of uncertain date, but their tenor coincides, on the whole, with the opinion of some traditionists that they were revealed in connection with the capture of Mecca.

When this was accomplished, it was celebrated in two special sermons which form the first portion of *Sûra* xlviii. (1-15).[67] To have become master of Mecca was, indeed, a "great victory" (v. 1), although it was won without bloodshed. Muhammed was, however, conscious that the way he had achieved this success was anything but straight, and this feeling interfered seriously with the logic of his speech. The next verse reads as if Allâh had given him the victory in *order* to grant him forgiveness for past and future sins, which seems like a premium put on his transgressions.[68] Muhammed evidently meant to imply that, being now in a position to fulfil the pious duties of pilgrimage, he had the opportunity to atone for his sins, or some such sophistry. — The verses 4 and 10 contain the reason, why this piece was connected with the older portion beginning with v. 18[69] to make one *sûra*. The tendency of the words spoken twice (vv. 4 and 7), that the hosts of heaven and earth were Allâh's,[70] is likewise unmistakeable. The conclusion to be drawn from this remark is that Allâh was free to give Mecca to the Believers. There is probably also an allusion to the large army fighting for Allâh in it. Nothing could have been more appropriate than for Muhammed, under very much altered circumstances, to proclaim himself once more on Meccan soil as Messenger, Witness, Harbinger of good tidings, and Warner (v. 8). The satisfaction he must have felt in recapitulating these words which had been nearly a score of years before uttered by him on the same spot at the peril of his life, is re-echoed in every sentence of this address, and his shrewdness is equally evident. Was it not possible that many who, at that period, became converts to Islâm, did so merely in deference to his personal power? He therefore hastened to assure the world that all new comers did not "swear allegiance" to the Prophet, but to Allâh (v. 10). The expression "become Moslim" is probably discarded here on purpose.

According to tradition another fear awoke in the breast of many Medinians, *viz.*, that Muhammed might now prefer living in his native town, instead of returning to Medina.[71] Should he decide that way, the loss would not only affect the faith, but the town to which the person of the Prophet attracted many deputations and visitors. The farther Islâm was spread, the larger became the area of which Medina was an important centre of people, trade, commerce and wealth. It seems to me, that

---

[64] Verse 187: Sedition is worse than slaughter.

[65] See Snouck Hurgronje, *l. c.*; — Nöldeke, p. 132, regards vv. 196-198 as Meccan, but the phrase وما له في الاخرة من خلاق is undoubtedly Medinian; *cf.* iii. 71. There exists therefore no reason to detach the verses in question from the context.

[66] See Nöldeke, p. 162.

[67] Nöldeke, p. 161, places this sermon immediately after the treaty of Ḥudeibiya, but v. 12 points to a time after the conquest.

[68] Beidhawi: for having performed the *jihâd* and checked idolatry.

[69] السكينة v. 4 اذ يبايعونك تحت الشجرة.

[70] جنود السموات vv. 4 and 7= צבאות השמים

[71] See Sprenger, III. 334.

these reasons had as much weight with the Medinians as any spiritual ones. Muhammed saw all this, as well as the ingratitude of which he would have been guilty, had he abandoned the town to which he owed so much. With his usual diplomacy he turned the tables, and charged those who deemed him capable of such a course of action, with "evil thoughts, and being people destitute of good" (v. 12).

The second, but short, thanksgiving address is contained in *Sûra* cx.[72] which, in a condensed form, reiterates the opening sentences of *Sûra* xlviii.[73] Since the *sûra* is so small, I reproduce it in full.

1. As the help of Allâh came[74] and victory.
2. And thou sawest men enter into the religion of Allâh by troops.
3. Then celebrate the praises of thy Lord and ask forgiveness of Him. behold He is forgiving.

These words describe the situation exactly, because after the conquest of Mecca Islâm was progressing by leaps and bounds.

According to tradition *Sûra* xlix. (1-5) was revealed when, after Muhammed's return to Medina, messengers of the Tribe of the Banu Tamîm arrived in the beginning of "the year of the embassies" (A. 9),[75] in order to negotiate with him about the redemption of some members of their tribe who had been taken prisoners by the Moslims. The embassadors are said to have shouted for Muhammed in a disrespectful manner, for which they are rebuked in the verses alluded to.[76] Other commentators think they refer to different incidents.

The next group of verses of the same *sûra* is said to allude to Al Walîd, son of Oqba b. Abi Moeit (who had been executed after the battle of Badr),[77] for having given information against the Banû Mostaliq who had refused to pay the tribute. Muhammed is said to have revealed the verses in which Al Walîd is styled a sinner (*fâsiq*).[78] The story which is not very well authenticated, although generally believed to be true, seems to me doubtful, and was probably invented to discredit the Omayyad party, or, at least, Al Walîd himself, who as Prefect of Kûfa[79] did not lead a very religious life, and was deposed by Othmân. It is not likely that Muhammed would thus have branded a new convert, member of a very influential family, and close relative to some of his nearest friends. Moreover as the whole affair, which was due to a misunderstanding, was subsequently cleared up, Muhammed would not have left so offensive an expression in the *Qorân*. I believe that the passage (the date of which I am, however, unable to fix) was placed here on account of verse 7 which also contains statements concerning the person of the "Messenger of Allâh" in juxtaposition to the messengers of the Banu Tamîm. The cause of the revelation of the verse in question seems to have been the same as in both the preceding groups (vv. 9-12), *viz.*, the petty quarrels and jealousies which prevailed among Arab tribes in general, and the Medinians (*Anṣâr*) on one side, and the Meccan Fugitives (*Muhâjirûn*) on the other in particular. These quarrels often threatened to assume dangerous dimensions. The two proverbial observations contained in verse 12[80] also tend to denounce suspicion and backbiting, so that they stand in direct connection with verse 6. Contrary to these, verse 13 teaches that not birth and family pride, but piety give, in the eyes of Allâh, the highest claim to distinction. The verse appears to imply a criticism of the haughty tone of the verses of Al Zibriqân,[81] the poet of the legation, and of this kind of poetry (*fakhr*) altogether.—In spite of the traditional explanation of v. 14,[82] *viz.*, that

[72] Nöldeke, p. 163, places the *sûra* prior to the conquest, but without valid reason. [73] cx. 1 = xlviii. 1-3.
[74] Palmer: *When there comes, etc.*, incorrect. [75] *Hish.* p. 239, Wâqidi, p. 386.
[76] See also Khamîs, II. p. 118. As regards the details see Sprenger, III. 365, and above, Ch. I. [77] See Ch. X.
[78] V. 6. On the authority of Yazîd b. Rûmân (died about 130) with no further *Isnâd*, related by I. I. p. 730; Al Beidhâwi, Khamîs, II. p. 120; Nöldeke, p. 164, v. 224; Sprenger, III. 363. I. I. seems to fix the incident prior to the expedition against the B. Muṣṭaliq.
[79] Ibn Ḥajar, No. 8657 (III. p. 1312). [80] See Ch. VIII.
[81] See Ḥassân b. Thâbit, *Divân*, p. 110 *sqq.* [82] Nöldeke, p. 165, adopts this explanation.

it refers to a certain Bedouin tribe which, in exchange for their conversion to Islâm, expected to receive provisions from the Prophet during a famine, I rather believe it to be a comment on the preceding verse, and for a good reason. As already intimated, many Bedouin tribes accepted Islâm after the conquest of Mecca; but, whilst finding the recitation of the formula of the creed very easy work, they found more difficulty in exchanging their modes of life for the practical duties of Islâm. Here we perceive the civilizing influence of Islâm better than anywhere else. Muhammed explained to the reluctant ones that it was not sufficient for Bedouins to say: "*We believe*"—which was no belief: but they were to say: "*we have become Moslims.*" In this sentence, he evidently contrasts theory with practice, and the passage also offers a valuable instance of Muhammed's own conception of Islâm at that stage.[33] As might have been expected he adds that it consists in obedience to Allâh and His Messenger, and sacrificing wealth and personality to the cause of the faith (vv. 15-16). Believers did not, by embracing Islâm, benefit either the Prophet or Allâh, but the latter benefitted them by his guidance (vv. 17-18). One cannot fail to perceive the altered tone in Muhammed's speech, assumed in the consciousness of his power. It was also quite justifiable in view of the rudeness of the Tamimite ambassadors, and fixes the date of the address decisively. The pieces of this exhortation seem to be simultaneous or very nearly so.

If Muhammed was able to adopt such language, it is small wonder that he dreamt of leading the now greatly increased forces of the Moslim army against the Emperor Heraclius, who shortly before had made himself master of Syria, and had several Arab tribes, as well as Jews, in his army. It was probably his brother Arabs, whom Muhammed was most anxious to induce to forsake their Christian patrons, since he could hardly hope to carry the Moslim arms beyond the borders of Asia. He was, however, fully alive to the dangers connected with an expedition against the better trained Greek troops. This meant warfare on a different scale from that to which he had hitherto been accustomed. As a tentative move he made two speeches, the first of which (*Sûra* ix. 23-27) in some respect resembles the one just discussed. Muhammed repeats that family ties or worldly interest must be second to the love for Allâh and His Prophet. Allâh had supported them in the past year at Ḥonein with a large though invisible army,[34] just as he had done at Badr, and given them the victory over the infidels.

When Muhammed set out to take Mecca, many Bedouin tribes had disappointed him. He severely censured those who were "left behind," and, as a punishment, they received none of the spoil gained in the expeditions against the Jewish clans (*Sûra* xlviii. 15). In order to give them an opportunity of redeeming their former laxity, Muhammed summoned them to join the forces which were sent against the Byzantines. I have little doubt that only these are meant by the expression "people of vehement valour" (*Sûra* xlviii. 16), and not the followers of Moseilima against whom Muhammed never intended sending an army. Considering the perils of this expedition Muhammed wished to have among his troops only able-bodied warriors who could cope with the Greek soldiers. In the less serious raids undertaken heretofore many had, no doubt, taken part who were not proof against the fatigues of real warfare, but underwent some hardship for the sake of the spoil. The next verse (17) seems to have been revealed in order to keep these people out rather than from purely humane motives. If such persons lost their share of the booty, it mattered little, because they would be rewarded for their obedience with the enjoyments of paradise.

The majority of voluntary and involuntary converts were not yet prepared to risk life and limb from sheer enthusiasm for Islâm, and did not respond to Muhammed's call to arms as willingly as he might have expected. He had to bring all his powers of eloquence to bear in order to overcome their reluctance. In a long speech (*Sûra* ix. 38-73) he charges Believers with preferring the comforts of this world to the next. He threatens them with heavy punishment.

[33] See Ch. I., App., Note 1. Al Beidhâwi فان الاسلام انقياد ودخول في السلم واظهار الشهادة وترك المحاربة يشعر به.

[34] Al Beidhâwi: five thousand angels, or according to others, six or eight thousand.

and recalls to their minds how Allâh had assisted him, when he, accompanied by a single friend,[85] had hidden himself during his escape from Mecca. While several phrases and expressions in this speech manifest its close relationship with the first part of this *sûra*,[86] it endeavours to re-kindle the zeal of the Moslims for religious war. The words: "He made the word *(kalima)* of the unbelievers the lowest (v. 40) are undoubtedly an allusion to the Christian faith of the enemy. If, he says, worldly gain were near at hand, and the march short, they would follow readily (v. 42), and in this manner he goes on blaming those who remained at home under various pretexts,[87] and were therefore classed among the "Hypocrites" (vv. 65, 68, 69).

During the expedition Muhammed returned to the same subject, and expressed his indignation against those who in spite of his entreaties stayed at home (v. 74-81). They were glad to remain behind for such paltry reasons as the heat of the season (v. 82). He declared that he would never again allow them to join any expedition (v. 84), and forbade praying at their graves[88] (v. 85). It grieved him to perceive that the belief of the newly converted tribes was very superficial.[89] He again laid down the rule for those who were exempt from military service, *viz.*, the weak, the sick, and those who were too poor to arm themselves.[90] Yet others who were [able-bodied and] wealthy asked leave to stay behind.[91]

If Muhammed was indignant against those lately converted, he was much more so against Medinians who were guilty of the same dereliction of duty, and set a bad example to others. In the address consisting of the verses 120-128 he censured that portion of the army which was under the command of Abd Allâh b. Ubeyy, and numbered many Jews among its ranks. The latter are alluded to in the usual term "of those in whose heart is sickness" (v. 126), and Believers are expected to fight them.

At any rate Muhammed's wish to overawe the Byzantine army by an overwhelming Moslim force was not fulfilled, and the expedition terminated in the bloodless demonstration of Tabûk, whence the army returned to Medina. No risk of life had been incurred, and those who had remained at home regretted it, being profuse in excuses which were entirely ignored. In an address on the matter (vv. 95-120) Muhammed was particularly severe against those Bedouins who were "the keenest in disbelief and hypocrisy and readiest to ignore the bounds which Allâh has revealed" (v. 98). Others, he said, gave their contribution unwillingly, and were only waiting for the fortune to turn against Muhammed (v. 99), though some of them were sincere Moslims (v. 100). Now here we may observe an interesting phenomenon. The social equality which had established itself during the iniatory stages of Islâm, commenced to undergo a slight change, as soon as the faith was supported by political power. Muhammed himself took the first step to create a kind of aristocracy by giving the "Fugitives" the foremost rank in the favour of Allâh. The rank next to them was occupied by the Medinian "Helpers"[92] (v. 101). This was but natural. It would have been an insult to those who nearly twenty years before had given up home and family, and in some cases fortunes, and cast in their lot with an outlaw, to rank them with Medinian traders and Bedouins who now ran after Islâm because it paid better than their former trade.

In the verses following these Muhammed describes the "hypocrite" penitents and those who had built a mosque with mischievous intentions[93] (v. 102-108). In opposition to the latter

---

[85] Abu Bakr.

[86] *Cf.* نصره v. 40 with نصركم v. 25 and انزل الله سكينته ...... وانزل جنودا لم تروها (v. 26).

[87] The verses 49 and 82 are said to refer to Al Jadd b. Qeis, *cf.* I. I. p. 894.

[88] The verse is said to refer to Abd Allâh b. Ubeyy, and Nöldeke, p. 167, regards it therefore as a later addition.

[89] *Cf. Sûra* 49 and above, rem. 83.

[90] No parallel to Deut. xx. 1-8.

[91] Palmer's translation (94): "Only is there a way against those, *etc.*," quite misses the point. السبيل means here *war* as usual. Verse 93 refers according to all authorities to the "Weepers," *viz.*, seven Ansâr who were too poor to procure camels, *cf.* Wâqidi, p. 392; I. I. p. 895.

[92] *Cf.* viii. 73.

[93] Wâqidi, *ibid.*, I. I. 913.

he places "the mosque founded on piety," as well as the position of the believers, and the fate awaiting them as laid down in Torâh, Gospel and *Qorân* (v. 109-113). The next portions of these rather incoherent speeches date from the same time. Verse 114 which refers either to the memory of Abu Tâlib, or Muhammed's mother,[94] is evidently in some way connected with verse 81, and seems to form the reply to a query based on *Sûra* xix. 46. The interpretation (given in verse 115) that Abraham only *promised*, but did not actually pray for his father, is cunning rather than dignified, because the tone of the verse alluded to impresses the reader with the idea that Abraham *did* pray. The word *tabarra'a* (verse 115) gives a clue why this sermon was joined to the one at the beginning so as to form one *sûra*.[95] Verse 119 standing alone, at length grants pardon to some of those censured in a former speech of the same *sûra* (vv. 38 *sqq*.).

Although the expedition to Tabûk did not bring the desired result, yet it added largely to the number of new converts, or at least subjects of Muhammed on the basis of a treaty. Finding the latter, however, not to his taste, Muhammed, in the following year, charged his cousin Aliyy to meet the pilgrims assembled at Mecca, and to read in their presence a proclamation which declared all compacts made with unbelievers null and void. Although this "Renunciation," which forms the first part of *Sûra* ix., does not appear in the usual form of revelations, it was embodied in the *Qorân*, but without the introductory formula "In the name of Allâh the Merciful, the Compassionate." This was, indeed, superfluous, since it is announced as a *barâa* (renunciation) and an *adân* (proclamation), both emanating from Allâh and His messenger (vv. 1-3). It is therefore not Muhammed who violates the treaty, but Allâh Himself, the Prophet being only his tool. Exempt were only the holders of a compact until a given term (vv. 4-6). After the elapse of the [four] sacred months infidels were to be regarded as outlaws, and Moslims were free to kill them by any means in their power, unless they confessed Islâm (vv. 5-12). In order not to leave any doubt which months were meant, he explains the matter in an appendix (vv. 36-37), and denounces the pagan custom of changing one of these months with another if more convenient. — There is, however, some uncertainty about the date of the piece vv. 13-22. Nöldeke, following Moslim interpreters, is inclined to retrodate these verses to the time before the conquest of Mecca, although the word *hammû* ("they solicited," *viz.*, to drive thee out, verse 13) speaks against such a theory.[96] It seems rather that this verse contains a reminiscence of the unsuccessful attempt undertaken by Muhammed two years before leaving Mecca to spread Islâm among the inhabitants of Tâif. His wrath against these people was all the greater, as even after the conquest of Mecca they entered into a coalition with the Hawâzin tribes to fight against Muhammed. Defeated at Ḥonein (Shawwâl A. 8), they retired into their city which the Prophet besieged in vain. It is, therefore, natural that he was not content to entrust their punishment to Allâh alone (v. 14),[97] but egged Believers on to continue fighting them with the assistance of Allâh. Like other infidels they must not be permitted to "visit"[98] the holy city even outside the sacred season, because this privilege is in future accorded exclusively to Moslims.

A further comment on the same prohibition is given in the section vv. 28-37, in which idolaters are declared to be "unclean,"[99] and must therefore not come near the sacred places after the termination of the present year. Such prohibition clashed, however, with the commercial interest of the believing population of Mecca. This was a rather serious objection, which Muhammed could not answer, except by the assurance that Allâh would compensate them for any loss of trade sustained in consequence of his command (v. 28).

---

[94] Nöldeke, p. 168. [95] See below.

[96] Al Beidhâwi refers v. 12 to the Jews who endeavoured to drive Muhammed out of Medina, but *cf.* v. 14.

[97] Tradition makes him pray for the conversion of the city, I. I. 188.

[98] To perform the *'umra* which means an occasional visit to Mecca for the purposes of performing the minor rites, but not accompanied by sacrificers.

[99] *Cf.* Levit. xxii. 3.

After their expulsion from Mecca many Jews had made common cause with Heraclius, and in Muhammed's eye still constituted some danger to Islâm. The Prophet seems to have feared that their spiritual influence might become harmful after his death. We have seen before that on several occasions Muhammed tried to foist upon the Jews the stamp of paganism.[100] Returning to this old charge, Muhammed enjoins Moslims again to fight those who held many things lawful which Allâh and His messenger had forbidden, but they did even not follow the law of their own faith (v. 29). In order to bear out the accusation of Jewish heathenism, Muhammed charged them with venerating Ezra as the son of God, in the same manner as the Christians did with Jesus (v. 30). The sole basis for this charge is the circumstance that Ezra was responsible for many institutions in the Rabbinical code, which appeared to differ from the written law, but this alleged sonship is an invention of Muhammed for the purpose alluded to above. If Moslims were to look upon Jews as upon polytheists, their influence in such quarters which stood outside the immediate control of Muhammed or any future head of the Moslim church, was not to be feared. Like unto Christians they took, he said, their Rabbis as *Lords* (*arbâb*, plural of *rabb*), and very shrewdly Muhammed described these "Lords" in the same term, as in his own first revelation. "They take their *Rabbis* and *monks* as Lords beside Allâh, and also the Messiah the son of Maryam, while they have been commanded only to worship *one* God, there is no God but He, exalted be he above those which they join with him" (v. 31). The theological observations attached to this disclosure explain themselves (vv. 32-33), *viz.*, that *Muhammed* is the true messenger. Rather sharp is the assertion that many of the Rabbis and monks eat the wealth of men for nought (v. 34), although as far as Jews are concerned it was in mediæval times not the custom to pay the spiritual heads of communities.

I place here the verse vii. 156 which refers to the conversion of some Jews and Christians. This is clear from the words: "They find written down *with them* in the Torâh and Gospel." Also the words "making lawful for them what is good and making unlawful evil things, and setting down for them their restrictions, and yokes which were upon them" are unmistakable. It seems to me that the verse was revealed chiefly in reference to the conversion of the Jew Abd Allâh b. Salâm which took place in the year 8.[1] The next piece, as far as verse 172, is a homily commenting on the same incident. The conversion of Abd Allâh to which Moslim traditionists attach the greatest importance, gave Muhammed an opportunity of proclaiming himself once more the Apostle of mankind in general, and of recalling several episodes of the history of Israel. He mentions the twelve tribes, the command given to Moses to strike the rock,[2] and other matters discussed in previous speeches.[3] The "Covenant of the Book" (168) bears a striking resemblance to the "Book of the Covenant" (Exod. xxiv. 7). The verses 171-172, speaking of the children of Adam bearing witness against themselves, seem to be based on, or at least influenced by, a *Midrâsh* (Canticles I. 4) according to which God, when about to reveal the law of Sinai, demanded from the people a pledge that they would observe it. After rejecting the Patriarchs and Prophets, God accepted the children as hostages.

There only now remains *Sûra* v. which, however, offers difficult problems for the arrangement of its portions in their proper places. Before attempting this task we must briefly survey the conditions under which they were revealed. In the 10th year of the Hijra Muhammed started, at the head of an immense crowd of pilgrims to pay the famous visit to his native city which is known as his last. The dogmas and rites of the Moslim church had then been already settled, not only in the outlines, but also in many details. Muhammed himself was so far advanced in years, as to make him think of his natural end. Knowing the character and prejudices of the Arabs, and being aware that the belief of a large number of believers was but superficial, his mind was filled with apprehensions about his future. Experience had taught him that but for his personal influence the differences of interest and temper would have caused splits in the community which endangered the safety of the faith. Tribal hostilities, so often quenched by

[100] *Cf.* iii. 73. [1] See Iṣâba and Ch. II. [2] See Geiger, *l. c.* p. 164. [3] *Cf.* ii. 54-61.

his exertions, might break out at any moment when he was removed, and end in civil war. Most of the ritual duties were a heavy burden on the masses, which were far from grasping their meaning. Not less undesirable was the moral code. It was hard that the smallest bit of pilfering was punishable. Wine and dice were to be abhorred, and the freedom of the chase to be restricted, not to mention other laws. Muhammed was well aware that his people could not be educated up to his ideal with one stroke. The warnings had to be repeated over and over again. Such speeches of a deuteronomic character form the framework of *Sûra* v., the bulk of which was preached on the occasion of the last pilgrimage in the presence of a huge congregation.

We can take it for granted that Muhammed was acquainted with the Jewish interpretation of the character of the Deuteronomy as a repetitional injunction of the Law *(Mishnêh Tôrâh)*. Why not follow this example? As an exterior deuteronomic feature in the first portion of our *sûra* I regard the three instances of *alyauma* ("today, " vv. 4, 5, 7), which in the same application is particularly frequent in the Biblical book of Deuteronomy.

Of this book the reader is already reminded in the opening words of verse 1 of our *sûra*,[4] corresponding to Deut. iv. 13, 23; xxix. 8, *viz.*, the injunction to keep covenants of which Muhammed had set such a good example by his *barâa*. The regulations with regard to forbidden articles of food (vv. 4-7) stand parallel to Deut. xii. 16, 20, 27; xiv. 3-21.[5] The verses 2-3 are regarded by Nöldeke as having been revealed before the conquest of Mecca, because they ordain that *pagan* pilgrims to the Ka'ba should remain unmolested. This is, however, hardly admissible. It is not to be assumed that Muhammed would have styled the deity to be worshipped by these heathen visitors as "their Rabb," because he employed just this term from the beginning in a strictly antagonistic sense. The verses refer to future pilgrimages. Muhammed warns Believers not to revive the old hatred, nor to bear grudge against those Meccan families which had been hostile almost to the last, but were now Moslims. The large meetings to be expected at Mecca inspired him with fear that old feuds might break out afresh to the desecration of the holy spot and season, and the same fear rings through a sermon shortly to follow. Verse 5 is the famous "verse of the *Dîn*," and reflects verses like Deut. iv. 8, and quite a host of others. As a supplement to the prayer ritual appears an ordination to wash the hands with water prior to the performance of the same, or if this should not be within reach, with sand[6] (vv. 8-9). Verse 10 is deuteronomic for *Sûra* ii. 285 and the parallel verses. The topic of verse 3 is with verbal repetition of the case,[7] taken up again in the verses 11 and 14.[8] The group 15-17 has a similar tendency. Nöldeke leaves a large margin for it between the years 2 and 7, but it seems that Muhammed had Moses' farewell speech in his mind. The "covenant" (v. 15) recalls Deut. xxxiii. 2, and the "twelve chiefs" are alluded to, *ibid.* v. 5. Allâh's word to the "children of Israel" recalls quite generally the blessing of verse 1 of the same chapter. As a matter of course the tone of Muhammed's imitation is on a level with his own taste, as well as the needs and intellects of his audience. The next verse (16) stating that the Banû Isrâil broke the compact, and were cursed, and hardened their heart, forged the law and forgot part of it (Deut. xxviii. 15-69), is trite enough, and served to give fulness to the speech. Less worn is the reproach addressed to the Christians that to their forgetfulness it was due that the church was split up in sects betwixt which there existed enmity and hatred "until the Day of Resurrection" (v. 17).

As a supplement to this criticism, the compilers of the *Qorân* have placed at the end of the *sûra* a narrative piece (vv. 109-120) which contains an admonition addressed by Allâh to Jesus. From the "table" mentioned in verse 112 the whole *sûra* has its name. The tendency

---

[4] The compound character of v. 1 has already been noticed by most Moslim interpreters, *cf.* Nöldeke, p. 169.

[5] وما ذبح علي النصب = Levit. xvii. 7; Deut. xxxii. 17.

[6] See Geiger, p. 89.

[7] ولا يجرمنكم شنآن قوم.

[8] *Cf.* ix. 13.

of the narrative is laid down in the verses 116-119, *viz.*, that Jesus commanded to worship only one God. He is, consequently, not responsible for the origin of the dogma of the Trinity which was only due to corruption and forgetfulness (see verse 17). Although it is hazardous to say anything definite with regard to the age of this piece, it seems somewhat older than verse 17 in which we may see a reference to it. Its Medinian origin is, however, beyond doubt on account of verse 110.

Now towards the end of this piece (verse 118) Jesus prays that Allâh may forgive his followers' sins, and to this the verses 18-19 seem to respond. The term "Possessors of the Writ" refers in this instance to Christians alone. It is noticeable that here as well as in verse 17 Muhammed regards the Christians with much complacency. He only reproaches them with *forgetfulness*, as we have seen, promises them that he, while explaining to them much of the Book made unintelligible by them, will also *forgive them much*. The following protest against the apotheosis of Jesus is strangely devoid of all sharpness. Even when commenting on the circumstance that [Jews and] Christians called themselves "Sons and beloved of Allâh" whilst they were only mortals (v. 21), he is not so bitter as usual. The reason seems to be that the failure of the expedition of Tabûk had taught Muhammed to abstain from reviling so large a Christian power. The effete Jews could be abused with impunity. Muhammed must certainly have feared that after his death the Moslim armies might be defeated by Christian ones, to the loss of many Arab tribes, which only a little while ago had been converted to Islâm. — Verse 22, of uncertain date, has been placed here on account of v. 18.

Deuteronomic are further the verses 44-55. Verse 45 repeats the idea of *Sûra* iv. 48, whilst verse 49 is a reiteration of *Sûra* ii. 173-175, yet modifying it in the way of clemency This furnishes some evidence that the piece v. 49-55 is later than the other. The verses 64-68 very conspicuously form a repetition of the scathing remarks in *Sûra* ii. 61, 257-258; iv. 54; ix. 34, reproducing the gist of these verses, as a comparison would show at a glance.

Of very late date is the sermon *Sûra* vi. 117-151 and partly of deuteronomic character, although nothing definite can be said with regard to the occasion on which it was revealed. The rather detailed denunciation of various heathen rites, such as the killing of children and the restriction observed with respect to using certain animals for food allow the suggestion that this speech also was addressed to the pilgrims assembled in Mecca.

The verse v. 69,[9] being evidently a misinterpretation of some words in Numb. xi. 23, reproaches the Jews with limiting the omnipotence of Allâh. The verse is one of those which on account of its strongly anthropomorphistic character caused Moslim theologians considerable diffiulties. But just this is an argument in favour of its late date, showing a time when Muhammed had ceased to see any danger in such figures of speech.

Deuteronomic are also the verses 89-90 which repeat, although perhaps not on the same occasion, prescriptions discussed at the beginning of the *sûra*. Verse 91 repeats in a somewhat extended form the command given in *Sûra* lxvi. 2. The verses 92-94 recapitulate as well as emphasize the prohibition of wine and gambling, warned against in *Sûra* ii. 216. The interdiction of statues and divining arrows is also added. The next verses (95-97) treat of the killing of game which is unlawful on sacred ground. The transgression of this command is to be expiated by an offering. In much more precise terms than in *Sûra* ii. 138 the Ka'ba is now appointed to form the "*Qibla* for men." Verse 101 is the reply to a query which, the traditionists assert, was asked with regard to the frequency with which Believers were expected to perform the pilgrimage. The angry tone of the answer is, however, unsuitable to the zeal of pious Believers. The query seems to have been of a perplexing nature, and I doubt the genuineness of the whole verse. Verse 102 abolishes the ancient custom of observing rules with regard to the eating of certain camels. One of these classes termed *baḥîra* will make it clear

[9] *Cf.* vii. 156, أغلال.

why Muhammed did not adopt the name *Baḥira*[10] for himself; the second part of the verse as well as verse 105 seems to refer again to Jews. Finally the regulations concerning wills and bequests (vv. 105-108),[11] and the warning to be truthful when giving evidence renew commands given long before (ii. 176; vi. 153).

I have still to mention several pieces which are of so uncertain date that it is not possible even to suggest anything as to their places. Of these are the three verses lxxxv. 9-11 which are evidently Medinian, but this is all that can be said about them with certainty. *Surâ* lxxiii. 20 is a very late repetition of the refrain of *Sûra* liv. (17, 22, *etc.*), but with a more practical aim. The verse is suggestive of Muhammed becoming advanced in years and more experienced as regards human nature. Long nightly devotions were not so essential for those who kept the chief duties of Islâm.

[10] See Ch. II.

[11] See ii. 175-176; iv. 1-45.

# CHAPTER XIII.

## Interpolations. Names of Suras. Initials.

Reason for and method of collecting the *Qorân* — Revelations omitted — Alleged integrity of the *Qorân* — Interpolated verses — The name "Muhammed" in the *Qorân* — Various theories on the initials — Synopsis of initials and conclusions.

Appendix : (Approximate) Chronological arrangement of revelations.

---

The *Qorân* is a comparatively small book, and for some time after the death of Muhammed it was not even a book, but the different pieces were scattered about in various private collections, all of which were incomplete. In most instances the revelations were committed to memory by the Believers. The condition of the *Qorân* faithfully reflected that of Islâm in the period immediately following the demise of the Prophet. Everything was out of joint. The Believers had no other guide in religious affair, which now permeated every action, than their individual knowledge of the *Qorân*, their recollections of how Muhammed had acted in certain emergencies, and the decisions of the *Imâm* or the *Khalifah* of the Prophet. This would, however, only describe how matters stood in Medina, the centre of Islâm, whilst the provinces were so badly provided with religious ministrations that Islâm only took root there with great difficulty.

Muhammed never had any intention of compiling a book. He did not even take any pains to have the revelations put down in writing till a considerable amount of those which were required for the spiritual guidance of the community were in existence. Besides the official oracles, there circulated in the memory of the people a mass of sayings, accessory to the *Qorân*, which were rightly or wrongly credited to Muhammed. Whenever a man, holding a prominent position, dies, a mass of *dicta* are attributed to him, and in good faith too, for which he is not responsible. This was the case in a much higher degree with a man like Muhammed, who was the very heart of Islâm, and whose most insignificant utterances were regarded as oracles. Official revelations and occasional supplementary remarks to the former lay stored up side by side in the memories of the Faithful, and Muhammed himself may not always have made it quite clear to which of the two classes words that had fallen from his lips, were to be reckoned. A short time after his death it was, therefore, impossible to draw a strict line between revelations and their appendage alluded to, even leaving the large class of fabricated sayings out of consideration.

Of the secretaries[12] whom Muhammed had appointed to jot down revelations for his own private purposes, Zeib b. Thâbit was known as the best authority on the matter. For this reason Muhammed's immediate successors charged him with the compilation of all the speeches he could gather. The history of this compilation is obscured rather than elucidated by a mass of traditions, and does not impress the student with the conviction that it was only composed of such speeches as Muhammed regarded as divine oracles. There are in this matter two facts to be kept in mind — (1) that the first impulse to undertake the task of collecting all available revelations was given by the circumstance that many of the oldest Moslims had passed away, and (2) that when Zeid set to work, he collected the revelations from those who had already started partial collections of their own from the sundry materials, on which he and his fellow secretaries had put them down, as also from the memories of the Believers. The work was superintended both by Abu Bakr and Omar, particularly the latter.

---

[12] See *Khamis*, I. p. 464.

From this way of proceeding we must draw our own conclusions. Omar is said to have accepted (on the instigation of Abu Bakr) only such revelations as genuine, as were supported by the evidence of two reliable witnesses,[13] or by two proofs if no living witness was forthcoming. This tradition, which is handed down on behalf of Omar, is so uncertain, that Ibn Ḥajar interprets the twofold evidence by "known by heart and written down by somebody."[14] Another authority[15] is of opinion that the "two witnesses" had to testify that such verses were written down in the presence of Muhammed, or at least, were revealed in one of the usual ways of revelation.

There is so much vagueness about all this that the tradition in question is scarcely trustworthy, especially as traditionists admit a case in which a verse was accepted on the authority of only one witness.[16] This being so, the memory of the Believers remains a prominent source of Qoranic verses, and we have to judge the matter accordingly. Tradition has, indeed, handed down quite a number of verses which were not accepted as genuine, because their authenticity was not sufficiently attested. A complete compilation of these verses has been made by Nöldeke.[17] Although they are, from religious reasons, placed in the class of "abrogated" revelations (which I have discussed at another place), it is clear that they were either overlooked by the compilers, or treated as merely casual remarks of Muhammed, and omitted on purpose. Considering the way in which the compilation was made, it would have been a miracle, had the *Qorân* been kept free of omissions, as well as interpolations.

Nöldeke denies emphatically that Zeid b. Thâbit or any of the Khalifahs responsible for the redaction of the *Qorân* had tampered with the book, and regards any view to the contrary as mistaken.[18] Now if omission was possible, why not addition? There was no hard and fast rule to distinguish between divine revelations and occasional utterances of Muhammed, especially as many of the latter are quite Qoranic in tone and style. The famous "verse concerning stoning"[19] may serve as an illustration. It reminds Believers to cling to their families, and to stone to death adulterers though they be advanced in years. Omar is stated to have treated this verse as genuine, but he refrained from inserting it in the *Qorân* for fear it might be said that he had interpolated it.[20] Here we have the complete contrast to the verse mentioned above, which, according to tradition *was* accepted on one authority alone. From this we may conclude that individual opinion was also a factor in accepting or rejecting doubtful verses, and it is possible that the "verse concerning stoning" was rejected for other reasons than the one mentioned. The affair which is said to have caused its revelation is closely connected with the tradition relating that the Jews in Medina brought before Muhammed a man who had committed adultery. On the Prophet's enquiry what punishment the Jews were accustomed to meet out for such crime, they answered: scourging. He then asked them whether the *Tôrâ* did not command stoning. This they denied. Abr Allâh b. Salâm had a copy of the *Tôrâ* brought, and requested the Jews to read it (*Qor.* iii. 87). The Rabbi (*Al Midrâs*) placed his hand upon the "verse concerning stoning" (Lev. xx. 10) in order to hide it, but Abd Allâh pushed it away, and showed the verse to Muhammed who thereupon sentenced the accused persons to death.[21] This tradition is most unreliable for various reasons. Firstly at the time Abd Allâh was converted, the Jews had been completely driven out of Medina, and could therefore not have made Muhammed judge in an affair which concerned them alone. Secondly the *Mishnah* (*Sanhedrin*, vii. 3) leaves no doubt as to what was to be done in such a case, even if we interpret the term '*Tôrâh*' by any religious code they might have brought to Muhammed. There is no other case mentioned in which Muhammed interfered with the jurisdiction of the Jews as long as they were externally on peaceful terms. As an outcome of Âisha's adventure, adultery was only to be punished with scourging (*Qor.* xxiv. 2), and Omar could therefore not accept as genuine a verse which demanded stoning. According to another version[22] Omar asked Muhammed when this verse was revealed, whether he should write it down "and it was as if he would not consent to such practice." We should think that, if this was an official divine revelation, the Prophet had no choice but to treat it as such, but it is pretty clear that the whole tradition was fabricated in order to justify Omar's course of action.

[13] *Itqân*, p. 133. [14] *Ibid.* [15] *Al Sakhâwi, ibid.* [16] *Ibid.* [17] *Q.* p. 174 *sqq.*

[18] *Orientalische Skizzen*, p. 56: "*Der Korân enthält nur echte Stücke.*"

[19] Nöldeke, *Q.* p. 185, gives the various readings of this verse. [20] *Ibid.* p. 194; *cf. Khamis*, I. 14; *Itq.* p. 527.

[21] *I. Hish.* p. 393; Bokh. III. p. 217. [22] *Itq.* 528; Beiträge, p. 52; *cf.* S. John viii. 3.

Moslim theology holds that the distance which separates the divine oracles of the *Qorân*, and the Prophet's other utterances is not very great. Al Shâfiî (died 204/820), author of an epoch making work on "the Principles of the *Fiqh*," and founder of the latest of the four orthodox Muhammedan law schools teaches that everything ordained by Muhammed is deduced from the *Qorân*, and there exists nothing which cannot be inferred from it, so much so,[23] that in the last verse of *Sûra* lxiii. ("Allâh will never respite a soul when its appointed time has come"), an allusion to the sixty-three years which Muhammed lived, is found.[24]

The declaration of Omar, recorded above, is very remarkable. Why should he have feared suspicion? The idea of the possibilty of anything creeping into the *Qorân* which originally did not belong to it, should have been inadmissible. Yet the notion of interpolations was so far from being out of the question that, according to Al Shahrastâni,[25] the Ajârida, a branch of the sect of the Khawârij, maintained that *Sûra* xii. did not previously form part of the *Qorân*, because it was only a tale — moreover a love story which could not be the subject of divine revelation. This is the most powerful attack ever made by Moslims against the divinity of the *Qorân*. Ibn Hazm, therefore, places these people outside the pale of Islâm.[26] From this denunciation of a whole *sûra*, consisting of 111 verses, we may at any rate conclude that there existed soon after the death of Muhammed a feeling that some persons had tampered with the holy Book.[27]

All this being taken into consideration, no serious objection can be made against the suggestion that the *Qorân* contains passages which were not *à priori* intended to be there. If I speak of interpolations, I chiefly mean the shifting of the line which separates the *Qorân* from the *Hadith*. This line has never been drawn by Muhammed himself, and it is hard to say, when and by whom it was fixed.

The first to suspect the genuineness of certain verses in the *Qorân* among European scholars was Silvestre de Sacy, who questioned the authenticity of *Sûra* iii. 138.[28] To this Weil[29] added verse 182; xvii. 1; xxi. 35-36; xxix. 57; xlvi. 14. Finally Sprenger has his doubts as to the genuineness of lix. 7.[30]

As regards xvii. 1 and xlvi. 14 there is not sufficient evidence for a verdict. Different is the case with iii. 138. Although the event which gave the occasion for the recitation of this verse is well known, I reproduce it for the sake of completeness. It is as follows: When Muhammed was dead, great consternation prevailed among the leaders of the community who apprehended great falling off of Believers. Omar said: "Some hyprocrites assert that Muhammed is dead, by Allâh, he is not dead, but was exalted to his Lord as Moses, who stopped away forty days, but returned though he was thought to be dead. Muhammed will also return and cut off the heads and legs of those whe believe him to be dead." Abu Bakr, who in the meanwhile had endeavoured to calm the fears of others, emphasised Omar's words, by saying: "Whoever serves Muhammed — well *he* is dead, but who serves Allâh — *He* never dies." Then he recited the verse alluded to,[31] the people listened attentively, but Omar said he felt as if he had never heard the verse before.[32]

It is rather strange that Omar should have confessed ignorance of a verse which, according to tradition, was revealed to Muhammed during the battle of Uhud when he was struck and lay apparently dead. The Moslims, relates Al Tabari,[33] seeing the Prophet on the ground, called: "If he

[23] Al Ushmûni, *Manâr, al hudâ*, p. 15. Ibn Burhân (*ibid.*) teaches that Muhammed has said nothing which cannot directly or indirectly be traced back to the *Qorân*.

[24] *Ibid.* [25] *Milal*, p. 95 *sq.* [26] *Milal*, fol. 136 vo. [27] *Cf.* Mewâqif. p. 357.

[28] *Journal des Savans*, 1832, p. 535 *sq.* [29] *Einleitung in den Korân*, 2nd ed. p. 52 *sqq.* [30] Vol. III. p. 164.

[31] Ibn Hish. p. 1012; Bokh. III. 191. Al Shahrastâni, p. 11, gives a somewhat different version according to which Omar threatened to kill anyone who said Muhammed was dead, and compared his ascension to heaven to that of Jesus.

[32] Al Ya'qûbi, ed. Houtsma, II. p. 127, gives the story with the following variation. When Muhammed had died, the people said: We thought that the Prophet would not die until he had conquered the earth. Omar made the speech quoted above, but Abu Bakr said: Allâh has announced his death in the revelation (xxxix. 31): Thou diest and they die. Omar then said: I feel as if I had never heard this verse. — Possibly Al Ya'qûbi confounds this verse with iii. 138. At all events the uncertainty as to which verse Omar's words refer, should not be overlooked.

[33] VI. p. 1316 *sq.*

be dead, [remember that] all Messengers before him have died." When Muhammed recovered consciousness, he revealed *Sûra* iii. 138.

I believe neither in the authenticity of this exclamation, nor of the verse in question. This alone, however, is not sufficient to advance us beyond the arguments brought by Weil. The verse contains yet another element which speaks against its authenticity, *viz.*, the name Muḥammed. I even go further and assert that all verses in the *Qorân* in which this name, or Aḥmad, occurs are spurious. The reasons on which I base my suggestions are the following.

In Chapter II. I have endeavoured to shew that the fabrication of the name *Muḥammed* stands in close connection with the elements of the Baḥira legend. If this be so, that name could not have come into practical use until a period of the Prophet's life, when the material of the *Qorân* was all but complete. Now it might be objected that the texts of the missionary letters which Muhammed commenced to send in the seventh year of the Hijra to unconverted Arab chiefs, as well as to foreign potentates,[34] were headed by the phrase: "From Muhammed, the Messenger of Allâh, to, *etc.*" — The authenticity of the majority of these letters, one of which will occupy our attention presently, is very doubtful, and besides, even if the genuineness of the texts of the documents be admitted, the superscription may have been added by the traditionists who took it for granted. At any rate I do not believe that *Muhammed* was an official name till after the conversion of Abd Allâh b. Salâm, or a year or two before his death. At the period of the battle of Uḥud (A. H. 3) there was certainly no trace of the name, and it is too superfluous to demonstrate how unlikely it was that Muhammed's friends, seeing him prostrate, should have uttered the words quoted above. If they had really thought him dead, they would have run away, as all would then have been lost. If, on the other hand, we assume that the name *Muhammed* was meant to signify something similar to *Messiah*, the verse in question is nothing but an imitation of the chief portion of another which was revealed *before* the battle of Badr (*Sûra* v. 79) and runs thus: "The Messiah the son of Maryam, is nothing but a Messenger, the messengers before him have passed away . . . ." The authors of iii. 138 simply replaced *almasîḥ b'nu' Maryama* by *Muḥammed*, and the verse was ready.

This is, however, not the only *Muḥammed*-verse which stands in connection with the Baḥira legend, as in *S.* xxxiii. 40 we find another reference to it. This revelation is appended to one of the paragraphs which deal with the affairs of Muhammed's wives, though it does not belong to it, the preceding sermon ending with verse 39. As each of these paragraphs commences with the words: O thou Prophet![35] we have seen that they refer to matters prior to the adoption of the name *Muhammed*. The verse in question runs thus: "Muhammed is no father of any of your men,[36] but [he is] the Messenger of Allâh and the Seal of the Prophets, Allâh knows everything." From its very place we can gather that the verse's only function is the condonation of the Prophet's marriage with the divorced wife of his adopted son,[37] which event took place in the year *four*. As to the "Seal of the Prophets," this is surely nothing but a skilful alteration of the "Seal of prophecy" in the Baḥira legend.

It is interesting that as a *third* variation of the Seal the traditionists tell us about a real seal which Muhammed used for his letters, and Weil[38] as well as Sprenger seem to regard it as historic. It is, however, just as mythical as the other two seals, at any rate, in the fashion in which it appears in tradition. Before despatching his missionary letters, we read, Muhammed was afraid that the persons to whom they were sent, would not accept them unless they were duly sealed. Muhammed, therefore, had a seal made of gold, and those of his companions who could afford it, followed his example. On the morrow, however, the Archangel Gabriel came and forbade Muhammed to use

---

[34] I. Isḥ. p. 971. Weil has shown that the letter to Khosrau must have been written prior to the treaty of Hudeibiya. Al Tabari, p. 1559, places it *after* the same. The authenticity of all these letters is questionable.

[35] Although this is not the case with verse 38, I am not at all convinced of its genuineness because it bears a striking resemblance to verse 62. Besides this the verse has the obvious tendency of freeing Muhammed from obligations which he considered binding for others. Finally, the passage "those who have passed away" must not be overlooked.

[36] Al Beidhâwi refers these words to Muhammed's two sons who had died in infancy, so that he was left without male offspring. "Even if they had lived," he adds, "they would have been *his* men, but not *yours*."

[37] See Ch. XI.

[38] *Muhammed*, p. 196.

gold. Thereupon they all discarded their seals, but Muhammed had one made of silver on which the words were engraved: "Muhammed [is] the Messenger of Allâh," each word on a separate line.[39]

The *third* verse containing the name *Muhammed* is xlvii. 2, placed in the introduction of a *sûra* which was revealed shortly after the battle of Uhud.[40] A closer examination, however, cannot fail to disclose the fact that the verse is wedged in between two which belong together, disturbing their logical connection. The translation of the verses in question will make this manifest in the following manner: (v. 1) Those who disbelieve and turn [others] from the [war] path of Allâh, He makes their works go wrong. (v. 3) This [is] because the infidels follow falsehood, and those who believe, follow the *truth from their Lord* — thus does Allâh set forth for men their parables. Between these two verses, which according to the usual logic of the *Qorân* fit exceedingly well together, stands the following: (v. 2) And those who believe and do right and believe on what is revealed upon *Muhammed* — and *it is the truth from their Lord*, may He forgive them their iniquities and set right their mind. Can anyone imagine that verse 3 forms a sequence to verse 2? On the other hand the words *the truth from their Lord* make it clear why the suspected verse was put in a place where it did not originally belong. This would, indeed, only prove that the verse is misplaced; but it is also so weak and invertebrate that we cannot tax Muhammed with its authorship. He is wont to assure Believers of their share in paradise, but not to *wish* that Allâh *may* pardon their sins. Besides, as the verse begins with "and," it could not have formed a detached revelation which the compilers did not know how to place. This circumstance is also much more easily explained, if we assume that the verse was fabricated.

There is one more verse containing the name *Muhammed, viz.*, xlviii. 29. It forms part of a letter which Muhammed is said to have dispatched to the Jews of Kheibar, although it is not stated in which year. It is, however, only necessary to cast a glance at the authorities on whose behalf the document was handed down, in order to recognise its untrustworthiness. It is preserved solely by Ibn Ishâq[41] who reproduces it on the authority of: A freed slave of the family of Zeid b. Thâbit from Iqrima *or* Sa'id b. Jubeir from Ibn Abbâs. The last name especially, augurs badly for the veracity of the letter. The verse itself, which is not given as a quotation from the *Qorân*, but as belonging to the text of the letter, has been discussed at the end of Chapter VIII. It stands in no connection whatever with the *sûra* to which it is appended, and the verse preceding it gives ample evidence why it was placed here. Finally it is to be observed that the words "in order to enrage the infidels" are borrowed from ix. 121 and lvii., 9, passages which are very late, having been revealed during the expedition to Tabûk. For so late a period the verse in question is much too clumsy and confused.

Now for what purpose were these four verses embodied in the *Qorân?* It appears that Muhammed had adopted the name too late to be addressed by it in a revelation, but it was considered necessary to have it officially recorded in the *Qorân*. The interpolators were sure of not meeting with opposition when offering verses which furnished a name for the mouth-piece of Allâh. One might, however, object that an appropriate name for the Prophet was to be found in one of the Hallelûjah addresses composed in celebration of the victory of Badr, *viz.*, lxi. 6, where Jesus announced to the children of Israel a messenger to come after him bearing the name *Ahmad*. But the genuineness of this verse is not beyond doubt. It is improbable that it was revealed at so early an epoch when there were enough Christians left in North Arabia to contradict it. After the surrender of the northern tribes this was not to be feared. The verse was, however, a convenient battle-cry for the army which was sent to Syria shortly after the death of Muhammed. The form *Ahmad* is nothing but a variation of *Muhammed*, and shews how little the latter name had then become settled in the minds of the Moslims.

There is less certainty about the spurious character of the following verse, but I cannot refrain from making a few observations as regards the suspicious elements of the same. *Sûra* v. 73 is,

---

[39] *Khamîs*, II. p. 29; Bokhâri, VIII. 457. [40] See Ch. X.

[41] Page 376, *cf.* Uyûn al Athâr. As to other letters of the similar character see *J. Q. R.* Vol. X. p. 113.

excepting a slight change in the wording, a verbal repetition of ii. 59:[42] "Verily those who believe, and those who are Jews, and the Baptists, and the Christians, whoever believes in Allâh and the last day, and does what is right,[43] there is no fear for them, nor shall they grieve." It seems to me that this verse owes its place not to any theological tendency, but to a mistake, and is actually identical with the other. Probably it was found in some collection with the words: *they have their reward at their Lord* missing, and was therefore regarded as a separate revelation. It is easy to see that the verse is out of place. The preceding one recalls to both Jews and Christians that they stood on nought until they fulfilled the *Tôrâ* and the Gospel. This being in reality only a variation of the old reproach of tampering with the holy books, it is difficult to understand, how so encouraging a revelation could follow immediately after it.

Verse 101 of the same *sûra*, alluded to on a formed occasion,[44] appears as if it had been composed after the death of the man who found a reply to every question addressed to him. It is quite natural that (before the *Sunna* was in anything like working order) many questions on religious matters were asked, especially by later converts. What can, therefore, be the meaning of the words: "And if you ask about them when the *Qorân*[45] is revealed, they are made manifest to you?" Evidently that it was too late now to ask questions beyond what was laid down in the *Qorân* itself. The growth of the *Hadîth* then supplemented what was wanting.

In conclusion there only remain a few observations to be made on the mysterious letters which stand at the head of twenty-nine sûras, and which have hitherto not found satisfactory explanation. The Moslim commentators of the *Qorân*, it is true, do not fail to give them all kinds of sacred interpretations, but these are without any foundation, and completely valueless. Yet these letters have not only occupied the minds of theologians, but no less a man than Ibn Sina[46] is supposed to have devoted a small treatise to their explanation. He moved, however, so entirely in the ways of scholastic philosophy, that he enlightens us no more than the theologians do. When the letters were put their places, Arab philosophy was yet unborn.

Of the endeavours of modern scholars to decipher those letters, the best known is Sprenger's who took the five letters standing at the beginning of *Sûra* xix. to mean I N R I.[47] This theory has been finally disposed of by Nöldeke. In my opinion the last named scholar made a successful beginning in the explanation of the letters. Unfortunately he gave it up, and adopted the older theory of the late Dr. Loth, who saw in these initials cabbalistic ciphers contrived by Muhammed after Jewish models.[48] In accordance with this view Nöldeke takes the letters as mystic signs which stands in relation to the heavenly archtype, and originated from Muhammed himself. This is, however, untenable. Jewish mysticism of this kind does not go back as far as the period in which these initials were written. On the contrary the oldest books of Jewish mystic literature show traces of Arab influence, and are at least 150 years later than the official text of the *Qorân*. Besides, there is no mysticism visible in the whole *Qorân*. Even *Sûras* cxiii. and cxiv. look like protests against magic practices, rather than magic formulas,[49] as they consistently place Allâh in sharp contrast to witchcraft.

If Muhammed were the author of those initials, he must have had an important share in the arrangement of the *sûras*, and this would contradict all we know of the compilation of the *Qorân*. We should also have traditions on the matter handed down by himself, but the few given by Al Bokhâri in the chapter headed *Kitâb tafsîr alqorân* do not go back far, and reveal a complete ignorance of the meanings of the letters in question. It is also strange that out

[42] *Cf.* xxii. 17, and Ch. XII.

[43] Verse ii. 59 has here the words: their reward is with their Lord.

[44] See Ch. XII.

[45] Palmer endeavours to meet the difficulty by inserting the word *whole*. He also translates: "they *shall* be shown," but it should be translated: "they *are* divulged."

[46] *Alrisâla Alneirûziyya*, Constantinople 1298 together with other small treatises.

[47] Vol. II. p. 18[illegible].

[48] *Encyclopædia Britannica*, IXth ed., article "Korân."

[49] The tradition given by Al Beidâwi is evidently late and fabricated, no authority is mentioned for it, and Ibn Hish. does not mention it at all.

of the more than two hundred addresses (of which the hundred and fourteen *sûras* of the *Qorân* are composed) only twenty-nine are preceded by initials, and that they are invariably found at the heads of compound *sûras*. No one will for a moment make Muhammed responsible for the arrangement of, *e.g.*, *Sûras* ii. and iii. Finally, if mystic relations existed between the *Qorân* and its heavenly architype, why were these restricted to so small a number only giving these a more sacred character than the majority of addresses?

Thus much is clear that the letters were added when the arrangement of the *Qorân* in its present form was completed. One can further not fail to observe that *sûras* with the same (or similar) initials stand in groups. *Sûras* ii., iii. and xxix. to xxxii. have [al]*M*; *Sûras* x. to xv. have [al]*R* except *Sûra* xiii. which has [al]*MR*; *Sûras* xxvi. to xxviii. have *ṬS* and *ṬSM* respectively; *Sûras* xl. to xlvi. have *ḤM*, except *Sûra* xlii. which has *ḤM'ASQ*; *Sura* vii. has [al]*MṢ*; *Sûra* xix. has *J* [or *N*] *'AṢ*; *Sûra* xx. has *ṬH*; *Sûra* xxxvi. has J [or *N*] *S*; *Sûra* xxviii. has *Ṣ*; *Sûra* l. has *N*, and lastly *Sûra* lxviii. has *Q*.

The *Sûras* ii., iii., xxix. to xxxi. evidently belong together, but had to be separated on account of their unequal length, and we know that the length of the *sûras* was an important factor in their final arrangement. This is alone sufficient to show that the initials have no sacred characters at all but are, as Nöldeke at first rightly suggested, monograms of private collectors or authorities prior to the official edition of the book. In one of the MSS. of al Dânîs' *Kitab altaisir* (Cod. Brit. Mus. Or. 3068, fol. 72ᵛ l. 2) the letters *ṬH* (*Sûra* xx.) are followed by the words *alaihi as salâm*[50] (peace upon him). From this we may conclude that Al Dâni (or the copyist) had a tradition that at least these two letters referred to a person, whilst the *sûra* to which they belong, has no other name or heading at all. Nöldeke, endeavouring to explain the letters has rightly hit upon Talḥa, but I believe that only the *Ṭ* refers to him, whilst *H*, which occurs again in *Sûra* xix., belongs to another person, probably Abu *H*ureira. The meaning of *ṬH* would, then, be that *Sûra* xx. was found in the collections of the two persons named. Such collections, we know, were made or kept by other people also, and probably marked with the name or initial of the collector or owner. At any rate, when Zeid b. Thâbit made use of these collections for the compilation of the *Qorân*, he incorporated them bodily into his volume, but from personal or other reasons kept the initials. This explains the fact that whole groups of *sûras* are headed by the same letters, and it is easily seen how such a manner of working facilitated the edition of the *Qorân*. Probably there was much less scrutiny used about it than tradition will have us believe. Even the best readers of the *Qorân* may not have mastered the whole book, but scanned a comparatively small part of it, so that it was quite possible to intersperse verses of very doubtful authenticity. Now when pieces found in sundry note books were united into one *sûra*, Zeid collected all initials belonging to them, and placed them together at the head. For the large majority of addresses which were not contained in any such collections, Zeid had his hand free to arrange on the lines dictated by Omar, or followed his own judgment. This portion, therefore, shows no initials at all, being understood to be Zeid's.

A parallel to this is offered by the superscriptions of the sûras. Some have none, and the initials attached to them are used as such, *viz.*, *Sûras* xx., xxxvi., xxxviii., l. *Sûra* lxviii. is named both after its initials and the first word. *Sûra* xlii. is titled after the initials and a word in verse 36, and many other *sûras* have two or more superscriptions. Different collectors probably chose different names, whilst the final compiler of the *Qorân* followed the same practice as he did with the initials, and preserved them all. Their inferior importance is, however, shown by the liberties which were taken with them in subsequent copies.

A very superficial enquiry into this matter will show that the word chosen as superscription is often quite trivial, but the piece serves as nucleus round which other, nameless, pieces are gathered.

[50] The Codd. Add. 7232 and 9485 have only طه.

Endeavouring now to substitute full names for the cyphers, I read with Nöldeke's *first* attempt — *Z* instead of *R*, but also *N* for *J* ( ﻧ for ﺟ ). If we further follow the Arabic custom of regarding cyphers not as representatives of the first letter only, but rather the most prominent of the word, we receive the following — of course only hypothetical — list: —

*M* = Al *M*ughîra.
*Ṣ* = Ḥaf*Ṣ*a.
*R* [*Z*] = Al *Z*ubeir.
*K* = Abu Ba*K*r.
*H* = Abu *H*ureira.
*N* = 'Othmâ*N*.
*Ṭ* = *Ṭ*alḥa.
*S* = *S*a'd [b. Abi Waqqâṣ].
*Ḥ* = *Ḥ*udaifa.
'— = *'O*mar [or '*A*liy, Ibn '*A*bbâs, '*Â*isha].
*Q* = *Q*âsim b. Rabî'a.
*Al* forms the article before Mughira and Zubeir, and is to be found with no other cypher.

## [APPROXIMATELY] CHRONOLOGICAL ARRANGEMENT OF THE REVELATIONS.

### A.—MECCAN REVELATIONS.

#### I. — First Proclamation.

*Sûra* 96, verse 1-5

#### II. — The Confirmatory Revelations.

*Sûra* 87
„ 68, verse 1-33
„ 112
„ 69, verse 40-52
„ 26 „ 221-228
„ 52 „ 29-49
„ 74 „ 1-30, 35-55
„ 73 „ 1-14
„ 76
*Sûra* 94
„ 96, verse 6-19
„ 111
„ 104
„ 79, verse 15-26
„ 53 „ 1-18, 24-62
„ 93 „ 1-8
„ 109

#### III. — The Declamatory Revelations.

*Sûra* 81
„ 82
„ 84
„ 99
„ 80
„ 86
„ 75
„ 83
„ 88
„ 79, verse 1-14
„ 77
„ 69, verse 1-39
„ 78
„ 56
„ 52, verse 1-28
„ 70
„ 100
*Sûra* 101
„ 106
„ 107
„ 108
„ 90
„ 92
„ 91
„ 105
„ 102
„ 97
„ 98
„ 89
„ 72
„ 85, verse 1-8, 12-22
„ 103
„ 95

### IV. — The Narrative Revelations.

*Sûra* 68, verse 34-52
,, 51
,, 26, verse 1-220
,, 54
,, 37
,, 44
,, 38
,, 27, verse 1-59
,, 28
,, 15
,, 18
,, 12
,, 19
,, 43, verse 25-89
,, 21
,, 14

*Sûra* 20
,, 11
,, 34
,, 7, verse 1-27, 57-155, 186-205
,, 17 ,, 1-8, 103-111
,, 73 ,, 15-19
,, 40 ,, 1-6, 24, 57
,, 29 ,, 13-42
,, 10 ,, 72-109
,, 23 ,, 23-52
,, 46 ,, 20-35
,, 5 ,, 23-38, 109-120
,, 2 ,, 200-210
,, 6 ,, 74-91
,, 1

### V. — The Descriptive Revelations.

*Sûra* 79, verse 27-46
,, 71
,, 55
,, 50
,, 45
,, 42
,, 41
,, 35
,, 32
,, 67
,, 25, verse 1-63
,, 23 ,, 1-22, 53-118
,, 16 ,, 1-115
,, 43 ,, 1-24
,, 13

*Sûra* 113
,, 114
,, 10, verse 1-57, 58-71
,, 31 ,, 1-10, 19-34
,, 36
,, 27, verse 60-95
,, 30
,, 39
,, 22, verse 1-13, 62-71
,, 40 ,, 7-23, 58-85
,, 2 ,, 158-162
,, 29 ,, 43-69
,, 17 ,, 87-102
,, 6 ,, 92-117

### VI. — The Legislative Revelations.

*Sûra* 6, verse 1-45, 46-73
,, 93 ,, 9-11
,, 25 ,, 64-72
,, 31 ,, 11-18
,, 7 ,, 28-56
,, 29 ,, 1-12

*Sûra* 46, verse 1-19
,, 17 ,, 9-86
,, 6 ,, 152-165
,, 9 ,, 129-130
,, 85 ,, 9-11

## B. — MEDINIAN REVELATIONS.

*Sûra* 2, verse 1-19a
,, 19b-37
,, 38-58
,, 59
*Sûra* 5, ,, 71-88
,, 2 ,, 60-97
,, 98-115
,, 116-147
,, 163-184

verse 211-223
,, 244-268
,, 269-281
*Sûra* 8 ,, 1-41 (after Badr)
,, 42-76
*Sûra* 3 ,, 1-29
,, 30-75
,, 76-90
*Sûra* 47

*Sûra* 3, verse 91-113 (?)
„ 114-137, 139-200
*Sûra* 57
„ 7, verse 174-185
„ 59
„ 61
„ 62
„ 16, verse 116-128 (?)
„ 64
„ 4, verse 1-45
„ 126-129
„ 46-72
„ 73-86 (after Uhud)
*Sûra* 2 „ 148-157
„ 87-95
*Sûra* 5 „ 56-63
„ 2 „ 282-284
„ 4 „ 96-105 (A. 4)
„ 106-125
„ 130-138 (?), 139 ?
„ 140-145
„ 146-151
„ 152-175
*Sûra* 33 (A. 5)
„ 2, verse 224-243 (?)
„ 65
„ 24
„ 66
„ 63
„ 58
„ 22, verse 14-61 (A. 6)
„ 72-78

*Sûra* 5, verse 39-44 (A. 7)
„ 2 „ 285-286
„ 48 „ 18-28
„ 2 „ 185-196[a], 196[b]-199 (A. 8)
„ 60
„ 110
„ 49 (A. 9)
„ 9, verse 23-27
„ 38-73
*Sûra* 48 „ 1-17
„ 9 „ 74-94 (A. 10)
„ 120-128
„ 95-119
„ 1-12
„ 36-37
„ 13-22
„ 28-35
*Sûra* 7 „ 156-172
„ 5 „ 1-4
„ 5-7
„ 8-14
„ 15-17
„ 109-120
„ 18-22
„ 45-55
„ 64-70
„ 89-104
„ 105-108 (?)
*Sûra* 6 „ 117 151 (?)
„ 73 „ 20 (?)
„ 74 „ 31-34 (?)

**Interpolated or uncertain.**

*Sûra* 53, verse 19-23
„ 3 „ 138
„ 33 „ 40
„ 47 „ 2

*Sûra* 48, verse 29
„ 61 „ 6
„ 5 „ 78 (?)
„ 101 (?)

## INDICES OF QUOTED PASSAGES.

### I.—Old Testament.

## II.—New Testament.



## III.—Qorân.

## IV.—Mishnâh.



## V.—Talmud.